English Silver

in the
Museum of Fine Arts
Boston

VOLUME I

English Silver

in the

Museum of Fine Arts, Boston

VOLUME I · SILVER BEFORE 1697

Catalogue by ELLENOR M. ALCORN

Museum of Fine Arts, Boston

Library of Congress catalogue card no. 93-78206
ISBN: 0-87846-373-9 (cloth)
ISBN: 0-87846-374-7 (paper)

Typeset by DEKR Corporation, Woburn, Massachusetts
Printed by Meridian Printing, East Greenwich,
Rhode Island

Designed by Cynthia Rockwell Randall
Edited by Troy Moss

Published with the assistance of the National
Endowment for the Arts and the Getty Grant Program

Cover illustration:
5. Ewer and Basin, London, 1567/8,
Silver, parcel gilt
1979.261-262

Table of Contents

7   Preface

8   Acknowledgments

10   Introduction

14   Abbreviations

21   Color Plates

39   Use of Catalogue

40   Catalogue

     OBJECTS, 40

     SPOONS, 196

     DOUBTFUL AUTHENTICITY, 220

228   Concordance

230   Index

Preface

THE ENGLISH SILVER IN THE collection of the Museum of Fine Arts, Boston—over 500 objects—has long been recognized by specialists as one of the finest in the world. The collection continues to grow and to improve in quality primarily due to the generosity and foresight of Miss Theodora Wilbour, who left to the Museum in 1947 a fund restricted to the purchase of English silver. Miss Wilbour's name will be found recurring in the credit lines of many of the finest objects in this book.

It is gratifying to be able to present our English silver of the sixteenth and seventeenth centuries in this handsome volume, which has been supported by generous awards from the National Endowment for the Arts and the Getty Grant Program. Preparation of the manuscript was funded by numerous patrons of the Museum of Fine Arts, especially Robert S. Pirie and Edith I. Welch. I want to express to them the gratitude of the Museum's trustees and staff for recognizing the value of such publications, not only to collectors and scholars, but also to the general public. The documentation and publication of its important holdings remains a basic commitment of art museums, one we carry out with great pleasure.

I also wish to thank Anne L. Poulet, Russel B. and Andrée Beauchamp Stearns Curator of European Decorative Arts and Sculpture, for supporting and overseeing the silver cataloguing project, and the author, Ellenor M. Alcorn, for her enthusiasm in undertaking this volume, which not only demonstrates her expertise and meticulous scholarship, but also her tremendous dedication to the field. The second volume, which will cover the eighteenth, nineteenth, and twentieth centuries, is in preparation as this volume goes to press.

ALAN SHESTACK
Director

Acknowledgments

A CATALOGUE OF A MUSEUM's permanent collection is never the work of a single person. I am fortunate to have had the sustained support of many colleagues, friends, collectors, and museum patrons, whose appreciation for the collection prompted them to maintain their interest in this project over several years. I hope I have done justice to the collection and that the people acknowledged here, and the many others whose names do not appear, feel that their trust and patience was not misplaced.

This book was initially conceived in 1975 and both Robert C. Moeller III and Leslie Campbell Hatfield contributed substantial preliminary research. I am grateful to Anne L. Poulet and Alan Shestack, whose commitment to the publication of the department's holdings afforded me the opportunity to work with this extraordinary collection. Gale Glynn, whose research on the engraved armorials is incorporated into the entries, was a most enlightening collaborator, frequently providing valuable observations on style and condition in addition to her expertise on heraldry. Rob Butler served as a consultant for the sections on construction, and shared his considerable insight on the issues of technique and condition. He also wrote the notes on technical terms included in the "Use of Catalogue" section. My colleagues in the Department of European Decorative Arts and Sculpture, Jeffrey Munger and Joellen Secondo, were unstintingly generous with their advice and support and extremely patient in carrying out many of my departmental responsibilities while the catalogue was being written. Nancy Eklund acted as midwife to the manuscript, and without her high standards and attention to detail it would never have come together. She also did preliminary research on the spoons.

Several former members of the department assisted with various aspects of the project. Diana Larsen devoted a great deal of time to the initial planning of the book, recording marks and measurements and arranging for the photography of the collection. Liana Paredes Arend and Susan Odell Walker offered assistance with bibliographic and mathematical details far beyond the call of duty. Cathy Modica and Matthew Alexander, and Erin Daley checked references and Museum records. Jennifer Lyn Karpf, Dale Pollock, Kippie Sala, and Ellen Tully kindly volunteered their time for this project.

Troy Moss edited the manuscript with boundless good humor, charity, and wisdom. I am grateful to Cynthia Randall, who is responsible for the handsome design of the volume.

Members of other departments in the Museum were also generous with their time. Martha Reynolds and her colleagues in the Development Department sought funding for the publication. The Department of Prints, Drawings, and Photographs gave me access to its collections and library, and the staff of the William Morris Hunt Library was resourceful and patient in accommodating my requests. Much of the information in this book is conveyed through the photographs. Jonathan Penfield Gill was an early and stimulating contributor. Nearly every member of the Department of Photographic Services was called upon in the various phases of this project; I am grateful to Janice Sorkow who not only orchestrated this long undertaking but provided moral support as well. I thank Tom Lang, Mary Lyons, Nicole Luongo, Karen Otis, Mary Sluskonis, Gary Ruuska, and John Woolf for their contributions. John Lutsch and Marty Wolfand deserve special thanks for producing the excellent photographs published here.

I am indebted to my colleagues in charge of other collections who made their objects available and shared their insights on many of the pieces published here. Among my colleagues in American institutions, I am especially grateful to Beth Carver Wees for her unstinting generosity and optimism. In addition I thank Roger Berkowitz, Martin Chapman, Christopher Hartop, Ian Irving, Jessie McNab, Anthony Phillips, and Kevin Tierney. I have benefited from the wisdom and hospitality of English colleagues, chief among them Philippa Glanville, who offered countless suggestions and much encouragement. Judith Banister, David Beasley, Alastair Dickenson, Susan Hare, Gareth Harris, Mrs. G. E. P. How, Brand Inglis, Titus Kendall, Timothy Kent, James Lomax, Timothy Schroder, Gerald Taylor, Eleanor Thompson, Charles Truman, Wynyard Wilkinson, and Timothy Wilson have also been most helpful.

The preparation of this manuscript was funded through several sources. A research grant was received from the National Endowment for the Arts when the book was conceived. I am deeply grateful for the confidence expressed by those friends of the Department of European Decorative Arts and Sculpture who under-wrote various aspects of the research and writing of this catalogue. Edith I. Welch, whose constant encouragement kept the project alive, has generously underwritten several phases of the preparation, including the technical review, the editing, and much of the photography; more than any other supporter, she has championed the cause of this catalogue. I thank John Axelrod, Annella Brown, Mr. and Mrs. I. W. Colburn, John L. Gardner, Harriet Carlton Goldweitz, John Lewis, Mrs. Caleb Loring, Jr., Jeffrey H. Munger, and especially Robert S. Pirie for their generous contributions. The publication of this catalogue has been made possible by awards from the National Endowment for the Arts and the Getty Grant Program.

ELLENOR M. ALCORN
Assistant Curator

Introduction

THE COLLECTION OF ENGLISH SILVER at the Museum of Fine Arts includes more than 500 objects ranging in date from the fifteenth through the early twentieth century. In scope and quality, it is among the foremost museum collections outside England. However, much of the collection is unpublished, and therefore relatively inaccessible to scholars and collectors in the field. This catalogue is intended to make the objects more widely available and to provide a concise history of the provenance, condition, and scholarship concerning each piece.

The literature on English silver is extensive. The consistency with which the London trade has been monitored by the Worshipful Company of Goldsmiths has long invited study. There are several surveys that treat the period covered by this catalogue, among them Sir Charles Jackson's *Illustrated History of English Plate*, Charles Oman's *Caroline Plate*, and Philippa Glanville's *Silver in England*. Articles on connoisseurship, terminology and usage, design, technique, and function have appeared regularly since the 1930s; many are included in the list of abbreviations, and more specialized citations are included in the footnotes. Philippa Glanville's recently published book *Silver in Tudor and Early Stuart England*, which includes a catalogue of the collection of the Victoria and Albert Museum, is a more ambitious study of the period than any previously undertaken. In addition to the visual evidence represented by the objects themselves, she has introduced a battery of documentary material from contemporary inventories and wills that sheds new light on our understanding of ownership, inheritance, patronage, terminology, and usage. While some of her material has been incorporated into this catalogue, it has not been possible to integrate many of her references. The present catalogue is not intended to realign our perception of the field, but rather to unveil a collection that is largely unknown and to provide as unbiased an account of its history as possible.

Because of the size and expense of a single volume covering the entire collection, it was decided to divide the catalogue into two parts, using the introduction of the Britannia standard (95.8 percent pure silver as opposed to the sterling standard, 92.5) in 1697 as a dividing line. In the study of English silver the reigns have traditionally been used to define broad categories; more recently stylistic groupings have been adopted to make the terminology more manageable. All such divisions are artificial, since the remarkable continuity of the history of English goldsmiths provides few landmarks to indicate dramatic change within the trade. The registers introduced by the Worshipful Company of Goldsmiths in 1697, when each maker was required to enter a new mark for the Britannia standard, provide access to a whole category of biographical information that is largely lacking for the sixteenth- and seventeenth-century makers. In addition, the last few decades of the seventeenth century saw the broad influence of immigrant craftsmen and imported designs on English production as well as the introduction of new types of wares to accommodate the new popularity of coffee and tea. For these reasons it was decided that 1697 was an appropriate cut-off point for the first volume. As with all such arbitrary limits, a few objects fell into a gray area—two pieces made in Ireland (which did not adopt the Britannia standard) around 1695–1697 will be included in the second volume. It was also decided not to include the seven pieces of silver in the Forsyth Wickes collection, which are listed in the catalogue published in 1992. This catalogue is otherwise a complete record of the Museum's holdings as of December, 1991.

For the pre-Britannia period only a handful of makers' marks have been identified with any certainty. In recent years it has been more widely acknowledged that the marks were not intended to credit the manufacturer of the object, but, more precisely, to indicate the sponsor who submitted the pieces for assay. Jackson's efforts to match makers' names as they appeared in the records of the Goldsmiths' Company and other documents with the initials represented on early makers' marks have not in general withstood closer scrutiny. More recently, Gerald Taylor, has applied a more scientific method and assigned names to several of the early marks. Considerable new information has come to light about provincial marks as well. For the purposes of this catalogue, only recently published attributions have been adopted, while the references to Jackson's index of marks are provided to assist in the comparison and interpretation of marks.

The Museum's holdings were established by the generous gifts of several private collectors. Frank Brewer Bemis, a Bostonian, first met Edwin Hipkiss, then Curator of Decorative Arts, in 1929. By that time, his collection had largely been formed. Bemis seems to have begun collecting in the early 1920s, relying mainly upon the New York dealer William E. Godfrey and the London dealer Walter H. Willson. The Museum already housed an important collection of American silver, including hundreds of pieces of early silver loaned by Boston area churches. Hipkiss immediately recognized the value of the Bemis collection for the Museum and arranged for a loan exhibition later that year. The entire collection, numbering ninety-two objects, came to the Museum as a bequest on the death of Bemis in 1935. Though many of the objects were modest domestic pieces, The Westbury Cup (cat. no. 14), and the pair of Bodendick candlesticks (cat. no. 75), among others, have proved more interesting than Bemis might have known.

Through her generous bequest of an endowment fund for acquisitions, Theodora Wilbour (d. 1947) continues to have an influence on the history of the collection. She was the daughter of Charles Edwin Wilbour (1833–1896), of Little Compton, Rhode Island, and Charlotte Beebe (1833–1914), of Springfield, Massachusetts. She and her sister, Zoë, named for Byzantine empresses, must have visited the Boston Museum as children, but Theodora never came to Boston in the long period during which she was avidly collecting Greek and Roman coins and

English silver. Her father had trained as a lawyer in New York, and worked under Horace Greeley on the *Tribune*. He later became president of the New York Printing Company, which was owned by William Marcy ("Boss") Tweed. At one point Wilbour held three city positions simultaneously, while his newspaper, *The Transcript*, netted a generous profit from highly priced city advertising. After the Tammany Hall scandal became public, Wilbour devoted himself to Egyptology, amassing a great collection over a period of twenty years. His collection descended to his only surviving daughter, Theodora Wilbour, who bequeathed it to the Brooklyn Museum. Miss Wilbour's association with the Boston Museum of Fine Arts seems to have begun in the 1920s; she made regular gifts to the collection from her own purchases, occasionally having pieces shipped directly from London to Boston. She bought from a slightly broader circle of dealers than Frank Brewer Bemis, including Tiffany's and Crichton Brothers. Like Bemis, she was interested in early domestic pieces, and seems to have admired particularly the more austere forms of Commonwealth or Queen Anne silver. Miss Wilbour's gifts were presented as anonymous gifts in memory of her mother, Charlotte Beebe Wilbour; her collection of coins came to the Museum in memory of her sister, Zoë, who had died at the age of twenty. The Director, George Harold Edgell, anxious to honor one of his most generous and shy patrons, persuaded her that after her death, the Museum should be allowed to use her name. Thus, the acquisition fund she endowed bears her name, and the gifts she made anonymously during her lifetime are identified in this catalogue as having belonged to her.

Richard C. Paine, who became a Trustee in 1932, was also an early benefactor of the collection. His high standards and commitment to the decorative arts are best shown by his collection of English eighteenth-century porcelain, which included the Hutton Collection. In 1946 he presented the Cholmondeley dish (cat. no. 18), a grander and more ambitious piece than any in the Wilbour or Bemis collections. The same year he gave the steeple cup (cat. no. 30). The two-handled cup and cover by the Hound Sejant maker (cat. no. 43) was purchased by the Museum from the sale of his collection.

When the Wilbour Fund became available for acquisitions in 1950, Edwin Hipkiss willingly accepted the mandate to build the collections. His collaborators on the staff were the American silver specialist Kathryn Clark Buhler, and the medievalist Hanns Swarzenski. The acquisitions made in the following two decades reflect the extraordinary wealth of objects on the market and the diverse approaches of the staff. The sixteenth- and seventeenth-century collections parallel in many ways those of the Victoria and Albert Museum. The predilection for mounted wares and for Germanic forms and decoration is conspicuous. Hanns Swarzenski, in particular, favored richly mounted objects, acquiring, for example, the hourglass (cat. no. 2) in 1957 and the mounted Ming flagon (cat. no. 19) in

1967. Kathryn Buhler advocated purchases more consistent with Miss Wilbour's taste. The growth of the collection followed the precedent established by Wilbour and Bemis—London silver of the late sixteenth and seventeenth centuries was emphasized, with consideration given to issues of quality of design and craftsmanship, rarity of form, condition, and provenance or documentary interest. In the 1970s Robert Moeller continued to purchase outstanding objects, most notably the Elizabethan ewer and basin engraved with portraits of the sovereigns (cat. no. 5), as well as several pieces by Jacob Bodendick. More recently, an effort has been made to strengthen the collection of neoclassical silver, and it is hoped that the late nineteenth and early twentieth centuries will eventually be well represented. On several occasions, duplicate or inferior objects have been sold with the proceeds used for further acquisitions. The purchase of the Elizabethan ewer and basin mentioned above was made possible for the Museum with funds raised from deaccessioning.

As might be expected in a relatively young collection, few pieces came to the Museum with any documented early history. It has been a primary consideration in this catalogue to record any evidence of alterations to the objects or doubts about their authenticity. In view of the malleable nature of the medium, however, many such alterations should be viewed as honest repairs. Several pieces that are substantially changed from their original appearance have been incorporated into the main section of the catalogue rather than relegated to the section headed "Doubtful Authenticity" since it is not clear that these changes were made with the intent to deceive. In many uncertain cases, further clues can be supplied by instrumental analysis, which requires the removal of a small sample of silver. Proper interpretation of this data requires a large body of comparative samples in which the trace elements may indicate a common source for the mineral and suggest a date of manufacture. To date there is no scientific publication providing an accurate and comprehensive guide to interpreting these figures. In view of the destructive nature of the process, it was decided not to undertake spectographic analysis until such a study is made public. In the future, it may be possible to draw firmer conclusions about the date of such pieces as the "College Cup" (cat. no. 136), or about the place of manufacture of several unmarked items. Special attention has been given to describing the construction of each object. Though there were no major technical innovations in the goldsmith's trade during the course of the period covered by this book, an accurate description of the structure and decoration of the object can answer many questions left unanswered by a photograph.

ELLENOR M. ALCORN
December, 1991

Abbreviations

BOOKS AND ARTICLES

Banister, 1969
Banister, Judith, *English Silver* (London, 1969).

Berliner, 1925
Berliner, Rudolph and Gerhart Egger, *Ornamentale Vorlageblätter des 15.–19. Jahrhunderts*, 3 vols. (Leipzig, 1925).

Brett, 1986
Brett, Vanessa, *The Sotheby's Directory of Silver, 1600–1940* (London, 1986).

Buhler, 1936
Buhler, Kathryn C., "The Frank Brewer Bemis Collection of Silver," *Bulletin of the Museum of Fine Arts* 34 (1936), pp. 78–83.

Buhler, 1952
Buhler, Kathryn C., "English Silver in the Frank Brewer Bemis Collection," *Connoisseur* 130 (1952), pp. 226–231.

Buhler, 1970
Buhler, Kathryn C., "Craftmanship in Silver," *Apollo* 91, no. 95 (1970), pp. 68–74.

Burns, 1892
Burns, Thomas, *Old Scottish Communion Plate* (Edinburgh, 1892).

Came, 1960
Came, Richard P., "A Notable Collection of English Silver," *Apollo* 71, no. 421 (1960), pp. 75–77.

Came, 1961
Came, Richard P., *Silver* (New York, 1961).

Carrington and Hughes, 1926
Carrington, John Bodman, and George Ravensworth Hughes, *The Plate of the Worshipful Company of Goldsmiths* (Oxford, 1926).

Clayton, 1971, rev. ed., 1985
Clayton, Michael, *The Collector's Dictionary of the Silver and Gold of Great Britain and North America* (New York, 1971, rev. ed. 1985).

Clayton, 1985a
Clayton, Michael, *Christie's Pictorial History of English and American Silver* (Oxford, 1985).

Clowes, 1957
Clowes, Laird, "The Rothermere Silver at the Middle Temple," *Connoisseur* 139 (1957), pp. 31–32.

Collins, 1955
Collins, A. Jeffries, *Jewels and Plate of Queen Elizabeth I* (London, 1955).

Cooper, 1977
Cooper, John K. D., "A Re-assessment of Some English Late Gothic and Early 'Renaissance' Plate I," *The Burlington Magazine* 119 (1977), pp. 408–413.

Dauterman, 1964
Dauterman, Carl Christian, "Dream Pictures of Cathay," *Metropolitan Museum of Art Bulletin* 23, no. 1 (1964), pp. 11–25.

Davis, 1976
Davis, John, *English Silver at Williamsburg* (Williamsburg, 1976).

Finlay, 1990
Finlay, Michael, *Western Writing Implements in the Age of the Quill Pen* (Wetheral, 1990).

Fontein, 1982
Fontein, Jan, *The World's Great Collections, 10, Oriental Ceramics, Museum of Fine Arts, Boston* (Tokyo, 1982).

Frederiks, 1958
Frederiks, J. W., *Dutch Silver: Wrought Plate of North and South Holland from the Renaissance until the End of the Eighteenth Century* (The Hague, 1958).

Frederiks, 1961
Frederiks, J. W., *Dutch Silver: Embossed Ecclesiastical and Secular Plate from the Renaissance until the End of the Eighteenth Century* (The Hague, 1961).

Glanville, 1985
Glanville, Philippa, "Tudor Drinking Vessels," *The Burlington House Fair* (Special Supplement to *The Burlington Magazine*) (London, 1985), pp. 19–22.

Glanville, 1987
Glanville, Philippa, *Silver in England* (Winchester, Massachusetts, 1987).

Glanville, 1987a
Glanville, Philippa, "Chinese Porcelain and the English Goldsmiths, circa 1550 to 1650," *Proceedings of the Silver Society, 1985* 3, no. 6 (1987), pp. 156–160.

Glanville, 1989
Glanville, Philippa, "Tudor or Tudorbethan," *The International Silver & Jewellery Fair and Seminar* (London, 1989), pp. 9–15.

Glanville, 1990
Glanville, Philippa, *Silver in Tudor and Early Stuart England* (London, 1990).

Glynn, 1983
Glynn, Gale, "Heraldry on English Silver," *Proceedings of the Silver Society 1979–1981* 3 (1983), pp. 6–10.

Grimwade, 1951
Grimwade, Arthur G., "A New List of English Gold Plate Part 1," *Connoisseur* 127 (1951), pp. 76–78.

Grimwade, 1982
Grimwade, Arthur G., *London Goldsmiths 1697–1837: Their Marks and Lives from the Original Registers at Goldsmith's Hall and Other Sources* (Boston, 1982).

Grimwade and Banister, 1977
Grimwade, Arthur G. and Judith Banister, "Thomas Jenkins Unveiled," *Connoisseur* 195 (1977), pp. 173–179.

Grimwade and Banister, 1982
Grimwade, Arthur G. and Judith Banister, "A Case of Mistaken Identity," *Proceedings of the Silver Society* 2, nos. 11–13 (1982), pp. 185–193.

Gruber, 1982
Gruber, Alain, *Silverware* (New York, 1982).

Hackenbroch, 1963, rev. ed. 1969
Hackenbroch, Yvonne, *English and Other Silver in the Irwin Untermyer Collection* (New York, 1963, rev. ed. 1969).

Hawley, 1984
Hawley, Henry, "An English Silver Dish," *The Bulletin of the Cleveland Museum of Art* 71, no. 10 (1984), pp. 334–340.

Hayward, 1965
Hayward, John Forrest, "The Mannerist Goldsmiths: 4: England, I," *Connoisseur* 159, no. 640 (1965), pp. 80–84.

Hayward, 1966
Hayward, John Forrest, "The Mannerist Goldsmiths: 4: England, II," *Connoisseur* 162 (1966), pp. 90–95.

Hayward, 1967
Hayward, John Forrest, "The Mannerist Goldsmiths: 4: England, III," *Connoisseur* 164, no. 659 (1967), pp. 19–25.

Hayward, 1969
Hayward, John Forrest, "The Goldsmiths Designs of Hans Holbein," *Proceedings of the Society of Silver Collectors* 1, no. 11 (1969), p. 22.

Hayward, 1976
Hayward, John Forrest, *Virtuoso Goldsmiths and the Triumph of Mannerism 1540–1620* (London, 1976).

Hernmarck, 1977
Hernmarck, Carl, *The Art of the European Silversmith, 1430–1830*, 2 vols. (London, 1977).

Hind, 1952
Hind, A. M., *Engraving in England in the Sixteenth and Seventeenth Centuries*, vol. 1 (Cambridge, 1952).

Hipkiss, 1929
Hipkiss, Edwin J., "British Silver of Three Centuries: a Loan Collection by Frank Brewer Bemis," *Bulletin of the Museum of Fine Arts* 27, no. 161 (1929), pp. 37–39.

Hipkiss, 1933
Hipkiss, Edwin J., "The Charlotte Beebe Wilbour Collection of English Silver," *Bulletin of the Museum of Fine Arts* 31, no. 184 (1933), pp. 25–30.

Hipkiss, 1951
Hipkiss, Edwin J. "English Silver Recently Acquired," *Bulletin of the Museum of Fine Arts* 49 (1951), pp. 11–17.

Honey, 1933
Honey, W. B., *English Pottery and Porcelain* (London, 1933).

How, 1952, 1953, 1957
How, Commander G. E. P. and Jane Penrice How, *English and Scottish Silver Spoons*, 3 vols. (London, 1952–1957).

Jackson, 1911
Jackson, Charles James, *An Illustrated History of English Plate, Ecclesiastical and Secular*, 2 vols. (London, 1911).

Jackson, 1921, rev. ed. 1989
Jackson, Sir Charles James, *English Goldsmiths and Their Marks: A History of the Goldsmiths and Plate Workers of England, Scotland, and Ireland* (London, 1921; revised by Ian Pickford, 1989).

Jones, 1907
Jones, Edward Alfred, *Catalogue of the Old Plate of Leopold de Rothschild, Esq.* (London, 1907).

Jones, 1907a
Jones, Edward Alfred, *Old English Gold Plate* (London, 1907).

Jones, 1908
Jones, Edward Alfred, *Illustrated Catalogue of the Collection of Old Plate of J. Pierpont Morgan, Esq.* (London, 1908).

Jones, 1908a
Jones, Edward Alfred, *The Old Royal Plate in the Tower of London* (Oxford, 1908).

Jones, 1909
Jones, Edward Alfred, *The Old English Plate of the Emperor of Russia* (London, 1909).

Jones, 1910
Jones, Edward Alfred, *The Old Plate of the Cambridge Colleges* (Cambridge, 1910).

Jones, 1911
Jones, Edward Alfred, *The Gold and Silver of Windsor Castle* (Letchworth, 1911).

Jones, 1929
Jones, Edward Alfred, "Some Early English Drinking Vessels in the Collection of Mr. William Randolph Hearst," *Connoisseur* 84 (1929), pp. 345–354.

Jones, 1938
Jones, Edward Alfred, *The Plate of Eton College* (London, 1938).

Kent, 1981
Kent, Timothy Arthur, *London Silver Spoonmakers 1500–1697* (London, 1981).

Le Corbellier, 1974
Le Corbellier, Clare, *China Trade Porcelain: Patterns of Exchange* (New York, 1974).

Lee, 1978
Lee, Georgina E., *British Silver Monteith Bowls Including American and European Examples* (Byfleet, Surrey, 1978).

Lightbown, 1968
Lightbown, Ronald W., "Christian van Vianen at the Court of Charles I," *Apollo* 87, no. 76 n.s. (1968), pp. 426–439.

Lightbown, 1975
Lightbown, Ronald W., *Catalogue of Scandinavian and Baltic Silver* (London, Victoria and Albert Museum, 1975).

Lunsingh Scheurleer, 1980
Lunsingh Scheurleer, D. F., *Chinesches und japanisches Porzellan in europäischen Fassungen* (Braunschweig, 1980).

Miles, 1976
Miles, Elizabeth B., *The Elizabeth B. Miles Collection: English Silver* (Hartford, 1976).

Moeller, 1974
Moeller, Robert C., "An English Silver Tray by Jacob Bodendick," *Bulletin of the Museum of Fine Arts* 72, no. 367 (1974), pp. 4–23.

Moffat, 1906
Moffat, Harold Charles, *Old Oxford Plate* (London, 1906).

ter Molen, 1984
ter Molen, Johannes R., *Van Vianen, een Utrechtse familie van zilversmeden met een internationale faam*, 2 vols. (Rotterdam, 1984).

Müller, 1986
Müller, Hannelore, *The Thyssen-Bornemisza Collection: European Silver* (London, 1986).

Nightingale, 1891
Nightingale, J. E., *The Church Plate of the County of Wilts* (Salisbury, 1891).

Oman, 1957
Oman, Charles C., *English Church Plate 1597–1830* (London, 1957).

Oman, 1961
Oman, Charles C., *The English Silver in the Kremlin 1557–1663* (London, 1961).

Oman, 1962
Oman, Charles C., *English Domestic Silver* (London, 1962).

Oman, 1962a
Oman, Charles C., "The Winchester College Plate," *Connoisseur* 149, no. 599 (1962), pp. 24–33.

Oman, 1965
Oman, Charles C., *English Silversmith's Work* (London, 1965).

Oman, 1970
Oman, Charles C., *Caroline Silver, 1625–1688* (London, 1970).

Oman, 1978
Oman, Charles C., *English Engraved Silver 1150–1900* (London, 1978).

Oman, 1978a
Oman, Charles, "Nicaise Roussel and the Mostyn Flagons," *Leeds Art Calendar*, no. 83 (1978), p. 4.

Oman and Rosas, 1950
Oman, Charles C. and José Rosas, Jr., "Portuguese Influence upon English Silver," *Apollo* 51, no. 304 (1950), pp. 162–164.

Owsley, 1966
Owsley, David T., "'Chinese' Designs on English Silver in Boston," *The Ellis Memorial Antiques Show* (Boston, 1965), pp. 33–39.

Penzer, 1961
Penzer, N. M., "The Plate at Knole I," *Connoisseur* 147 (1961), pp. 84–91.

Penzer, 1961a
Penzer, N. M., "The Plate at Knole II," *Connoisseur* 147 (1961), pp. 178–184.

Read, 1928
Read, Sir Hercules, *Catalogue of the Silver Plate, Medieval and Later, Bequeathed to the British Museum by Sir Augustus Wollaston Franks* (London, 1928).

Rupert, 1929
Rupert, Charles G., *Apostle Spoons* (Oxford, 1929).

Schroder, 1983
Schroder, Timothy, *The Art of the European Goldsmith: Silver from the Schroder Collection* (New York, 1983).

Schroder 1983a
Schroder, Timothy, "Sixteenth Century English Silver, Some Problems of Attribution," *Proceedings of the Silver Society* 3, nos. 1 and 2 (1983), pp. 40–46.

Schroder, 1988
Schroder, Timothy, *The Gilbert Collection of Gold and Silver* (Los Angeles, 1988).

Schroder, 1988a
Schroder, Timothy. *The National Trust Book of English Domestic Silver, 1500–1900* (Harmondsworth, 1988).

Smith, 1968
Smith, Georgina Reynolds, *Table Decoration, Yesterday, Today, and Tomorrow* (Rutland and Tokyo, 1968).

Tait, 1964
Tait, Hugh, "The Stonyhurst Salt," *Apollo* 79, no. 26 (1964), pp. 270–278.

Taylor, 1956
Taylor, Gerald, *Silver* (Harmondsworth, 1956).

Taylor, 1984
Taylor, Gerald, "Some London Platemakers' Marks, 1558–1624," *Proceedings of the Silver Society, 1983* 3, no. 4 (1984), pp. 97–100.

Wark, 1978
Wark, Robert R., *British Silver in the Huntington Collection* (San Marino, 1978).

Watts, 1924
Watts, W. W., *Old English Silver* (New York, 1924).

Wenham, 1931
Wenham, Edward, *Domestic Silver of Great Britain and Ireland* (London, 1931).

EXHIBITIONS

Amsterdam, Rijksmuseum, 1986
Amsterdam, Rijksmuseum, *Kunst voor de beeldenstorm,* 1986.

Antwerp, Rockoxhuis, 1988
Antwerp, Rockoxhuis, *Zilver uit de Gouden Eeuw van Antwerpen,* 1988.

Austin, University of Texas at Austin Art Museum, 1969
Austin, University of Texas at Austin Art Museum, *One Hundred Years of English Silver 1660–1760,* 1969.

Birmingham, Alabama, Museum of Art, 1990
Birmingham, Alabama, Museum of Art, *The Stuart Legacy: English Art 1603–1714,* 1990. Catalogue by Walter R. Brown, E. Bryding Adams, S. Katherine Estes, Douglas K. S. Hyland, and Frances C. Somers.

Boston, Museum of Fine Arts, 1933
Boston, Museum of Fine Arts, *An Exhibition of English Silver, 1571–1800; The Charlotte Beebe Wilbour Collection,* 1933. (No catalogue).

Boston, Museum of Fine Arts, 1982
Boston, Museum of Fine Arts, *New England Begins: The Seventeenth Century,* 1982. Catalogue in three volumes by Jonathan Fairbanks and Robert F. Trent.

Cambridge, Fitzwilliam Museum, 1975
Cambridge, Fitzwilliam Museum, *Cambridge Plate: An Exhibition of Silver, Silver-Gilt, and Gold Plate Arranged as a Part of the Cambridge Festival 1975,* 1975.

Cambridge, Massachusetts, Fogg Art Museum, 1937
Cambridge, Massachusetts, Fogg Art Museum, Harvard University, *The Art of the Renaissance Craftsman,* 1937.

London, British Antique Dealers Association, 1928
London, British Antique Dealers Association, *Exhibition of Art Treasures*, 1928.

London, Burlington Fine Arts Club, 1901
London, Burlington Fine Arts Club, *Exhibition of a Collection of Silversmith's Work of European Origin*, 1901.

London, Chrichton Brothers, 1898
London, Chrichton Brothers, 1898, *A Collection of Early English Spoons of the 15th, 16th, and 17th century*, 1898.

London, Christie's, 1990
London, Christie's, *The Glory of the Goldsmith: Magnificent Gold and Silver from the Al-Tajir Collection*, 1990.

London, Goldsmiths' Hall, 1951
London, Goldsmiths' Hall, *Catalogue of the Exhibition of the Historic Plate of the City of London*, 1951.

London, Goldsmiths' Hall, 1952
London, Goldsmiths' Hall, *Catalogue of Corporation Plate of England and Wales*, 1952.

London, Park Lane, 1929
London, Park Lane, *Loan Exhibition of Old English Plate and Decorations and Orders*, 1929.

London, St. James's Court, 1903
London, St. James's Court, *Old Silver Work, Chiefly English, from the XVth to XVIIIth Centuries*, 1903. Catalogue by John Starkie Gardner.

London, Seaford House, 1929
London, Seaford House, *Queen Charlotte's Loan Exhibition of Old Silver*, 1929.

London, Sotheby's, 1991
London, Sotheby's, *English Silver Treasures from the Kremlin*, 1991.

London, South Kensington Museum, 1862
London, South Kensington Museum, *Catalogue of the Special Exhibition of Works of Art of the Medieval, Renaissance, and More Recent Periods on Loan to the South Kensington Museum June, 1862* (cat. revised, 1863). Catalogue by J. C. Robinson.

London, Spink & Son, Ltd., 1980
London, Spink & Son, Ltd., (arranged by the National Trust for Scotland), *Beckford and Hamilton Silver from Brodrick Castle*, 1980. Catalogue by Malcolm Baker, Timothy Schroder, E. Laird Clowes.

Minneapolis, Minneapolis Institute of Arts, 1956
Minneapolis, Minneapolis Institute of Arts, *French, English and American Silver: a Loan Exhibition in Honor of Russell A. Plimpton*, 1956.

New York, Britain Salutes New York, 1983.
New York, Britain Salutes New York, 1st New York International Arts Festival, *Heritage of England: Silver through Ten Reigns: in Aid of the Royal Oak Foundation*, 1983. Catalogue by James Charles.

New York, China House Gallery, 1980
New York, China House Gallery, China Institute in America, *Chinese Porcelains in European Mounts*, 1980–1981. Catalogue by Sir Francis Watson.

New York, Cooper-Hewitt Museum, 1985
New York, Cooper-Hewitt Museum, *Wine: Celebration and Ceremony*, 1985.

New York, Frick Collection, 1986
New York, Frick Collection, *Mounted Oriental Porcelain*, 1986–1987. Catalogue by Sir Francis Watson.

Oxford, Ashmolean Museum, 1928
Oxford, Ashmolean Museum, *Catalogue of a Loan Exhibition of Silver Plate Belonging to the Colleges of the University of Oxford*, 1928.

Richmond, Virginia, Museum of Fine Arts, 1964
Richmond, Virginia, Museum of Fine Arts, *The World of Shakespeare 1564–1615*, 1964.

San Francisco, Fine Arts Museums of San Francisco, 1966
San Francisco, Fine Arts Museums of San Francisco, *Cathay Invoked: Chinoiserie, A Celestial Empire in the West*, 1966.

San Francisco, Fine Arts Museums of San Francisco, 1977
San Francisco, Fine Arts Museums of San Francisco, *The Triumph of Humanism: A Visual Survey of the Decorative Arts of the Renaissance*, 1977–1978.

Toronto, Royal Ontario Museum, 1958
Toronto, Royal Ontario Museum, *Seven Centuries of English Domestic Silver*, 1958.

University Park, Pennsylvania, Pennsylvania State University Museum of Art, 1982
University Park, Pennsylvania, Pennsylvania State University Museum of Art, *William Penn's England*, 1982.

Utrecht, Centraal Museum, 1985
Utrecht, Centraal Museum, *Zeldaam Zilver uit
de Gouden Eeuw: De Utrechtse edelsmeden Van Vianen,* 1985.

Washington, National Gallery of Art, 1985
Washington, National Gallery of Art, *The Trea-
sure Houses of Britain,* 1985.

**Worcester, Massachusetts, Worcester Art
Museum, 1969**
Worcester, Massachusetts, Worcester Art Mu-
seum, *The Virtuoso Craftsman: Northern European
Design in the Sixteenth Century,* 1969. Catalogue
by David Farmer.

Works Consulted for Armorials

Balfour, Sir Paul, *An Ordinary of Arms Contained in the Public Register of all Arms and Bearings in Scotland,* 2nd ed. (Edinburgh, 1903).

Balfour, Sir Paul, *An Ordinary of Arms Contained in the Public Register of all Arms and Bearings in Scotland,* vol. 2, edited at the Lyon Office (Edinburgh, 1977).

Betham, William, *The Baronetage of England* (Ipswich, 1801–5).

Burke, Arthur Meredyth, *The Prominent Families of the United States of America* (London, 1908, reprint 1975).

Burke, John, *A Genealogical and Heraldic Dictionary of the Peerage and Baronetage of the British Empire,* 8th ed. (London, 1846).

Burke, John, *Genealogical and Heraldic History of the Landed Gentry* (London, 1838).

Burke, John, and Sir Bernard Burke, *A Genealogical and Heraldic History of the Extinct and Dormant Baronetcies of England, Ireland, and Scotland* (London, 1841).

Burke, Sir Bernard, *A Genealogical and Heraldic Dictionary of the Peerage and Baronetage together with Memoirs of the Privy Councillors and Knights,* 61st ed. (London, 1899).

Burke, Sir Bernard, *A Genealogical History of the Dormant, Abeyant, Forfeited, and Extinct Peerages of the British Empire* (London, 1883, facsimile edition, 1969).

Burke, Sir Bernard, *Genealogical and Heraldic History of the Colonial Gentry,* vol. 2, edited by Ashworth P. Burke (London, 1891, 1895, reprint 1970).

Burke, Sir Bernard, *A General Armory of England, Scotland, and Ireland* (London, 1884, 4th reprint, Gloucester 1969).

C[okayne], G[eorge] E[dward], *The Complete Baronetage* (London, 1900–1909, reprint 1983).

C[okayne], G[eorge] E[dward], *The Complete Peerage of England, Scotland, Ireland, Great Britain, and the United Kingdom, Extant, Extinct, or Dormant* (London, 1910–1959, reprint 1980).

Collins, Arthur, *Peerage of England,* ed. by Sir E. Bridges (London, 1812).

Debrett, *The Peerage of England, Scotland and Ireland* (London, 1790).

Elvin, Charles Norton, *A Handbook of Mottoes* revised by R. Pinches (London, 1971).

Fairbairn, James, *Fairbairn's Book of Crests of the Families of Great Britain and Ireland* (London, 1905, reprint 1968).

Fox-Davies, Arthur Charles, *Armorial Families, a Directory of Gentlemen of Coat-Armour,* 7th ed. (London, 1929).

Fox-Davies, Arthur Charles, *The Book of Public Arms: A Complete Encyclopaedia of All Royal, Territorial, Municipal, Corporate, Official, and Impersonal Arms* (London; Edinburgh, 1915).

Guillim, John, *A Display of Heraldry* (London, 1724).

Leeson, Francis L., *A Directory of British Peerages from the Earliest Times to the Present Day* (London, 1984).

Maclean, Sir John, *The Parochial and Family History of the Deanery of Trigg Minor in the County of Cornwall* (1876).

MacLysaght, Edward, *Irish Families; Their Names, Arms, and Origins* (Dublin, 1972).

Matthews, John, *Complete American Armoury and Blue Book* (New York, 1903, 1907, 1911–23, reprint 1965).

Nisbet, Alexander, *A System of Heraldry Speculative and Practical with the True Art of Blazon* (Edinburgh, 1722).

O'Hart, John, *The Irish and Anglo-Irish Landed Gentry* (Dublin, 1884, reprint Shannon, 1969).

Papworth, John Woody, *An Alphabetical Dictionary of Coats of Arms Belonging to Families in Great Britain and Ireland* (London, 1874, reprint, 1968).

Pinches, J. H. and R. V., *The Royal Heraldry of England* (London, 1974).

Pine, L. G., *Burke's Genealogical and Heraldic History of the Landed Gentry of Ireland* (London, 1958).

Ruvigny, Henry de Massué, *The Jacobite Peerage* (London and Edinburgh, 1904, reprint 1974).

Townsend, Peter, *Burke's Peerage and Baronetage,* 105th ed. (London, 1975).

Vivian, J. L., *The Herald's Visitations of Devon Comprising The Heralds' Visitations of 1531, 1564 and 1620* (Exeter, 1895).

Vivian, J. L., *The Visitation of Cornwall, Comprising the Herald's Visitations of 1530, 1573, and 1620* (Exeter, 1887).

Color Plates

PLATE I. 2. Sandglass
English or German, ca. 1550

PLATE II. 4. Flagon
English or German, ca. 1560–70

PLATE III. 5. Ewer and Basin
London, 1567/8

PLATE IV. 10. Architectural Salt
London, 1577/8

PLATE V. 14. The Westbury Cup
London, 1585/6

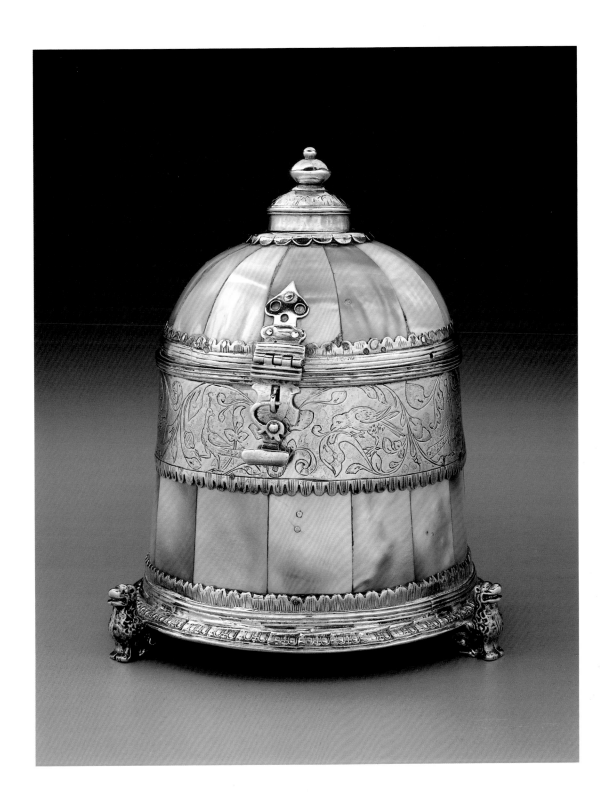

PLATE VI. 16. Casket
Probably London, ca. 1590

PLATE VII. 18. Basin
London, 1599/1600

PLATE VIII. 19. Flagon
Probably London, ca. 1600

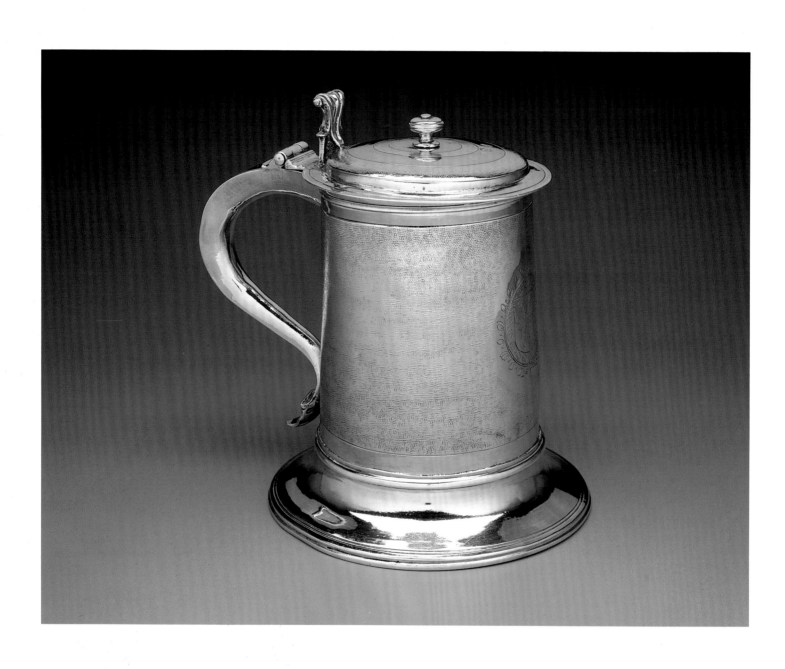

PLATE IX. 38. Tankard
London, 1639/40

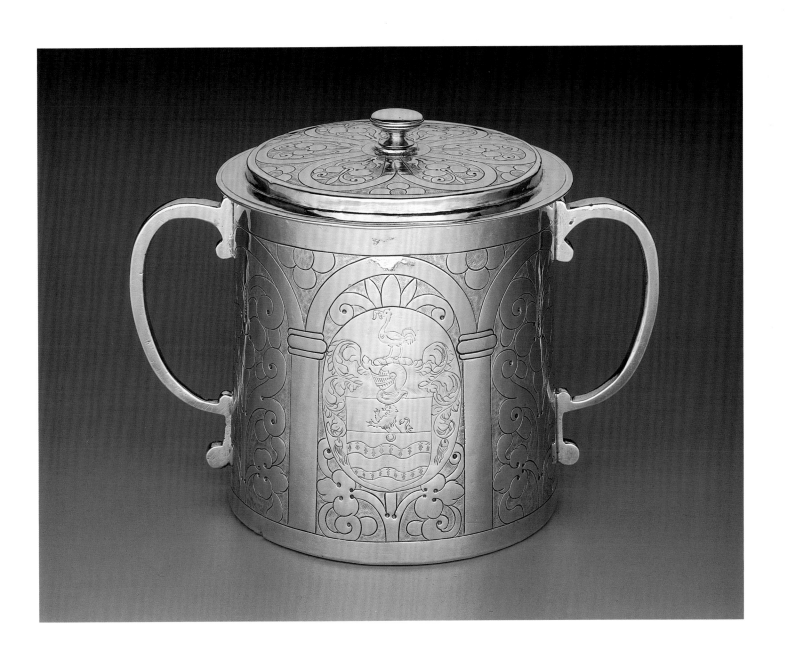

PLATE X. 45. Two-handled cup and cover
London, 1653/4

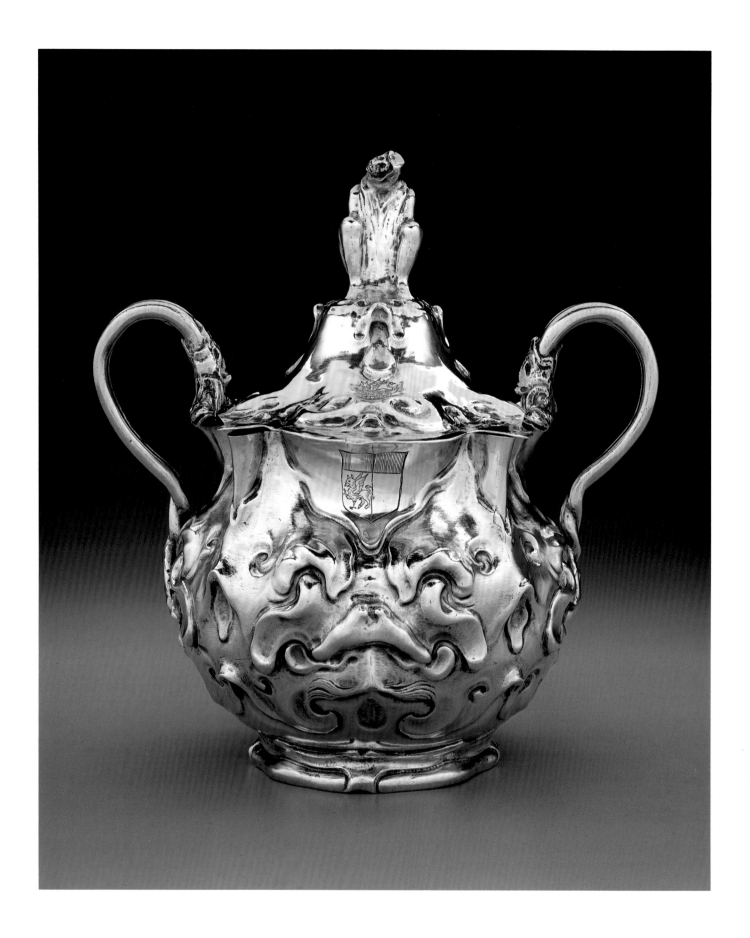

PLATE XI. 52. Two-handled cup and cover
Probably London, ca. 1660

PLATE XII. 58. Two-handled cup and cover
London, ca. 1665

PLATE XIII. 59. Tankard
London, Jacob Bodendick, ca. 1665

PLATE XIV. 66. Pair of andirons
London, Jacob Bodendick, 1671/2

PLATE XV. 71. Wax jack
London, ca. 1675/1685

PLATE XVI. 89. Teapot
London, ca. 1690

Use of Catalogue

The objects are catalogued in chronological order, followed by spoons and objects of doubtful authenticity. The conventional term "maker's mark" has been used in place of the less familiar "sponsor's mark." Marks are recorded as they appear on the object, from left to right or clockwise. Dimensions are listed in centimeters followed by inch equivalents. Unless otherwise indicated, the maximum dimension is recorded. The following abbreviations are used: H. = height; W. = width; d. = depth; diam. = diameter; L. = length.

Weights are listed in grams followed by troy equivalents. Weights are not provided for mounted wares or objects in which silver is not the primary medium.

Provenance cited is limited to documented owners; armorials are not taken as evidence of previous ownership, but are listed separately. The Museum's acquisition of an object is recorded on the date of the vote of the Trustees. A dealer bidding on behalf of the Museum of Fine Arts at auction is listed in square brackets following the sale date. A comma between the names of two former owners indicates that the piece passed directly from the first to the second. A semi-colon indicates a gap in documentation.

Observations on condition are incorporated into the section headed "construction."

References in the footnotes to objects in other collections include date, maker's mark, dimensions, and accession or inventory number whenever possible. Unless otherwise indicated, the place of manufacture is London, and the material is silver.

The following technical terms are used:

RAISING: A specific technique to achieve a hollow vessel form from flat sheet by hammering over iron or wooden stakes (anvils). The metal is gradually raised up and drawn in by hammering from bottom to top (a "course" of raising) in successive concentric circles. Stress created by the hammering is relieved by annealing after each course.

PLANISHING: The final hammering that smooths the rough marks made by raising. The planishing hammer is light and has a highly polished surface.

CAULKING: The gradual thickening of the rim of a hollow raised vessel. Made by hammering down evenly on the top edge after each course of raising.

FORMING: Used to create a small hollow object that is not raised but sunk with a round hammer or punched into a depression.

FABRICATING: Any technique used to make hollow geometric shapes from flat sheet, such as scoring, cutting, bending, filing, and soldering.

CHASING: Manipulating the exterior surface of an object with various hand-held hammer-struck punches. Pitch generally supports the piece. The result varies from a single fine line (flat chasing) to low relief. Matting punches create a textured or matt surface.

EMBOSSING (repoussé): Working a flat surface from the back with chasing punches to achieve higher relief. Usually the front is then chased to sharpen the design.

ENGRAVING: A surface decoration made by hand-held gravers or burins that remove a small amount of metal. The depth and angle of the cuts and the shape of the graver affect the quality of the engraved line. Pouncing (or pricking) and wriggle-work are variations.

CASTING: Two methods of casting have traditionally been used. For sand casting a model in wood, wax, lead, or other material is pressed into a bed of a compressed mixture of sand and binders and then removed. The molten silver is poured into the cavity. For lost wax casting a wax model is invested in clay or plaster and then "burnt" or melted out. The empty cavity is then filled with hot metal. Both techniques usually required some finishing work including filing, sanding, chasing, and polishing.

SWAGED: A plain wire or sheet that has been shaped by passing through molded iron or steel swage blocks in a screw frame. As the screw is turned the silver is compressed to conform to the profile of the swage blocks.

DRAWN WIRE: Similar to swaged wire, but the wire is pulled through an iron or steel drawplate with tapered holes. The wire is drawn through successively smaller holes until it reaches the desired diameter.

PUNCHING: A surface decoration created by hammering a hand-held steel punch usually to achieve a repeating pattern.

DIE-STAMPING: Similar to punching, but implying a more mechanical application using a carved iron or steel die into which the wire or sheet is hammered.

CUT-CARD WORK: Flat sheet cut into decorative outlines and soldered to the surface of an object.

I

• I •

MAZER
Probably London, ca. 1500–1525 with later
alterations
Burl maple with silver and silver-gilt
mounts
67.1017

Unmarked
H. 6 cm (2⅜ in.); diam. of rim 17.9 cm (7¹⁄₁₆
in.)

PROVENANCE: Sotheby & Co., London, November 17, 1966, lot 106, purchased by S. J. Phillips, London; purchased from John Hunt, Dublin, December 13, 1967, Theodora Wilbour Fund in Memory of Charlotte Beebe Wilbour.

EXHIBITED: New York, Cooper Hewitt Museum, 1985 (not in catalogue).

DESCRIPTION: The shallow bowl of finely burled wood has a low plain foot. The rim is fitted with a flaring silver-gilt band that is stamped with two bands of crosses formed of tiny pellets. Between the bands is a wrigglework pattern of a wavy line and semicircles with rays resembling sunflowers. At the center of the bowl is a gilt-silver molded boss, or "print," that is fitted in the center with a white silver disk engraved with the sacred monogram, IHS, enclosed in two interlocking squares.

CONSTRUCTION: The wood bowl is turned. There is a large crack near the rim and worm damage under the "print." The silver rim, which is formed and seamed, is pinned to the bowl in several places. The decoration on the rim is chased, stamped, and engraved. The gilding has been renewed.

Inventory records show that turned wood mazers, both plain and silver mounted, were owned in large numbers by religious houses, livery companies, and colleges in the first half of the sixteenth century, but by about 1550 they had fallen from favor. These relatively modest functional drinking vessels were never highly valued, and those that survive were probably preserved for sentimental reasons.[1] The two bands of stamped crosses and the engraved chevrons around the border of the rim of this mazer are similar to those on an example in the Gilbert Collection,[2] though the workmanship on the present example is cruder. As Timothy Schroder points out, precise dating of these pieces is difficult because of the absence of marks. The motif of the stamped crosses appears as early as 1380–1400 on the Studley Bowl[3] and is commonly used on mazers of the first quarter of the sixteenth century similar to the present example. In particular, see the mazer published by Evan-Thomas,[4] and the mounted coconut cup in the Ironmongers' Company, probably made about 1490–1510.[5]

Several features indicate that this mazer has been altered. The wriggle-work pattern of wavy lines around the rim does not have a parallel in sixteenth-century silver, and is more in keeping with nineteenth-century design. In addition, the seam on the rim is badly joined, suggesting that the rim may have been repaired or transferred from a slightly larger bowl. The silver collar around the "print" at the center of the bowl was either fabricated or reshaped by spinning.

1. Glanville, 1990, pp. 225–233. For a discussion of the use and origin of the term mazer, see Glanville, 1987, p. 16; Schroder, 1988, pp. 32–33; W. H. St. John Hope, "On the English Medieval Drinking Bowls Called Mazers," *Archaeologia* 50, no. 11 (1886), pp. 8–193; Edward H. Pinto, "Mazers and Their Wood," *Connoisseur* 123 (1949), pp. 33–36.
2. Schroder, 1988, cat. no. 1, p. 32.
3. Victoria and Albert Museum, acc. no. M.1-1914. See Oman, 1965, pls. 1, 2.
4. Owen Evan-Thomas, *Domestic Utensils of Wood* (London, 1932), pl. 1, p. 4.
5. The Ironmongers' Coconut Cup, unmarked, bequeathed to the Company in 1526, h. 21 cm, ill. Cooper, 1977, p. 413, fig. 36.

• 2 •

SANDGLASS
English or German, ca. 1550
Silver gilt, blown glass, silk, gold thread
57.533

Unmarked
H. (wall mounted, open) 22.1 cm (8 11/16 in.); w. 17.9 cm (7 1/16 in.); d. 6.5 cm (2 9/16 in.)

WEIGHT: 620.9 gm (19 oz 19 dwt)

PROVENANCE: purchased from John Hunt, Dublin, June 5, 1957, Theodora Wilbour Fund in Memory of Charlotte Beebe Wilbour.

EXHIBITED: Worcester, Massachusetts, Worcester Art Museum, 1969, cat. no. 8, p. 31; San Francisco, Fine Arts Museums of San Francisco, 1977, p. 54, fig. 72.

PUBLISHED: L. G. G. Ramsey, "A Holbein Hour-glass?," *Connoisseur* 134 (1954), p. 117[1]; Hayward, 1966, p. 90; Buhler, 1970, p. 74, fig. 12; Hayward, 1976, p. 366, pls. 301–302; Klaus

Maurice, "Wie Zeit lange verrinnt," *Kunst und Antiquitäten*, (1986), no. 3, p. 37; Glanville, 1987, p. 31; Schroder, 1988a, p. 35.

DESCRIPTION: The sandglass is mounted horizontally on a wall bracket with a reversible hinge. The bracket is surmounted with a cast crest composed of scrolls terminating in acanthus leaves and dolphins flanking the head of an angel. The molded edge of the bracket is dentiled, and triangular braces with pierced hanging mounts form the support. The circular ends of the sandglass are embossed with lobes alternately plain and chased with acanthus. The glass is enclosed by four columns, each with a central section composed of applied scrolling brackets joining the acanthus foliage on the column.

CONSTRUCTION: The elements of the bracket support are formed from wrought sheets. The cresting and the columns are cast, and the scrolls at the centers of the columns are composed of wires, chased and soldered together. The ends of the sandglass are formed from assembled wrought pieces, embossed, chased, die-struck, and flat-chased.

This is the only known silver sandglass of this design to have survived. Three C-shaped brackets allow the sandglass to be dropped to a vertical position from either side of the mount. Four other wall mounted sandglasses with a similar reversible hinge are known; all, however, are painted iron.[2] The construction and proportions of these glasses are very close to the present example, in particular, the four baluster supports enclosing the glass, and the scalloped edges of the hinge mechanism. There is a reference in the 1574 inventory of royal plate to a set of sandglasses, "four litell howre glasses in a Case of mother of pearle and in a box of Crimsen silke enbrauderid with golde and siluer gevon by Mrs. West."[3] They probably ran for fifteen minutes each; the present glass runs approximately one hour. Other silver sandglasses of the sixteenth century are of traditional construction, not wall mounted: one bears the arms of the King of Portugal, and a second bears the arms of Bavaria and the initials of Herzog Maximilian.[4]

L. G. G. Ramsey and John Hayward have pointed out similarities between this sandglass and designs for metalwork by Hans Holbein II (ca. 1497–1543). Hayward compares the columns of the sandglass and the acanthus foliage terminating with a dolphin's head to those in Holbein's sketch for a mirror frame.[5] A further comparison might be made in the asymmetrical treat-

2 (Color Plate 1)

ment of the putti adorning each object. Other Holbein images that repeat specific decorative features of the sandglass are the title page for Coverdale's English Bible, published in 1535 with woodcuts designed by Holbein.[6] A cresting composed of scrolling acanthus leaves surmounted by the head of a putto is used on an architectural molding similar to the bracket of the sandglass. The expressive modeling of the dolphin termini of the acanthus scrolls may also be seen on the brackets supporting a cup in a design by Holbein for a cup presented by Henry VIII to Jane Seymour.[7] Ramsey refers for comparison to Holbein's drawing of the clepsydra (waterclock) and sundial presented to Henry VIII by his Chamberlain, Sir Anthony Denny in 1544.[8] He correctly points out, however, that all the classicizing motifs used on the sandglass were common elements in the ornamental vocabulary of the early northern Renaissance. All of Holbein's designs for goldsmith's work are more ambitious in scale and more densely ornamented than the sandglass. The few surviving objects known to be after a Holbein design are much more finely worked, incorporating enamels, rock crystal, and precious and semiprecious stones.[9] The relative simplicity of this sandglass suggests that the association with Holbein is indirect and extremely tentative.

While the ornament and mechanism of the sandglass may be difficult to localize precisely, several distinctive features of the ornament may be assigned to either English or German traditions. The center sections of the columns are formed of applied brackets decorated along the spine with dentils or beads. This feature does not appear in marked English silver of the mid-sixteenth century, but is quite commonly used on German metalwork of the period.[10] Another ornamental motif that is uncommon on English silver appears on the ends of the sandglass. Between each raised lobe is a single chased line with a punched dot at each end. There are several German vessels on which this technique is used.[11] The sole ornamental feature on the sandglass that is more typical of English than German silver is the use of a punch to decorate the bands that form the ends of the glass. The question of whether the sandglass is of German or English manufacture must remain open; indeed, the exchange of designs, artisans, tools, and even molds between the two countries was so extensive in the middle decades of the sixteenth century that a definitive answer is probably impossible.

1. Ramsey does not indicate the ownership of the hourglass in this publication.
2. See A. J. Turner, *The Time Museum, Volume I, Time Measuring Instruments,* Part 3 (Rockford, 1984), cat. no. 8, pp. 86–89 for the early seventeenth-century example in The Time Museum, Rockford, Illinois. Three others are attributed by Turner to the same workshop; the first in the Victoria and Albert Museum, illustrated in W. C. Harford, "The Hour-Glass," *Connoisseur* 91 (1933), p. 164, no. 8, another in the Österreichische Museum für Angewandte Kunst, Vienna, illustrated in Henry René d'Allemagne, *Les Accessoires du Costume et du Mobilier,* vol. 2 (Paris, 1928), pl. 178, no. 1, and a third of about 1550 surmounted by figures of Adam and Eve, ill. Anton Lübke, *Das grosse Uhrenbuch* (Tübingen, 1977), p. 112, fig. 202.

3. Collins, 1955, p. 552.

4. Museu Nacional de Arte Antiga, Lisbon, acc. no. 109, Sandglass, first quarter of the sixteenth century, ill. Leonor B. S. d'Orey, *Ourivesaria Portuguesa no Museu de Arte Antiga* (Lisbon, 1984), p. 6, pl. 4; Schatzkammer der Residenz, Munich, Sandglass, ca. 1596–1600, German, parcel gilt, h. 9.5 cm, ill. Helmut Seling, *Die Kunst der Augsburger Goldschmiede 1529–1868* (Munich, 1980), cat. no. 246, p. 258.

5. See Hayward, 1976, p. 366. He refers to a pen and ink drawing in the Öffentliche Kunstsammlung, Basel, ill. Paul Ganz, *Handzeichnungen von Hans Holbein dem Jüngeren* (Berlin, 1923), fig. 45.

6. Ill. Hind, 1952, pl. 5.

7. Hayward, 1976, pl. 41, p. 341. Glanville (1987, p. 31) points out that the dolphin brackets appeared on other English wares of the first half of the sixteenth century; compare the handles of a covered cup of 1555/6 at Corpus Christi College, Cambridge, ill. Hayward, 1976, pl. 304, p. 366.

8. L. G. G. Ramsey, "A Holbein Hour-glass?," *Connoisseur* 134 (1954), p. 117. The drawing to which he refers is in the British Museum, and is illustrated in Ganz, op. cit., fig. 49.

9. Hayward, 1976, pls. 645–647, p. 400.

10. See, for example, a cup of about 1540 attributed to Erasmus Krug, Strasbourg, in the Schroder Collection (Schroder, 1983, cat. no. 7, pp. 43–46) which has similarly decorated brackets applied to the stem and finial.

11. See, for example, a Nürnberg flagon of about 1540, on which the lines and dots are used in the center of raised lobes on the body, cover, and foot. See H. Kohlhaussen, *Nürnberger Goldschmiedekunst des Mittelalters und der Dürerzeit* (Berlin, 1968), cat. no. 485, fig. 711. A similar motif appears on a Stuttgart beaker of about 1570 at Brodrick Castle, exhibited London, Spink & Son, 1980, cat. no. 11.

· 3 ·

MALLING JUG
London, 1550/1
Tin-glazed earthenware (English or Netherlandish, ca. 1550) with silver-gilt mounts
49.475

MARKS: on top of cover, maker's mark crowned cross moline (Jackson, 1921, p. 96; rev. ed. 1989, p. 92); date letter *N*; lion passant; on foot, underside of hinge, and hinge near thumbpiece, French import mark used after 1738, boar's head in a triangle

ARMORIALS: engraved on inside cover, the arms of Powlett, Dukes of Bolton

H. 18.1 cm (7⅛ in.); diam. of base 9.9 cm (3⅞ in.); w. 11.9 cm (4¹¹⁄₁₆ in.)

PROVENANCE: Samuel Montagu (Lord Swaythling), sold Christie, Manson & Woods, London, May 6, 1924, lot 109; William Randolph Hearst; Joseph Brummer, sold Parke Bernet, New York, April 20–23, 1949, lot 452, purchased May 12, 1949, Theodora Wilbour Fund in Memory of Charlotte Beebe Wilbour.

EXHIBITED: London, St. James's Court, 1903, pl. 48, fig. 1 (not in catalogue).

PUBLISHED: Bernard Rackham and Herbert Read, *English Pottery* (London, 1924), pl. 49, fig. 85; Jones, 1929, p. 345, fig. 2; Honey, 1933, p. 36, fig. 4; Edward Wenham, "Silver Mounted Pottery," *Connoisseur* 97 (1936), p. 253, no. 6; Robert J. Charleston and D. F. Lunsingh Scheurleer, *Masterpieces of Western and Near Eastern Ceramics 7 English and Dutch Ceramics* (Tokyo, 1979), p. 295, fig. 4.

DESCRIPTION: The body of the jug is a light gray earthenware. The bulbous body rises to a short neck, with a C-shaped handle joining the shoulder. The mottled glaze ranges in color from a medium to a dark cobalt with traces of manganese near the handle. There are numerous chips and flaws in the glaze. The silver foot rim is decorated with a stamped wire. The silver collar has a large stamped decoration in a cross pattern. The cover has a reeded flange with decorative punching. It is attached to the handle by a hinged strap, which has worn away much of the glaze from the handle. There is a high open hinge with a thumbpiece formed of twisted fruits and foliage. The slightly domed cover is engraved with an interlacing pattern of serpents, strapwork, and bunches of fruit and foliage suspended from the strapwork. At the center is a baluster finial.

CONSTRUCTION: The jug is wheel thrown from a light, finely grained earthenware, and glazed with a thick, opaque tin glaze that is cobalt in color with flecks of manganese. The interior has an opaque white glaze. The silver cover is raised and engraved and has an applied wire rim. The seamed collar on the pottery is die-stamped. The foot rim is also formed of several pieces of stamped wire. The finial and thumbpiece are cast. The cover has been extensively repaired, especially around the top rim. The gilding has been renewed.

The term "Malling jug" refers to a group of short-necked, bulbous jugs traditionally thought to represent the earliest tin-glazed earthenware made in England and named after a single jug found in the parish of West Malling, Kent, now in the British Museum.[1] The form is related to Rhenish stoneware jugs which, by the third quarter of the sixteenth century, were being im-

44

glazes which includes, in addition to the dark cobalt used here, a powdered blue and manganese[4] and a bright blue or turquoise.[5] Like the present example, most seem to have a colored exterior with a white glazed interior.

A number of features raise the possibility that the cover of the present jug may have originally belonged to another piece. It is too large for the neck, and the angle of the thumbpiece prevents the cover from being lifted. The dentiled tooling on the rim of the cover does not match that used on the foot.[6] Though the style of the engraving on the cover is unusual, there are numerous other parallels for the thumbpiece and the finial.[7] A second unusual feature is the broad band of stamping on the collar mount; the only other example of this of which I am aware appears on a jug in the Gilbert Collection.[8]

1. British Museum acc. no. MLA 1987,7-2,1. Exhibited London, St. James's Court, 1903, pl. 47, fig. 2.
2. F. H. Garner and Michael Archer, *English Delftware* (London, 1972), p. 4. See also Ivor Noël Hume, *Early English Delftware from London and Virginia* (Williamsburg, 1977), pp. 2–3, for a summary. Hume proposes, in the absence of archaeological evidence, a Continental origin for the jugs.
3. See the jug from the Franks Bequest in the British Museum (Read, 1928, cat. no. 28, p. 12) and another in the Victoria and Albert Museum, acc. no. M33-1929.
4. See, for example, the jug from the Rous Lench Collection, sold at Sotheby's, London, July 1, 1986, lot 69. (The illustration is incorrectly numbered 70.)
5. See, for example, the mounted jug of about 1580 sold at Christie, Manson & Woods, London, October 3, 1984, lot 430. See also cat. no. 32.
6. They would have been assembled, however, before the application of the French import mark, which appears on both the hinge and the foot.
7. For other examples of the thumbpiece, see the Malling jug from the Rous Lench Collection, sold at Sotheby's, London, July 1, 1986, lot 69, cited above, and the mounted stoneware jug in the Vintners' Company, illustrated in Watts, 1924, pl. 24b.
8. Schroder, 1988, cat. no. 40, pp. 40–43. The mounts of the jug are not hallmarked, and the band of stamped ornament appears on the foot rim, an unusual use of such decoration. The body of the vessel is marked by Benjamin Pyne, and Schroder suggests that it was made to replace a glass original.

3

ported to England in large numbers. Until recently, the pottery was thought to have been produced in or near London, though the specific kiln sites have never been identified.[2] Since three mounted jugs were found in Kent, it was theorized that a potter, probably a Flemish immigrant, had established a kiln in Sandwich. The tradition is much disputed, however, and it has also been suggested that these tin-glazed pieces were imported from Germany or the Low Countries, to be mounted in London. The earliest mounted tin-glazed jugs bear hallmarks of 1549/50,[3] and the latest examples date from the first decade of the seventeenth century. There is a broad variety of

4 (Color Plate II)

FLAGON
English or German, ca. 1560–70
Marble with silver-gilt mounts
49.476

Unmarked
H. 24.5 cm (9⅝ in.); w. 14.9 cm (5⅞ in.); diam.
of foot 12.1 cm (4¾ in.)

PROVENANCE: by tradition Great Stukeley Hall, Huntingdon, collection of Captain C. Torkington (unverified),[1] until ca. 1852; sold Christie, Manson & Woods, London, June 13, 1907, lot 66; Samuel Montagu (Lord Swaythling), sold Christie, Manson & Woods, London, May 6, 1924, lot 124, purchased by Crichton Brothers, London; Estate of Joseph Brummer, sold Parke Bernet, New York, April 20–23, 1949, lot 453, purchased May 12, 1949, Theodora Wilbour Fund in Memory of Charlotte Beebe Wilbour.

EXHIBITED: Worcester, Massachusetts, Worcester Art Museum, 1969, cat. no. 64, p. 124; San Francisco, Fine Arts Museums of San Francisco, 1977, cat. no. 63.

PUBLISHED: Jackson, 1911, vol. 2, p. 778, fig. 1011; Jones, 1929, p. 348; Wenham, 1931, pl. 41; Glanville, 1985, p. 22, fig. 8.

DESCRIPTION: The cylindrical body of the flagon is of highly polished gray marble with dark red, brown, and green inclusions. It rests on a molded silver-gilt foot embossed with strapwork and engraved on the rim with a reeded pattern. The rim of the flagon is mounted with a broad band of embossed strapwork with clusters of fruit. Immediately below is a narrow molded band chased with strapwork; two identical bands are applied to the rim of the domed cover and to the base of the flagon, serving as an attachment for the base of the handle. The handle is ear shaped with a scrolled terminus decorated with a mask and a lion's foot. The spine of the handle is engraved with a scrolling vine, and the thumbpiece is cast in the form of two profile masks within addorsed scrolls. The baluster finial rests on a domed collar that is embossed with clusters of fruit; the interior fitting for the finial is in the form of an embossed rose.

CONSTRUCTION: The stone vessel is turned from a single piece of marble. The domed silver foot is raised, joined to several molded wires, and fixed to the marble body with a serrated bezel. The two bands at the bottom and top of the body of the vessel are formed and secured with a hinge attachment behind the handle. The upper part of the handle is formed and assembled; the terminus, thumbpiece, and finial are cast. The collar at the top of the vessel and the rim on the cover are embossed; the latter is attached to the marble with a serrated bezel.

The marble of which this flagon is composed may be an ancient piece of "Africano" marble, quarried in Teos in Asia Minor and shipped to Rome.[2] Ancient architectural fragments or pieces of sculpture excavated during the Renaissance were often recut and embellished with silver or gold mounts.[3] Occasionally these vessels are hallmarked, but more often the attribution and dating must be based on the style of the mounts.

Certain features of the silver mounts on this flagon are uncharacteristic of English design in the mid-sixteenth century, particularly the complex terminus of the handle and the broad bands of strapwork embossed in high relief without stamped borders. The close connections between English and German goldsmiths' work during the third quarter of the sixteenth century have only been explored in a preliminary way,[4] and it is impossible to know if the present flagon is the work of an English or German goldsmith. The richly textured mounts are similar to those on a serpentine standing cup in the Schroder Collection that is thought to have been made in Aachen or Frankfurt.[5] The pattern of the strapwork on the embossed bands is more complex and is worked more precisely and in higher relief than that found on most English pieces of the period. Even in the context of German silver, the prominence of the individual pieces of fruit, regularly spaced in the strapwork, is unusual. Comparison might be made to a flagon marked by the Hamburg maker Peter Henninges I before 1591, on which a band of large apples or melons is enclosed in simplified strapwork with detailing similar to that of the present example.[6] In the Gilbert Collection there is a rock-crystal tankard with Strasbourg mounts of about 1560 that has similar embossed motifs as well as a band of laurel leaves around the edge of the foot, as on the present example.[7] Related English objects include a mounted marble tankard bearing London marks for 1575 that was exhibited at Seaford House in 1929.[8] This cylindrical marble tankard is fitted with broad gilt bands that are heavily chased, and the terminus of the thumbpiece, though more elaborate than the present example, also features a lion's foot. While a firm attribution remains impossible, the balance of evidence leans slightly towards a German origin.

1. A note written by Captain C. Torkington (1847–d. after 1910) accompanies the object. "With regard to the Tankard I regret to say that I have never been able to trace its history, but I know that it has been in my family for a great number of years. It was removed from Great Stukeley Hall, Huntingdon about the year 1852 when the house was dismantled." Stukeley Hall was built about 1830 for James Torkington, and the tankard is not listed in a sale of property from the house on April 27–29, 1852, following his death.

2. I am grateful to John Herrmann for his observations on this subject. See Raniero Gnoli, *Mormora Romano* (Rome, 1971), fig. 133.

3. For examples see Hans R. Hanloser and Susanne Brugger-Koch, *Corpus der Hartsteinschliffe des 12.–15. Jahrhunderts* (Berlin, 1985), especially nos. 497–499.

4. See Hayward, 1966, p. 94.

5. See Schroder, 1983, cat. no. 29, pp. 99–102. The stem of the Schroder cup is identical in design to a group of pieces marked in London; Schroder (1983a, pp. 40–46) discusses this complex group. See also Hayward, 1976, pp. 301–303, and Glanville, 1987, pp. 223–228.

6. Museum für Kunst und Gewerbe, acc. no. 1916.163. See Renate Scholz, ed., *Goldschmiedearbeiten: Renaissance und Barock* (Hamburg, 1974), cat. no. 8, pp. 80–81.

7. It bears the mark of the Strasbourg maker Diebolt Krug. See Schroder, 1988, cat. no. 133, pp. 492–496.

8. The tankard, with the maker's mark of a bird, was lent by Lord Shelborne. Exhibited London, Seaford House, 1929, no. 60, pl. 22.

· 5 ·

EWER AND BASIN
London, 1567/8
Silver, parcel gilt
1979.261–262

MARKS: on underside of basin, maker's mark a pick or sythe (similar to Jackson, 1921, p. 101), lion passant, leopard's head crowned, date letter *k* with a difference

INSCRIPTIONS: engraved twice in central medallion of basin, engraver's monogram *P* over *M*

1979.261 (ewer): H. 33.8 cm (13⁵⁄16 in.); diam. of foot 10.9 cm (4⁵⁄16 in.)

1979.262 (basin): H. 5.4 cm (2⅛ in.); diam. 50 cm (19¹¹⁄16 in.)

WEIGHT: 1979.261: 1,247.4 gm (40 oz 2 dwt). 1979.262: 3,047.7 gm (98 oz)

PROVENANCE: Philip Herbert, fourth Earl of Pembroke and Montgomery (1584–1650), Anne Clifford, Dowager Countess of Dorset, Pem-

broke, and Montgomery (1590–1676), Nicholas Tufton, third Earl of Thanett (1631–1679); Crichton Brothers, London, J. P. Morgan (1867–1943), sold Parke Bernet, New York, November 1, 1947, lot 466,[1] purchased by C. Ruxton Love, New York; purchased from S. J. Shrubsole, New York, May 16, 1979, The G. H. and E. A. Payne Fund; Anonymous Gift in Memory of Charlotte Beebe Wilbour; Bequest of Frank Brewer Bemis; Theodora Wilbour Fund in Memory of Charlotte Beebe Wilbour; The M. & M. Karolik Collection of 18th century American Arts; Gift of G. Churchill Francis; Gift of the Trustees of Reservation, Estate of Mrs. John Gardner Coolidge; Gift of Phillips Ketchum in memory of John R. Macomber; Gift of Mrs. Richard Cary Curtis; Gift in Memory of Dr. William Hewson Baltzell by his wife, Alice Cheney Baltzell; Gift of Mr. and Mrs. Richard Storey in memory of Mr. Richard Cutts Storey; Gift of Mrs. John B. Sullivan, Jr.; Gift of Mrs. Heath-Jones; Bequest of Mrs. Thomas O. Richardson; Bequest of Charles Hitchcock Tyler; Gift of Miss Caroline M. Dalton; Bequest of Clara Bennett; Maria Antoinette Evans Fund; Gift of Miss E. E. P Holland, by exchange.

PUBLISHED: Yvonne Hackenbroch, "A Mysterious Monogram," *Bulletin of the Metropolitan Museum of Art* (1960), pp. 18–24; Came, 1961, p. 24; Clayton, 1971, p. 132 (mentioned), rev. ed. 1985, p. 181 (mentioned); Oman, 1978, p. 143; Museum of Fine Arts, Boston, *Masterpieces from the Boston Museum* (Boston, 1981), no. 42; Thomas E. Norton, *100 years of Collecting in America* (New York, 1984), p. 147; S. J. Shrubsole Corp., *50 Years on 57th Street* (New York, 1986), cat. no. 75; Glanville, 1987, p. 211 (mentioned); Glanville, 1990, p. 153, fig. 70.

DESCRIPTION: The circular basin has a broad rim with a molded wire edge, a deep depression, and a raised boss. The center of the boss is engraved with a scene of Joshua's battle with Amelek (Exodus 17). Around the boss is the engraved inscription: *SANGUIS IESU CHRISTI FILY DEI EMVNDAT NOS AB OMNI PECCATO IOHANNIS I CV.* (The blood of Jesus Christ, Son of God, cleanseth us from all sin.) The well of the basin is engraved with four portrait roundels framed by laurel garlands. Depicted are: Elizabeth I, Mary I, Edward VI, and Henry VIII. Between the roundels are engraved scenes of Abraham's journey through Canaan (Genesis 12), Lot seduced by his daughters (Genesis 19), the sacrifice of Isaac (Genesis 22), and Rebecca at the well (Genesis 24). The outer rim of the basin is divided by eight roundels depicting Edward V, Edward IV, Henry VI, Henry V, Henry IV, Edward II, Henry VII, and Richard III. Between the roundels are engraved scenes of the birth of Jacob and Esau (Genesis 25), the worship of the golden calf (Exodus 32), the Israelites departing for Egypt (Exodus 13), Passover

5 (Color Plate III)

(Exodus 12), Aaron casting his rod before the Pharoh (Exodus 7), Joseph interpreting the Pharoh's dream (Genesis 41), Joseph and Potiphar's wife (Genesis 39), and Joseph cast into the pit (Genesis 37).

The ewer is vase-shaped, with a domed molded foot, a spool-shaped stem, and a tapering neck flaring to a broad, shaped lip with a gadrooned edge. The handle is ear-shaped with a scrolling terminus. The body of the ewer is decorated with portraits of the sovereigns in two registers. Around the shoulder are five circular medallions with portrait profiles of Edward III, Edward II, Edward I, Henry III, and John. Around the body of the vessel in elliptical panels are engraved standing portraits of Richard I, Henry II, Stephen, Henry I, William Rufus, and William I. On the basin and the ewer, the engraved panels are left white, and the enframing garlands are gilt.

CONSTRUCTION: The basin is raised, with a molded wire applied to the rim. The central boss is composed of a raised rim with a flat disk let in to the center; it is riveted to the basin. The body of the ewer is formed from two raised sections, with a molded wire covering the join. The foot is assembled from a raised domed section with a wire rim, a raised stem, and a fabricated collar. The handle is formed of two pieces. The lip of the ewer has been damaged.

The ewer and basin are engraved with portraits of all the sovereigns of England from William the Conquerer to Elizabeth I and with biblical scenes illustrating passages from Genesis and Exodus.[2] In the central medallion the engraver placed his monogram *P* over *M* on the shield of one of the slain soldiers and again on a banner held above the battle, where it is flanked by the date *1567*. The date letter *k* is marked with a difference, a pellet under the letter, used after Christmas 1567, when Thomas Keelynge succeeded Richard Rogers as Assay Master, until May 19, 1568. The ambitious iconographic scheme and the fine quality of the engraved decoration are unique in the context of Tudor silver.

Charles Oman identified six groups of objects decorated with finely engraved scenes and attributed them all to the monogrammist *P* over *M*. In addition to the present ewer and basin, he recorded a set of twelve plates engraved with Old Testament subjects in the Metropolitan Museum of Art,[3] a set of twelve plates engraved with the Labors of Hercules in the Fowler Collection,[4] a set of twelve plates engraved with the parable of the Prodigal Son in the collection of the Duke of Buccleuch,[5] a

ewer and basin decorated with Old Testament subjects in the Toledo Museum of Art,[6] and a set of six bowls engraved with Old Testament subjects and sea monsters in the Victoria and Albert Museum.[7] The plates in the Fowler Collection and the Metropolitan Museum and the present ewer and basin bear the engraver's monogram; the bowls in the Victoria and Albert Museum, the plates in the Buccleuch Collection, and the ewer and basin in Toledo are unsigned. Philippa Glanville has recently observed that the style of the engraving on the Victoria and Albert bowls has little in common with the work of *P* over *M,* and suggested that the bowls are by another hand.[8]

The identity of the monogrammist *P* over *M* has not yet been established. As Yvonne Hackenbroch pointed out, Pieter Maas must be ruled out since he was only active after 1577.[9] The absence of comparable work in England in the second half of the sixteenth century[10] strongly suggests that he was a Continental engraver; it is possible that he was active in London for a short period or that finished pieces of plain silver were sent abroad for decoration. The selection of printed designs used as sources for this group of objects is not revealing; Bernard Salomon's woodcuts that served as the model for the engraved scenes on the present ewer and basin, on the Toledo ewer and basin, and on the Metropolitan Museum's plates were widely distributed and adopted by craftsmen in many media.[11] The designs have been altered as needed to fill the irregular spaces of the objects, and the engraver has inserted details and extended the landscapes in many scenes with confidence.

The graphic source for the series of royal portraits on the present ewer and basin has puzzled historians. It is likely that the engraver based the designs on a series of woodcuts published in London in 1562/3 by Giles Godet.[12] The series depicts the genealogy of the kings of England, showing their descent from Noah, with each portrait accompanied by a short text. The scale and design of the portraits change with the end of the Saxon kings. This may be attributed to the fact that Godet's designs were based on a series of English royal portraits from William the Conquerer to Henry VII published in Antwerp by Dirick Vellert (active ca. 1511–1544) in 1534.[13] Godet borrowed Vellert's compositions, grouping the sovereigns in threes, alternating between profile and three-quarters views, placing a coat of arms above, and a translation of Vellert's text below.

Charles Oman discounted the possibility that Godet's *Genealogie of Kynges* was the model for *P* over *M*'s portraits, pointing out that the early kings in particular did not resemble the woodcuts.[14] With only a few exceptions, however, the facial types and attributes are identical, and the variations may be attributed to the silver engraver's need to fill a larger, sometimes asymmetrical, space. Vellert's series ended with Henry II, and Godet has filled in the remaining figures after various sources in a stiffer, less decorative style. His portrait of Elizabeth, printed on a separate sheet of paper, is related to a type attributed to Hans Huys and published by Hieronimus Cock, in which the queen wears a dark robe slashed and trimmed with fur.[15] On the ewer and basin *P* over *M* has followed Godet's formula for his portraits of Henry VIII, Edward VI, and Mary I. The source for his portrait of Elizabeth remains uncertain. The queen is shown wearing a gown with a patterned bodice, slashed sleeves, and a square neckline with a gathered partlet and a small ruff. The design does not appear in the recorded portraits of Elizabeth, except the engraving by Remigius Hogenberg.[16]

The ewer and basin are not recorded in the 1574 inventory of the Jewel-house. The earliest reference to them is in the 1674 will of Anne Clifford, Dowager Countess of Dorset, Pembroke, and Montgomery (1590–1676) where they are bequeathed to her grandson the Earl and Countess of Thanett and described as "my silver bason and ewer, with the Scripture history, and some of the kings of England, curiously engraven upon them, and 12 silver plates of the same workemanshipp, which were my last lord's the Earle of Pembroke's."[17] The plates referred to are almost certainly those in the Metropolitan Museum. Anne Clifford married first Richard Sackville, second Earl of Dorset (d. 1624) and second Philip Herbert, fourth Earl of Pembroke and first Earl of Montgomery (1584–1650). Pembroke, who is thought to have been named for his maternal uncle, Sir Philip Sidney, was the younger son of William Herbert, first Earl of Pembroke (1501?–1570), whose extensive holdings of plate are recorded in an inventory of 1561 with additions to 1567. Included in the list of 127 items were twenty-nine pieces of gold; the present ewer and basin are not recorded.[18] It is possible that it was given by the queen to the first Earl of Pembroke, or it may have been accepted from the royal collection in exchange for a loan.[19] The dynastic imagery on the set suggests that it must have been made for presentation to or by the queen. Since the piece was completed after Christmas 1567, it is tempting to assume that it was a New Year's gift, but the 1567 Gift Rolls do not include a reference to it.[20] There remains the possibility that the piece came into the hands of the fourth Earl of Pembroke through another source. Anne Clifford's description of it in her will, however, makes clear that it was a treasured family heirloom.

1. The sale catalogue indicated that the ewer and basin had descended in the Hyde family, but this cannot be substantiated. A similar claim was made of the set of twelve plates now in the Buccleuch Collection when sold from Strawberry Hill (April 24, 1842, lot 88).

2. An error was made in the decoration of the rim of the basin, and Edward II is shown in place of Richard II.

3. Acc. no. 65.260.1–12, Set of plates, probably London, ca. 1565–1570, marked Strasbourg, diam. 20 cm, ill. Oman, 1978, fig. 30, see also Yvonne Hackenbroch, "A Mysterious Monogram," *Bulletin of the Metropolitan Museum of Art* (1960), pp. 20–24. Nine of the plates are engraved with scenes after Bernard Salomon's *Quadrins Historiques de la Bible* (Lyons, 1553); the remaining scenes may be represented in an earlier edition.

4. Set of twelve plates, 1567, maker's mark a hooded falcon, diam. 20 cm, ill. Oman, 1978, pl. 32, p. 38. Three of the plates bear the *P* over *M* monogram. The scenes of the Labors of Hercules are based on a series of designs by Heinrich Aldegraver (1502–ca. 1558). See also John Hayward, "English and Irish Silver in the Francis E. Fowler Jr. Museum in Beverly Hills, California: Part 1," *Connoisseur* 178, no. 716 (1971), pp. 115–118.

5. Set of twelve plates, 1568, maker's mark of Roger Flynt, diam. 19 cm, ill. Oman, 1978, figs. 36–37.

6. Acc. no. 83.80, 81, Ewer and basin, German, 1575, maker's mark *BI* in an oval, diam. of basin 48 cm, ill. Oman, 1978, figs. 40–41, p. 44. The engraved scenes on the ewer depict the story of Joseph after Virgil Solis. The scenes of the story of Abraham are based on Bernard Salomon's *Quadrins Historique de la Bible*.

7. Acc. no. M55a-1946–M55f-1946, Set of six bowls, 1573/4, maker's mark for Roger Flynt, diam. 25.2 cm, ill. Oman, 1978, figs. 38–39. See also Glanville, 1990, cat. nos. 72a–f, pp. 444–445.

8. Glanville, 1990, p. 444.

9. Hackenbroch, *op. cit.,* p. 23.

10. As Philippa Glanville has pointed out, there are numerous inventory references to elaborately engraved plate, but the survival of such pieces is limited to the present group. See Glanville, 1990, p. 217.

11. Salomon's designs were used most frequently on Limoges enamels, but they also appear in silver; see for example the repoussé medallion in the center of the standing bowl from St. Michael's Church, Southampton, exhibited New York, *Britain Salutes New York*, 1983, p. 36.

12. Giles Godet (Godett or Godhed) was granted denization in 1551. (Ernest James Worman, *Alien Members of the Book Trade During the Tudor Period* [London, 1906], p. 25.) The *Genealogie of Kynges* is his best known work; the copy at the British Library has a note bound in stating "I have heard of no other copy of this book except one at Althorp."

13. British Library, Dirick Vellert, *Prologhe van allen den Coninghen in Enghelant,* Antwerp, 1534.

14. Oman, 1978, p. 54 note 6.

15. See Hind, 1952, p. 41a–b.

16. Ill. Janet Arnold, *Queen Elizabeth's Wardrobe Unlock'd* (Leeds, 1988), fig. 11, p. 15.

17. George C. Williamson, *Lady Anne Clifford* (Kendal, 1922), p. 467. I am very grateful to Philippa Glanville for this reference.

18. Manuscript in the Victoria and Albert Museum; transcript in the Department of Metalwork, Victoria and Albert Museum.

19. The Earl of Pembroke received a "folding table covered all over with silver plate ingraven" from the Jewel-house in 1649. See Hervey George St. John Mildmay, "Account of Papers Relating to the Royal Jewel-house in the Sixteenth and Seventeenth Centuries," *Archaelogia* 48 (1884) p. 215.

20. British Museum Add. 9772.

6

JUG

London, 1569/70
Salt-glazed stoneware (Frechen [near Cologne], ca. 1560–1590) with silver-gilt mounts
49.581

MARKS: on edge of neck, on cover, and on foot rim, date letter *m*; lion passant; leopard's head crowned; maker's mark *WC* above a grasshopper (Jackson, 1921, p. 103; rev. ed. 1989, p. 95).

H. 23.2 cm (9⅛ in.); w. 13.3 cm (5¼ in.); diam. of base 10.6 cm (4³⁄₁₆ in.)

PROVENANCE: J. Toovey, Esq., by 1862 (?),[1] by descent to Charles James Toovey, Esq., London, sold Christie, Manson & Woods, London, February 9, 1926, lot 117; purchased from Spink & Son (Canada), September 15, 1949, Theodora Wilbour Fund in Memory of Charlotte Beebe Wilbour.

EXHIBITED: London, South Kensington Museum, 1862, cat. no. 5,729.

DESCRIPTION: The reddish brown pottery jug has a bulbous body, a tall neck, and a C-shaped handle. The broad silver-gilt mount on the neck is engraved with interlacing strapwork enclosing foliage. It is joined to the handle by a hinged mount supporting a box hinge. The domed cover has a flat rim and is embossed in high relief with clusters of fruit alternating with lions' masks. The baluster finial rests on a disk with engraved rays. The thumbpiece is in the form of two oak branches with acorn terminals. The molded foot rim is stamped with ovolo and beaded decoration.

CONSTRUCTION: The pottery jug is wheel thrown from a light colored gray stoneware and salt glazed. The silver foot rim is composed of three molded and stamped wires with a serrated bezel attachment. The edge of the mount on the top of the handle is broken off in a straight line; it was probably originally finished with a cut edge in the shape of an acanthus leaf. The neck rim and box hinge are formed and engraved; the thumbpiece is cast. The cover is raised, embossed, and chased, with a molded wire supporting the engraved rayed disk and cast finial. There are two small areas of trial engraving; one section of hit-and-miss decoration on the bands of strapwork on the collar, and an acanthus leaf sketched on the inside of the hinge below the thumbpiece.

The history of mounted stoneware pots has recently been the subject of considerable research prompted by concerns about the authenticity of the numerous surviving examples.[2] Salt-glazed stoneware was exported to England in large quantity from several Rhenish sites from the fourteenth century. The steady flow of stoneware continued through the first half of the seventeenth century. A number of these objects were mounted with silver that was usually, though not always, gilt.

Although there are inventory references to mounted stoneware pots from the first half of the sixteenth century, most surviving examples with marked mounts date from the years between 1560 and 1590. At least nine bear the maker's mark described by Jackson as *WC* above a grasshopper,[3] although the device is sometimes interpreted as a pig. These range in date between 1567 and 1577. A jug of 1568 bears mounts that are virtually identical to the present example with a similar box hinge engraved with a panel of foliage and a strap mount affixing it to the handle.[4]

1. Lender to the 1862 South Kensington Museum exhibition. The catalogue description is general enough to leave some doubt as to whether this was the object shown; the maker's mark is not included, and the height is listed as 9 inches.
2. See Glanville, 1990, pp. 329–338, for a discussion of the documentary evidence regarding the ownership and usage of these pieces. Problems of authenticity are discussed in Glanville, 1989.
3. Jackson, 1921, p. 103.
4. Jug, 1568, maker's mark *WC* above a grasshopper, h. 22.9 cm, with Spink & Son, London, ill. *Antique Dealer and Collector's Guide* (August 1978), p. 56.

· 7 ·

Coconut cup
Probably Hugh Kayle (first mentioned 1569, d. 1604)
London, 1574/5
Coconut shell with silver-gilt mounts
33.60

MARKS: on rim near handle, on cover near finial, and on underside of base, maker's mark *HK* conjoined an ermine spot below in a shaped shield (similar to Jackson, 1921, p. 98; rev. ed. 1989, p. 95); leopard's head crowned; lion passant; date letter *r* (struck twice on base)

H. 24 cm (9⁷⁄₁₆ in.); w. 17 cm (6¹¹⁄₁₆ in.); diam. of rim 10.5 cm (4⅛ in.)

PROVENANCE: Colonel Legh, High Legh Hall, Cheshire, sold Christie, Manson & Woods, London, March 22, 1906, lot 90, purchased by Molineux; Crichton Brothers, London, by 1928; Anonymous Gift in Memory of Charlotte Beebe Wilbour (1833–1914), March 2, 1933.

EXHIBITED: London, British Antique Dealers' Association, 1928, cat. no. 924 (lent by Crichton Brothers, London); Boston, Museum of Fine Arts, 1933 (no catalogue); Cambridge, Massachusetts, Fogg Art Museum, 1937, cat. no. 18.

PUBLISHED: Hipkiss, 1933, pp. 25, 27.

DESCRIPTION: The coconut shell is supported by a flaring fluted stem on a domed foot that is embossed with strapwork, fruit, and flowers. Projecting moldings have punched egg-and-dart decoration. The mount is secured with three hinged straps depicting caryatid figures that are attached at the top to a flaring rim engraved with birds entwined in foliage. The S-shaped handle is joined to the stem with a hinged strap and is soldered to the rim. It is engraved with birds and foliage on the spine and with cross-hatching on the terminus. The domed cover is embossed with strapwork enclosing heads and clusters of fruit and has a punched rim. The baluster finial rests on a raised, rayed disk and is attached to the cover with later rivets. The cast thumbpiece depicts a grotesque face in symmetrical strapwork.

CONSTRUCTION: The foot, stem, and cover are raised, fabricated, and embossed. The handle is formed and engraved. The thumbpiece, finial, and straps are cast. The foot has been reattached, and the finial is secured by later rivets. The surface is worn and pitted overall, and the gilding is flaking in several places on the cover. The short strap extending from the foot to the base of the handle has been repaired and may be a restoration.

By the third quarter of the sixteenth century, mounted coconut cups were no longer considered exotic, especially when compared to the rarer mounted wares available such as porcelain, ostrich eggs, nautilus shells, or rock crystal.[1] Though the style of the mounts of this example is quite ambitious, the execution is somewhat crude, and the form of the cup appears to have been altered. The squat proportions and relatively large handle are unusual.[2] Other examples of coconuts or ostrich eggs with ornate mounts and cast straps such as this generally have a high foot with a baluster stem and cast brackets.[3] These examples do not have handles or hinged covers. Physical evidence suggesting the extent of the alterations to the present cup may be found in the spool-shaped section of the stem, which has crudely punched dots around the edges that are uncharacteristic of sixteenth-century workmanship and do not match the matted ground of the foot or cover. The cover has been altered by the addition of a rim and flange that serve as a foundation for the hinge and thumbpiece mount; here too, the stamping is of cruder quality than on other parts of the cup. Finally, the engraving around the rim of the vessel seems to have been removed in the area where the handle is now soldered on, suggesting that the handle may be an addition.

The maker's mark is similar to one attributed by Gerald Taylor to Hugh Kayle, one of the Queen's goldsmiths from 1586 to 1599, and Prime Warden for 1595/6.[4] It has previously been described as *HR* conjoined.

7

1. For a history of earlier coconut cups, see Glanville, 1990, pp. 325–326.
2. The closest parallel appears to be a cup of 1566 in the Metropolitan Museum of Art, which has a similarly short stem and large handle, though the proportions are narrower. See Hackenbroch, 1963, no. 2, p. 3, pls. 2–3. A Dutch example in the Schroder Collection has a similarly short stem, high collar, and large handle. See Schroder, 1983, no. 30, pp. 102–104.
3. See, for example, the mounted ostrich egg in the Lee Collection, Toronto, published in W. W. Watts, *Works of Art in Silver and Other Metals Belonging to Viscount and Viscountess Lee of Fareham* (London, 1936), cat. no. 16. The design of the caryatid straps on the Toronto cup is identical to that of the present example. Also see the mounted coconut in the same collection (cat. no. 22) which does not have caryatid straps or brackets but has a taller baluster stem.
4. Taylor depicts a pellet below; this mark seems to represent an ermine spot. See Taylor, 1984, p. 99.

8

COMMUNION CUP AND PATEN COVER

Probably Carmarthen, Wales, 1577
Silver
35.1548

MARKS: on side of cup and on dome of cover, four ovals (Jackson, rev. ed. 1989, p. 513)

INSCRIPTIONS: engraved around side of cup, *POCULUM ECLESIE DE MELINE*; engraved on top of paten, *1577*

H. 18.2 cm (7³⁄₁₆ in.); diam. 8 cm (3⅛ in.)

WEIGHT: 223.6 gm (7 oz 7 dwt)

PROVENANCE: H. D. Ellis by 1911; William E. Godfrey, New York, purchased by Frank Brewer Bemis, 1923, Bequest of Frank Brewer Bemis, November 7, 1935.

PUBLISHED: Jackson, 1911, vol. 1, p. 406, fig. 448.

DESCRIPTION: The domed foot stands on a plain molded rim. The spool-shaped stem has a molded knop with hit-and-miss engraving and a border of stamped dentils at the top and bottom. The body of the cup has a slightly flaring rim and is engraved around the middle with an inscription and around the rim with foliage and strapwork. The domed cover has a spool-shaped finial that is engraved on the top with the date *1577*.

CONSTRUCTION: The domed foot is raised and the rim strengthened by an applied wire. The stem is formed of two raised pieces, joined at the center by a seamed ring. The body of the cup is a seamed cylinder with an applied base. The cover is raised with a seamed finial. There is evidence of repair on the interior rim of the cup as well as at the join of the stem to the base of the body.

Edward VI mandated the destruction of all "prophane cuppes, bowles, dishes, or chalices heretofore used at masse," requiring their replacement with a "comely Communion Cup of silver, and a cover of silver for the same, which may serve for the ministration of the Bread."[1] Charles Oman identified seventy-three Welsh communion cups from the archdeaconries of Cardigan, Carmarthen, and Pembroke bearing the maker's mark of four ovals.[2] Upon the consecration of Matthew Parker and Edmund Grindal to the sees of Canterbury and London in 1559, a campaign was undertaken to replace each parish's chalice with a communion cup.[3] In Wales, the first commissions for new plate were made in the diocese of St. David's, under the juris-

9

diction of Bishop Davies. Oman proposed that a native goldsmith probably established his shop in Carmarthen, near the Bishop's seat in Abergwili.[4] The engraved dates on his cups range from 1573 to 1587, with the largest number belonging to the year 1574. The parish of Meline is in the Diocese of St. David's, Pembrokeshire.

1. Quoted in John Thomas Evans, *The Church Plate of Gowerland* (Stow-on-the-Wold, 1921), p. 58.
2. Oman, 1957, p. 142; see also Evans, op. cit., pp. 58–67, which includes a list of church plate bearing the mark of four ovals. See also idem, *The Church Plate of Cardiganshire* (Stow-on-the-Wold, 1914), pp. x–xii.
3. Oman, 1957, p. 133.
4. Oman, 1957, p. 142.

• 9 •

COMMUNION CUP
London, 1577/8
Silver
33.61

MARKS: near rim, maker's mark *AH* in a rectangle (Jackson, 1921, p. 104; rev. ed. 1989, p. 100); leopard's head crowned; lion passant; date letter *u*

H. 16.8 cm (6⅝ in.); diam. of rim 7.8 cm (3 1/16 in.)

WEIGHT: 232.5 gm (7 oz 10 dwt)

PROVENANCE: Christie, Manson & Woods, London, December 9, 1913, lot 104, purchased by The Goldsmiths' and Silversmiths' Company, Ltd., London; Anonymous Gift in Memory of Charlotte Beebe Wilbour (1833–1914), March 2, 1933.

EXHIBITED: Boston, Museum of Fine Arts, 1933 (no catalogue).

DESCRIPTION: The cup rests on a stepped foot rising to a baluster stem with dentiled borders at each end and around the central knop. The body of the cup has tall straight sides, a flat base, and a flaring rim. There is a band of engraved foliage and strapwork around the center of the vessel.

CONSTRUCTION: The body of the vessel is raised. The stem is formed of two raised sections, joined in the middle with a knop composed of three molded sections. The foot is raised, with an applied molded and stamped rim. The body of the cup appears to have been rehammered.

10 (Color Plate IV)

ARCHITECTURAL SALT
London, 1577/8
Silver gilt, rock crystal
51.1618

MARKS: on underside of base, maker's mark, a bird in a shaped shield (Jackson, 1921, p. 104; rev. ed. 1989, p. 93); lion passant; date letter *u* (struck twice); leopard's head crowned

INSCRIPTIONS: engraved on underside of flange, *London 1577*[1]

H. 17.9 cm (7$\frac{1}{16}$ in.); w. 7.6 cm (3 in.)

WEIGHT: 345.9 gm (11 oz 2 dwt)

PROVENANCE: sold Christie, Manson & Woods, London, December 11, 1902, lot 62, purchased by Crichton Brothers, London; John Augustus Holmes, Renfrewshire, Scotland by 1903; John Crichton-Stuart, 4th Marquess of Bute (1881–1932); purchased from How (of Edinburgh), London, September 13, 1951, Theodora Wilbour Fund in Memory of Charlotte Beebe Wilbour.

EXHIBITED: London, Burlington Fine Arts Club, 1901, p. 26, cat. no. 25, case C, pl. 39, fig. 3; London, St. James's Court, 1903, pp. 49–50, pl. 44; San Francisco, Fine Arts Museums of San Francisco, 1977, p. 38, fig. 40.

PUBLISHED: J. W. Caldicott, *The Values of Old English Silver and Sheffield Plate* (London, 1906), p. 42, pl. 4; Jackson, 1911, vol. 2, p. 551; Collins, 1955, p. 453 (mentioned); Glanville, 1990, p. 288, fig. 170.

DESCRIPTION: The square base of the salt rests on four claw feet, each grasping a crystal ball; the edge is stamped with two bands of ovolo decoration. On the corners of a cushion-shaped base, embossed with fruit clusters surrounding applied masks, four pedestals rise to caryatid figures supporting the upper section of the salt. In the center stands a figure of Venus holding a wreath above her head. She is flanked by two putti, encircling her with joined hands. The group is enclosed by a rock crystal cylinder that is fitted into a collar above and below; the lower fitting is stamped with an egg-and-dart pattern and a fluted border; the upper fitting repeats the egg-and-dart decoration. The top section of the salt is composed of a square flange with a dentiled rim, the underside of which is stamped with an egg-and-dart pattern. The receptacle for salt is set within a square that is engraved on the corners with scrolling foliage. The removable cover is square, with a raised dome chased with fruit and strapwork flanking an applied mask on each side. The edges are finished with a textured applied wire, and the corners are engraved with scrolling foliage and set with glass beads. The finial is composed of a crystal ball supported on a calyx, surmounted by a figure of a putto holding a bagpipe.

CONSTRUCTION: The square base of the salt is formed, embossed, and chased, with moldings composed of die-struck wires applied to the rim. The cast claw feet with crystal mounts are soldered to the corners of the base; a pin with a decorated rivet secures each crystal foot. The central section of the salt is composed of the cast sculptural group centered in the rock crystal cylinder that is supported on moldings composed of die-struck and formed wires. The four cast and chased caryatid pillars rest on fabricated bases; they are soldered at the top to the die-struck upper molding. The well for salt is raised and engraved. The cover of the salt is formed of a single sheet that is embossed, chased, and engraved, with applied cast masks and cut wire borders. The cast finial is riveted to the rock crystal ball; the supporting calyx has been repaired with soft solder, and the three faceted glass beads on the corners of the cover are replacements. The fourth is lacking.

The form of the "architectural" salt, usually composed of four columns supporting a canopylike cover, recalls Italianate fountain designs that echoed the classical temple. The Gibbon Salt in the Goldsmiths' Company is the closest surviving example to this standing salt.[2] Made in 1576, it is of a similar square architectural design, though nearly twice the size of the Boston salt, with columns in the middle of each side, rather than at the corners. A faceted rock crystal cylinder in the center encloses a gilt figure of Neptune. The architectural form survived into the first decade of the seventeenth century, as shown by the Butleigh salt in the Barber Institute, Birmingham, and the related example in the Boston collection (see cat. no. 25). As Hugh Tait has observed, the large number of objects incorporating rock crystal in Renaissance goldsmiths' work suggests that this rare material was salvaged from monstrances and other medieval ecclesiastical objects that had been seized from churches and monasteries.[3] Newly carved rock crystal was also being provided for silver mounted objects.[4]

The present salt is one of a very few surviving examples that suggest the rich surface and complex composition of several objects listed in the 1574 inventory of royal plate. Variations on the design include a piece incorporating a clock, described as "oone Sault being a Clocke with a Christall with viij pillers of siluer guilt enamelid blew and standing vpon like blew balles the toppe being a Sault of Christall with a rounde balle blewe in the Couer. . . ."[5]

The maker's mark, a bird, has been tentatively attributed to Affabel Partridge, one of the Queen's goldsmiths, who was active about 1550–1577.[6] It appears on about twenty pieces, all of the highest technical quality.[7] Among the most ambitious of these is the so-called "Queen Elizabeth Salt" of 1572 in the Tower of London, which features several of the same crisply modeled details as the present salt.[8] It is cylindrical in form and finely chased with figures of three Virtues. The association with the queen is undocumented. Related to the "Queen Elizabeth Salt" is a square example of 1569 by the Bird maker in the Vintners' Company.[9] Timothy Schroder has pointed out the internationalism of some of the motifs used on this maker's pieces, particularly the applied masks that appear on the baluster stems of a group of four cups, two by the Bird maker, one marked in Strasbourg, and a fourth made in Frankfurt or Aachen.[10]

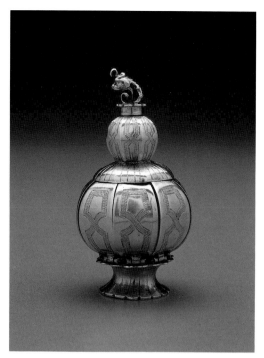

11

1. This inscription must have been added by J. A. Holmes. The West Malling jug, now in the British Museum and formerly in the Holmes Collection, bears a similar inscription. See *The Burlington Magazine* 130 (1988), p. 399.

2. Goldsmiths' Company, The Gibbon Salt, 1576, maker's mark three trefoils slipped, h. 35 cm, ill. Carrington and Hughes, 1926, pp. 37–38, pls. 17–18.

3. Hugh Tait, "The Stonyhurst Salt," *Apollo* 70, no. 26 n.s. (1964), pp. 270–278.

4. See, for example, the crystal cup and cover in the Schroder Collection, with mounts by the Bird maker. The crystal was probably carved in Freiburg im Briesgau. Schroder, 1983, p. 191.

5. Collins, 1955, p. 451.

6. Glanville, 1987a, p. 157. The mark is discussed in the sale catalogue entry for a Nautilus Cup, now in the Victoria and Albert Museum (acc. no. M 117–1984), Christie, Manson & Woods, London, December 12, 1983, lot 198.

7. Schroder (1988, p. 53) provides references to eleven.

8. Tower of London, "Queen Elizabeth Salt," 1572, silver gilt, maker's mark a bird, h. 34.9 cm, ill. Jones, 1908a, pl. 2.

9. Vintners' Company, Salt, 1569/70, silver gilt, maker's mark a bird, h. 31.7 cm, ill. Glanville, 1990, p. 289.

10. Schroder, 1983a pp. 40–46.

• I I •

POMANDER
Probably England, ca. 1580
Silver gilt
35.1547

Unmarked

H. 6.4 cm (2½ in.); w. 3.4 cm (1⁵⁄₁₆ in.)

WEIGHT: 50.2 gm (1 oz 11 dwt)

PROVENANCE: Walter H. Willson Ltd., London, purchased by Frank Brewer Bemis, 1929, Gift of Frank Brewer Bemis, November 7, 1935.

EXHIBITED: Worcester, Massachusetts, Worcester Art Museum, 1969, cat. no. 65, p. 124.

PUBLISHED: Buhler, 1936, p. 78; Buhler, 1952, p. 227, no. 3.

DESCRIPTION: The spherical pomander rests on a spool-shaped foot with a fluted upper and lower rim. An eight-sided central container is attached to the removable finial, which has eight facets and is surmounted by a grotesque figure. The body of the pomander is composed of eight wedge-shaped pieces, each hinged to the base on the lower edge. In the closed position, the upper edges of the wedges are held in place by the tightened finial; when opened, the sections fan out around the central post. Each section is engraved on the outer face with wriggle-work, and on the interior has an engraved sliding cover. The inscriptions read: *ROSE;*

CEDRO; GESMINI; AMBRA; MOSCHETE; VIOLE; NARANSI; GAROFOLI. The underside of the base is engraved with a cartouche from which the armorials have been removed, surmounted by an archbishop's hat with tassels.

CONSTRUCTION: Each wedge of the pomander is assembled from five flat pieces, with the top section left open to accommodate the sliding cover. The foot is composed of three formed pieces, and the central section is a faceted and seamed sheet. The finial is cast.

By the late middle ages, aromatic spices were often carried in richly decorated pierced spherical pendants that were worn around the neck. Pomanders in the form of a segmented orange, with several compartments for various scents, appear as early as the fourteenth century.[1] Dutch, Italian, French, English, and German examples of this type are known. Often unmarked, English examples have not survived in large numbers, but they are recorded as gifts along with other items of personal adornment.[2] The wriggle-work decoration is the only feature by which the present example can be dated, and there remains the possibility that it may be Continental. The arms have been removed from the engraved cartouche on the base, and the archbishop's hat which surmounts it appears to be later than the manufacture of the piece. The latin inscriptions on each compartment refer to the following scents: rose, cedar, jasmine, ambergris, musk, violet, orange, clove.

1. Günther Schiedausky, "Vom Bisampfel zur Vinaigrette," *Kunst und Antiquitäten* (1985) no. 4, pp. 28–38; W. Turner, "Pomanders," *Connoisseur* 32 (1912), pp. 151–156.
2. Glanville, 1990, p. 143.

· 12 ·

JUG WITH BRIDGE SPOUT
London, ca. 1580
Salt-glazed stoneware (Raeren, ca. 1570)
with silver mounts
62.1166

MARKS: on cover, maker's mark fleur-de-lys incuse (similar to Jackson, 1921, p. 104; rev. ed. 1989, p.95[1])

INSCRIPTIONS: scratched on underside of foot rim, *vii oz*

ARMORIALS: in boss on cover (enamel largely missing), arms of Wyatt quartering Wyatt, Balife alias Clark, Hawte, and Sheluing for George Wyatt of Hautbourne, Kent (d. 1623); in relief on stoneware, the arms of Cologne

H. 25.1 cm (9⅞ in.); w. 17.9 cm (7¹/₁₆ in.); diam. of base 9.5 cm (3¾ in.)

PROVENANCE: Sir Andrew Noble, John Noble, and Michael Noble, sold Christie, Manson & Woods, London, March 28, 1962, lot 128B; Sotheby & Co., London, October 25, 1962, lot 14 [Garrard & Co., London], purchased December 12, 1962, Theodora Wilbour Fund in Memory of Charlotte Beebe Wilbour.

PUBLISHED: Hermes, "Old English Domestic Silver," *Apollo* 77, no. 11 (1963), p. 73.

DESCRIPTION: The pottery jug has a bulbous body, a tall neck, a C-shaped handle, and a tall straight spout that is joined to the top of the neck by a "bridge" in the shape of an arm. It is decorated around the rim with a band of busts in low relief, and, on each side of the body of the pot, with the arms of Cologne in elaborate mantling. At the base of the spout is a silver collar engraved with foliage. The molded silver foot rim is attached with a serrated bezel. The broad seamed collar around the neck of the jug is engraved with birds entwined in foliage. It is attached to the handle of the jug with a box hinge that has an engraved diaper pattern on three sides. The domed cover, engraved with birds in foliage, has a plain rim and a circular boss with an engraved coat of arms (formerly enameled) applied to the center. Only the base of the thumbpiece remains.

CONSTRUCTION: The jug was wheel thrown from a pale gray stoneware and salt glazed; the decoration was incised and molded. The pottery "bridge" to the spout has been broken and repaired. The silver foot rim is formed of three drawn wires. The silver collar is formed of two seamed pieces and is engraved on the exterior. The raised and engraved cover has an applied wire bezel. The central boss is set within an applied molded wire. Traces of black and red enamel are left in the engraved fields. The box hinge is formed of three pieces. The cast thumbpiece has been broken off.

Philippa Glanville has discussed the abundant supplies of salt-glazed stoneware shipped from several factories in the vicinity of the Rhine to London.[2] This vessel is related to two examples associated with the Raeren workshop of Jan Emens. One of these bears silver mounts dated 1585, with an inset boss on the top of the domed cover similar to the present example.[3] While the body of the present vessel and the silver foot rim are in keeping with

wares of the 1580s, several features suggest that the mounts on the jug may have been altered. The collar does not fit the pottery neck properly, and the cover and hinge are tilted unevenly on the rim. The gap between the silver neck rim and the pottery body is filled with an unfired material. There is also a coarse patch secured with lead solder on the underside of the join of the box hinge to the handle, suggesting that the mount may have been moved from another, larger jug. The engraving on the cover and on the rim appears to be by the same hand, however, and is similar to that on pieces marked in about 1580–1590.

1. Jackson records a fleur-de-lys on a stoneware (*sic*) Malling jug of 1581; the earthenware jug, which has a tin glaze, is now in the British Museum, acc. no. MLA 1987-7-2,1. The mark on the present jug is smaller and less complex. See Timothy Wilson, "Recent Acquisitions of Postmedieval Ceramics and Glass in the British Museum's Department of Medieval and Later Antiquities (1982–1988)," *The Burlington Magazine* 130 (1988), p. 399.
2. Glanville, 1990, pp. 329–337. See also cat. no. 6.
3. See the example of about 1570–1580 with pewter mounts in the Kunstgewerbemuseum, Cologne (Gisela Reineking-von Bock, *Kataloge des Kunstgewerbemuseums Köln IV, Steinzeug* [Cologne, 1971], cat. no. 356) and another, sold at Sotheby Parke Bernet in 1982, advertised in *Die Weltkunst* 22 (1982), p. 3328. Reineking-von Bock suggests that the Emens workshop was influenced by the Siegburg potter Anno Knütgen, who had used a similar form. I am grateful to David Gaimster for his observations about the pottery.

12

13

• 13 •

PAIR OF STANDING BOWLS
London, 1582/3
Silver gilt
52.1835–1836

MARKS: on rim of each, date letter *E;* lion passant; leopard's head crowned; maker's mark *WH* a pellet and a crescent (?) below (unrecorded)

ARMORIALS: engraved on side, near rim, of each, the arms of the town of Boston, Lincolnshire

INSCRIPTIONS: engraved, on underside of foot (52.1835), *B No. 2 14=15;* (35.1836), *B No. 1 14=16*

52.1835: H. 12.9 cm (5⅟₁₆ in.); diam. 17.2 cm (6¾ in.); diam. of foot 9.9 cm (3⅞ in.).
52.1836: H. 13 cm (5⅛ in.); diam. 17.2 cm (6¾ in.); diam. of foot 9.9 cm (3⅞ in.)

WEIGHT: 52.1835: 453.6 gm (14 oz 12 dwt). 52.1836: 453.6 gm (14 oz 12 dwt)

PROVENANCE: bought with funds bequeathed by Christopher Audley to the Corporation of Boston, Lincolnshire, sold at auction by George Miller, June 1, 1837, lot 74–75, purchased by Thomas Hopkins, Esq.; they descended in his family and were sold at Christie, Manson & Woods, London, May 3, 1906, lot 68, purchased by J. Wells; Crichton Brothers, London, J. P. Morgan (1867–1943), sold Parke Bernet, New York, November 1, 1947, lot 459, purchased by Winston F. C. Guest, Gift of Mr. and Mrs. Winston F. C. Guest, December 11, 1952.

EXHIBITED: Richmond, Virginia, Museum of Fine Arts, 1964, cat. no. 72, p. 45; Cooper-Hewitt Museum, New York, 1985, p. 122.

PUBLISHED: Pishey Thompson, *The History and Antiquities of Boston* (Boston, 1856), p. 305; Jackson, 1911, vol. 2, pp. 695–696; Arthur Grimwade, "Shrewsbury and Boston Plate," *Apollo* 54 (1951), p. 106; Edwin J. Hipkiss, "Strange Turns in English Silver," *Bulletin of the Museum of Fine Arts* 51 (1953), pp. 20–23; *Connoisseur* 132 (1953), pp. 208–209; Collins, 1955, p. 33 (mentioned); Glanville, 1990, p. 242 (mentioned).

DESCRIPTION: The bowls stand on a high domed foot embossed with clusters of fruit and masks in strapwork. The foot rim is stamped with ovolo decoration. The spool-shaped stem, chased with strapwork against a matted ground, has a flattened central knop that is chased with

fruit. The broad flat bowl has a plain exterior, and on the interior, a raised central boss that is embossed with a bust in profile against an irregularly shaped matted ground. On 35.1835, the figure is a female facing right; on 35.1856, a helmeted man is shown facing left. The rim and bottom of the bowl are engraved with a band of arabesques. The style of the engraved coats of arms of the city suggests that they were added about 1670.

CONSTRUCTION: The feet of the bowls are constructed of several die-stamped wires, joined to a raised section that makes up the dome. The stem is composed of two raised sections, with the seam covered by the raised knop. The bowl is made from a single sheet, raised, embossed, and engraved. The gilding has been renewed.

Christopher Audley, in his will proved July 10, 1576, provided for ". . . the Mayor and the Burgesses of Boston for the use of saide Mayor and his successors syx drinkinge pottes to the value of twentie markes to be provided by my executors."[1] Audley held various official positions in the city from 1564, and was appointed Alderman in 1571. In 1568 he was dispatched to Norwich to "view and peruset howe and after what maner certen fflemings and other strangers be used and occupied there. . . ." In 1573 he was given responsibility for the "order and Govern^mt of the Bekonage of the haven And Deepes of Boston," and the following year he was called to account for "certen grete Somes of mony" he had received. He was also brought before the counsel and Mayor to confess "with a penitete heart and lowlie submission that he had comitted advowtrie and fornicacion" for which he was dismissed from the board of aldermen. In view of "what slannders might ensew," if he were openly punished, it was decided that he should be required to donate £5 to the poor. He appeared before the counsel three months later wishing "to marrye and to take to wife one Mis Busshe who cannot as yet be wonne to inhabite within this Borough unles the said Cristopher Audley can obtayne oure grannte . . . to be discharged of the maioraltye and of all other offyce beringe within the saide Boroughe duringe her naturall life." The counsel reluctantly conceded in view of "the many and grete benifitts and tokens of favor and good will as by noo inhabitante more . . ." bestowed by Audley.[2]

Christopher Audley's brother and executor, Walter, apparantly never commissioned the six drinking pots specified in the will, however. An entry in the corporation records for May 25, 1580, indicates that the city brought suit against Walter Audley to recover £20 "to be imployed in plate geven to this corporation by Christopher Audeley merchant deceased by his laste will." The 1582 hallmarks on the surviving pair of cups suggests that Walter Audley eventually complied, but it is not certain how large the original set was. In the 1837 sale of Corporation plate, only two "antique plattens" were listed, with their weights recorded as 14 oz 13 dwts.

The broad shallow bowl on a short stem appears in Dutch and German silver; it was also produced in Venetian glass.[3] The question of whether such bowls or wine cups were routinely provided with covers has been debated. Philippa Glanville has suggested that most Tudor drinking vessels were supplied with covers; sets sometimes came with only one.[4]

1. Will of Christopher Audley of Boston, Public Record Office Prob. 58/21, 152.
2. Boston Corporation records, typescript in the Borough of Boston Municipal Buildings, pp. 160–246. I am grateful to Ernest Coley for his assistance.
3. See, for example, the glass bowls in the collection of the Corning Museum of Glass, exhibited New York, Cooper Hewitt Museum, 1985, p. 122.
4. Glanville, 1987, p. 35.

· 14 ·

STANDING CUP AND COVER (THE WESTBURY CUP)
London, 1585/6
Silver gilt
35.1550

MARKS: on cover near finial, maker's mark *M* a line across (Jackson, 1921, p. 105; rev. ed. 1989, p. 101); leopard's head crowned; lion passant; date letter *H*

INSCRIPTIONS: engraved around rim, *Given to the Church of Westbury by Collonel Wancklen & Mary Contes of Malbrōū 1671*; engraved on cover, *TW, MM*

H. 26.2 cm (10⁵⁄₁₆ in.); diam. of foot 10.3 cm (4¹⁄₁₆ in.)

14 (Color Plate V)

WEIGHT: 787.7 gm (25 oz 6 dwt)

PROVENANCE: All Saints' Church, Westbury, Wiltshire, until 1845; Estate of F. W. Rummens, Esq., sold Christie, Manson & Woods, London, April 17, 1896, lot 27; sold Christie, Manson & Woods, London, June 27, 1898, lot 78, purchased by Corbett; Sir John Charles Robinson, Dorset by 1904; A. M. S. Smedley, Esq., by 1915; Frederick Bradbury, London; sold to Frank Brewer Bemis, 1927, Bequest of Frank Brewer Bemis, November 7, 1935.

EXHIBITED: Minneapolis, Minneapolis Institute of Arts, 1956, cat. no. 113, p. 30, fig. 13; New York, Cooper Hewitt Museum, 1985 (not in catalogue).

PUBLISHED: Nightingale, 1891, p. 99; John Charles Robinson, "The Westbury Cup, an Ancient Scandal," *The Ancestor* 9 (1904), pp. 187–190; Jackson, 1911, vol. 2, p. 662, fig. 871; Arthur Hayden, *Chats on Old Silver* (London, 1915), pp. 97–98, fig. 95; Hipkiss, 1929, p. 39; Buhler, 1952, p. 228, no. 5.

DESCRIPTION: The body of the cup is in the form of an acorn, with high straight sides, a domed cover, and a rounded textured base. The cover has an interior bezel fitting and a baluster finial. The cup stands on a detachable stem with a flattened knop and a spreading base with a stepped molded foot.

CONSTRUCTION: The body of the vessel is composed of two pieces: a raised, barrel-shaped closed cylinder and a raised sleeve that fits over a threaded post at the base. The sleeve is decorated with a circular punch. The stem is assembled from several raised and formed sections with a drawn wire foot. The raised cover of the cup seems to have been repaired.

This cup in the form of an acorn belongs to a popular category of drinking vessels in the form of fruits or gourds. Philippa Glanville cites inventory references to an apple cup, a strawberry cup, and a pear cup as evidence that the form was well established by the early sixteenth century, considerably earlier than the surviving examples would suggest.[1] The only surviving acorn cup comparable to the present example is a gold cup from Stapleford Church, Leicestershire, now in the British Museum.[2] The precise form is otherwise unknown in English silver, but there are a number of Dutch glasses of the late sixteenth century of a similar shape.[3] A contemporary manuscript describes the glasses as ciboria, but as with the silver examples, this may have been a later use for a domestic vessel. Though unmarked, the Stapleford cup is considered to date from the first decade of the seventeenth century. It has more delicate proportions than the Westbury cup, largely because of its high twisted stem in the form of a branch. The spreading foot and flattened knop of the Westbury cup are more typical of the mid-seventeenth century than of the late six-teenth, suggesting that the original foot, probably similar in proportion to that of the Stapleford cup, was replaced in 1671 when the cup was presented to the church. The broad short foot would make the cup more practical for use as a communion vessel. In the absence of marks on the body of the vessel, the foot, and the tex-tured sleeve that forms the "cap" of the acorn, however, there remains the possibil-ity that the entire cup is of seventeenth-century manufacture, utilizing for the cover a previously marked piece of plate.

The cup has an interesting history. The inscription *Given to the Church of Westbury by Collonel Wancklen & Mary Contes of Malbroū* was presumably added when it was presented to the church in 1671.[4] The Westbury Churchwardens' accounts and vestry minutes do not survive from the pe-riod, and the first record of the cup is an entry in the Vestry Book of 1750.[5] Mary, Countess of Marlborough, and daughter of Sir Arthur Capell of Little Hadham, Hert-fordshire, was the widow of Henry Ley, second Earl of Marlborough (1595–1638), and mother of the third Earl who was killed at sea in 1665.[6] Little is known about the Colonel Wanklin referred to in the inscription; he does not appear to have served in the army. The Oxford antiquar-ian Anthony Wood (1632–1695) recorded the Countess's death on June 2, 1670: "The countess of Marlborough, mother to that earl that was killed in the sea fight, 1666 (*sic*), died. Buried by her second husband (Thomas Wanklin, son of a smith) in her garden, between two boards, under a tur-nip plot, because Mr. Ash who was to en-ter upon her joynter should not know it. About Michelmas following she was taken up and buried by her husband at West-bury-on-the-plaine Wiltshire."[7] Wanklin was named in the third Earl's will where he is entrusted with "twenty pounds [to] be given to the poore of the parish of Westbury by the old wife of Coll: Wank-lin."[8] It must be assumed that the "old wife of Coll: Wanklin" referred to in the will of the third Earl is not the testator's mother, and that Mary, Countess of Marl-borough, married Colonel Wanklin some-time after the death of her son in 1665. The cup must have been bequeathed to the church by the countess or presented in her memory by her husband.[9]

1. Glanville, 1990, pp. 166–167; 246–249.
2. The Stapleford Cup, ca. 1600–1610, gold, unmarked, h. 20.3 cm, ill. Grimwade, 1951, part 1, no. 1, p. 76.
3. One example, exhibited at the Rijksmuseum, Amsterdam, is compared to a drawing in a manuscript of about 1550–1560 where it is de-scribed as a ciborium. Amsterdam, Rijksmu-seum, 1986, cat. no. 293.
4. The style of the engraved date differs from the rest of the inscription, and may be a later addition.
5. Wiltshire Record Office, reference number 1427/7. I am grateful to Mr. K. H. Rogers, County Archivist, for having provided these references.
6. See cat. no. 61 for a cup made in the third Earl's memory.
7. Andrew Clark, *The Life and Times of Anthony Wood* (Oxford, 1892), p. 194. The Westbury burial register (Wiltshire Record Office 1427/4) records the following entry for the year 1670/1: "The Righ Honnorable the Countes of Marel-bough was Buried the 26 of February."
8. Will of James Ley, Earl of Marlborough PRO Prob 3/7/64.
9. Her will is not listed in the index of the dioc-esan court.

· 15 ·

PEDESTAL SALT
London, 1587/8
Silver, parcel gilt
33.62

MARKS: on corner of base, repeated in bowl (rubbed): indistinct maker's mark (possibly *IS* in monogram, Jackson, 1921, p. 99; rev. ed. 1989, p. 95); leopard's head crowned; lion pas-sant; date letter *k*

ARMORIALS: engraved on each side of upper flange, the crest of Morrice[1]

H. 12.4 cm (4⅞ in.); w. 10.2 cm (4 in.)

WEIGHT: 289.7 gm (9 oz 6 dwt)

PROVENANCE: Spink & Son, London, by 1928; Anonymous Gift in Memory of Charlotte Beebe Wilbour (1833–1914), March 2, 1933.

EXHIBITED: Boston, Museum of Fine Arts, 1933 (no catalogue); Cambridge, Massachusetts, Fogg Art Museum, 1937, cat. no. 17.

15

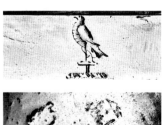

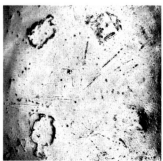

PUBLISHED: Edward Wenham, "Salt Cellars and Superstitions," *The Antiquarian* 11, no. 5 (1928), p. 34; Wenham, 1931, pl. 25; Hipkiss, 1933, pp. 25, 27; Gruber, 1982, p. 159, fig. 214.

DESCRIPTION: The salt is in the form of a square pedestal and stands on four scroll feet. The four sides of the middle section are embossed with a lion's head framed by strapwork with guilloche and ovolo panels above and below against a matted ground. The base and upper rim rest on inverted cushion-shaped moldings embossed with fluting and lions' heads with a border of rectangular punching. The receptacle for salt is formed of a separate piece fitted into a square flange and is engraved on the corners with hatched floral strapwork.

CONSTRUCTION: The body of the salt is formed in three sections; two cushion-shaped moldings each formed of an embossed sheet, and a central section seamed on one corner. The upper and lower rims are formed of stamped and engraved wires. Each foot is cast in two sections. The surface of the salt is extremely worn and is flaking extensively, particularly on the edges of the matted ground in the center section. The well for salt has been corroded and scratched from use, and the gilding in that area, possibly original, is thin. There is some evidence of alteration, particularly on the corners of the top, where the engraving has been reinforced, and on the edges of the flanges supporting the top, where the heads of the engraved birds have been cut off.

The design of this salt is closely related to four examples, each of a similar light guage. The best-preserved example is the Cosway Salt,[2] recently purchased by the British Museum. It varies in design from this example only in the strapwork surrounding the central lion's mask and in the omission of the two broken bands of guilloche ornament above and below. It has cast feet in the form of crouching lions, and retains its domed cover, surmounted by a figure. The scroll feet on the present example are certainly restorations and must have replaced similar animal figures. A second salt of 1573 published by Jackson[3] is similar in design to the Cosway salt, but the feet have grotesque faces. A third salt is in the Adelaide Art Gallery of South Australia. Dated 1584, the design follows the same formula, and it has a high domed cover and ball-and-claw feet.[4] A fourth related example was exhibited in 1901 at the Burlington Fine Arts Club; its embossed decoration is a simplified form of geometric strapwork and the feet and finial are lacking.[5] A variation in the treatment of the embossed side panels may be seen in a much larger example of 1594 in the Kremlin Armory Museum, Moscow. Instead of a geometric pattern of lions' masks and strapwork, the panels are filled with figures in classical dress.[6]

This salt belongs to a group of coarsely executed salts that in all probability have not survived in a quantity proportionate to their manufacture. Philippa Glanville mentions inventory references to small salts weighing under five ounces.[7] The large cylindrical salts at the Victoria and Albert Museum,[8] the Metropolitan Museum of Art,[9] and the two salts in the Gilbert Collection[10] are similarly chased and suggest the more ambitious application of this style.

1. There is a variation in that Fairbairn (1905, vol. 1, p. 399) does not record the falcon as guardant.
2. The Cosway Salt, 1587, h. 21.6 cm, now in the British Museum, ill. G. E. P. How, *Notes on Antique Silver* no. 6 (1948–49) pl. 20, p. 28.
3. Pedestal salt, London, 1573, ill. Jackson, 1911, vol. 2, p. 549, fig. 760.
4. I am grateful to Timothy Wilson for providing this information. Illegible maker's mark, London date letter for 1583/4, h. 27.9 cm. Formerly in the Leopold de Rothschild Collection, and illustrated in Jones, 1907, p. 2, pl. 2.
5. Collection of Jeffery Whitehead, Salt, 1562, maker's mark a bird, exhibited London, Bur-

lington Fine Arts Club, 1901, no. 12, case D, p. 33, pl. 38.
6. Silver-gilt salt, 1594/5, maker's mark a daisy between *AS*, h. 40.96 cm, ill. Oman, 1961, pl. 45.
7. Glanville, 1987, p. 43.
8. Acc. no. M146.1886, The Mostyn Salt, 1586/7, maker's mark *T*, h. 41 cm, ill. Oman, 1965, pls. 27–28.
9. Standing salt, 1581, maker's mark a bull's head, h. 25.4 cm, ill. Hackenbroch, 1963, no. 73, pl. 86, p. 44.
10. Standing salt, 1572/3, maker's mark an eagle (?), h. 26.8 cm; Standing salt, 1581/2, maker's mark *RM*, h. 27.7 cm, ill. Schroder, 1988, cat. nos. 8–9.

· 16 ·

CASKET
Probably London, ca. 1590
Mother-of-pearl with silver mounts
63.1252

Unmarked

H. 13.7 cm (5⅜ in.); w. 12.4 cm (4⅞ in.)

PROVENANCE: Dukes of Norfolk, Arundel Castle (unverified); purchased from How (of Edinburgh), London, September 18, 1963, Theodora Wilbour Fund in Memory of Charlotte Beebe Wilbour.

EXHIBITED: Toronto, Royal Ontario Museum, 1958, cat. no. B18, p. 15.

PUBLISHED: Glanville, 1990, fig. 188.

DESCRIPTION: The cylindrical body of the casket is composed of vertical strips of mother-of-pearl pegged into a broad silver collar with a dentiled border. The collar is engraved with scrolls of foliage enclosing exotic birds. The silver foot has a flaring rim with stamped egg-and-dart ornament. The three feet are formed by cast figures of seated lions. The domed cover is made of strips of mother-of-pearl secured with a silver wire rim, rising to a boss with a bun-shaped finial. It is attached to the body by an exterior hinge that is pierced with a pattern of arabesques. A hinged clasp with a hook and eye secures the cover at the front.

CONSTRUCTION: The strips of shell are pegged to the silver frame with brass rivets. The broad center section of silver is formed from a strip seamed near the hinge. The feet, hinge, and upper section of the finial are cast. The surface of the silver collar shows considerable flaking and corrosion.

Among the objects assembled from pieces of lustrous nautilus shell are basins, ewers, spoons, flagons, and salts. Numerous sixteenth-century references to these pieces

16 (Color Plate VI)

show that while they were included in the royal collections in some quantity, and occasionally presented as gifts, they were not generally owned outside aristocratic circles.[1]

The dating of this casket is based on the style of the engraving, which is similar in spirit to ornament panels published by the Nürnberg engraver Virgil Solis (1514–1562) in the mid-sixteenth century.[2] The cast hinge with openwork arabesque decoration was also probably designed after a printed source.[3] Other details, such as the cast feet in the form of lions, are features that appear on a variety of objects made between about 1570 and 1600. The closest comparison to the present example is a covered hemispherical box with an engraved hinged cover in the Victoria and Albert Museum.[4] A large bowl, fully

marked by the Trefoil Slipped maker for 1621/2, is indicative of the longevity of the taste for these luxurious items.[5] By about 1610, the shells used were being imported from India by the British East India Company, and the supply increased as the century progressed.[6]

1. Glanville, 1990, pp. 319–320.
2. Berliner, 1925, pl. 181, nos. 5–7, p. 51.
3. For example, the engravings of Thomas Geminus, published in London in 1548. See Hind, 1952, pls. 26–27.
4. Acc. no. M245–1924, Casket, mother-of-pearl with silver-gilt mounts, ca. 1600, h. 8.5 cm, ill. Glanville, 1990, cat. no. 109, p. 477.
5. Victoria and Albert Museum, acc. no. M17-1968, Bowl, mother-of-pearl with silver-gilt mounts, maker's mark a trefoil slipped, diam. 24 cm, ill. Glanville, 1990, cat. no. 75, p. 448.
6. Glanville, 1990, p. 321.

· 17 ·

TANKARD
London, ca. 1590–1600; hallmarked 1618/9
Silver, parcel gilt
56.1183

MARKS: on underside of base and on cover, maker's mark *IP* above a bell in a shaped shield (Jackson, 1921, p. 114; rev. ed. 1989, p. 110); leopard's head crowned; date letter *a*; lion passant

H. 17.5 cm (6⅞ in.); w. 22.9 cm (9 in.); diam. of foot 11.3 cm (4⁷⁄₁₆ in.)

WEIGHT: 556 gm (17 oz 17 dwt)

PROVENANCE: Samuel Montagu (Lord Swaythling), sold Christie, Manson & Woods, London, May 6, 1924, lot 98, purchased by Crichton Brothers, London; sold anonymously (William Randolph Hearst) at Sotheby & Co., London, October 9, 1947, lot 152; Christie, Manson & Woods, London, June 30, 1954, lot 160; purchased from Thomas Lumley, Ltd., London, December 13, 1956, Theodora Wilbour Fund in Memory of Charlotte Beebe Wilbour.

EXHIBITED: London, Burlington Fine Arts Club, 1901, case C, no. 25, pp. 26–27, pl. 39, fig. 3; London, St. James's Court, 1903, pl. 44 (not in catalogue).

PUBLISHED: Jones, 1929, p. 345, fig. 3; Wenham, 1931, pl. 42; Clayton, 1985a, p. 37, fig. 9.

DESCRIPTION: The tapered body of the tankard rests on a domed foot that is embossed with strapwork and clusters of fruit against a punched ground. The body is divided into three registers by two applied molded bands that are stamped with ovolo decoration. The central register is engraved with birds resting on swags, foliage, and clusters of fruit. The upper and lower registers are engraved with strapwork and foliage. The domed cover has an embossed design similar to that on the foot. The flange is stamped with egg-and-dart decoration, and the baluster finial rests on a rayed disk on a patterned rim. On each side of the thumbpiece is a mask in a cartouche. The S-shaped handle is engraved along the spine with foliage and at the terminus with a cross-hatched pattern. The sides of the vessel and the underside of the handle are white; all other areas are gilt.

CONSTRUCTION: The foot of the tankard is raised and strengthened at the rim with an applied wire. The body and the cover are raised. The applied ribs and the handle are formed. The thumbpiece, finial, and rayed disk are cast. The finial and the rim of the cover have been repaired, and the gilding has been renewed.

About twenty tankards of a similar form are known, ranging in date from 1571 to 1607. They have in common tapered sides, two horizontal ribs around the body, and a domed cover and foot. The earliest known are those given by Archbishop Parker in 1571 to Trinity Hall and to Gonville and Caius College, Cambridge.[1] The form seems to have undergone few modifications during the last quarter of the sixteenth century, though the earlier examples are distinguished by cast masks in roundels on the sides and by scrolled thumbpieces. Most have flat-chased and matted decoration, a treatment characterized by Timothy Schroder as typical of less expensive wares produced for the middle range of the market.[2] Six, however, are decorated with engraved strapwork, foliage, and fruit, in a manner similar to the present example.[3]

The design of the engraved decoration on this example incorporates birds and clusters of fruit into strapwork and swags. Certain details are particularly close to the tankards in the Schroder Collection and in the Huth Collection, suggesting that they may have been engraved after a common source.[4] The swags of fabric are pulled through notches in the upper edge of the frame, clusters of fruit are suspended from ribbons, and naturalistically rendered birds balance on the foliage. The decoration on the tankard in the Schroder Collection has been attributed to the Flemish engraver Nicaise Roussel by Schroder, who likened the style to Roussel's early work, also found on the Magdalene Cup in the Manchester City Art Gallery.[5] Schroder concluded that the tankard must have been made in the early 1570s, but not submitted for assay until 1599.[6] While the engraving style of the Boston tankard cannot be firmly tied to any work as early as the 1570s, it was certainly out of date by 1619, the year in which the tankard was hallmarked. Mannerist and grotesque motifs can be found on English silver as late as about 1610, but by the following decade the conventions of naturalistic clusters of fruit and foliage had been superseded by a more schematic decoration of highly stylized flowers in scrolling foliage, often chased against a matted ground.[7] Significantly, there are no other surviving tankards of this form later than 1607.[8] It is possible, therefore, that this tankard was not submitted for assay until it changed hands in 1619, and that its date of manufacture was considerably earlier, perhaps about 1600.

17

1. Archbishop Parker presented each college with one of a pair of tankards, maker's mark *FR* in monogram, 1570/1; Trinity Hall, Cambridge, and Gonville and Caius College, Cambridge. See Jones, 1910, p. 28, pl. 31; p. 33, pl. 37.

2. See Schroder, 1988, p. 78.

3. Private Collection, Tankard, 1578, ill. Watts, 1924, pl. 27a; Collection of L. Huth, Tankard, 1573, maker's mark a crab, exhibited London, Burlington Fine Arts Club, 1901, p. 9, case B, no. 3, pl. 40, fig. 2; Schroder Collection, Tankard, hallmarked for 1599/1600, maker's mark *IA,* for John Acton, ill. Schroder, 1983, cat. no. 21, p. 86; Swaythling Collection, Tankard, 1591, maker's mark a double-headed eagle, sold Christie, Manson & Woods, London, May 6, 1924, lot 108; Ashmolean Museum, Oxford, Tankard, 1574, maker's mark *CP* an axe between, exhibited Oxford, Ashmolean Museum, 1928, cat. no. 85, fig. 38; Sterling and Francine Clark Art Institute, Williamstown, Tankard, 1574/5, ill. Hernmarck, 1977, vol. 2, p. 80, no. 219.

4. See the engraved designs by Virgil Solis of about 1550, ill. Berliner, 1925, vol. 1, pl. 181, nos. 5–7.

5. See Schroder, 1983, p. 86; see also Schroder, 1983a, pp. 44–45. The Magdalene Cup is illustrated in Jackson, 1911, vol. 1, p. 186, fig. 205.

6. Both the design and execution of the Schroder tankard, however, are less sophisticated than the published engravings after Roussel or the engraving on the Magdalene Cup or the St. Mary Woolnoth flagon. See Oman, 1978 p. 47.

7. See, for example, cat. no. 23.

8. Victoria and Albert Museum, acc. no. M.I-1923, Tankard, 1607/8, maker's mark *RM,* h. 21 cm, ill. Oman, 1965, pl. 35. There is an inexplicable absence of surviving tankards from the period 1610–1635; Clayton (1985, p. 398) suggests that this fact reflects the decision to melt relatively modern silver during the Civil War.

· 18 ·

BASIN

London, 1599/1600
Silver gilt and *basse-taille* enamel on silver
46.845

MARKS: on rim, date letter *B*; lion passant; leopard's head crowned; indistinct maker's mark

ARMORIALS: in central boss in *basse-taille* enamel, the arms of Cholmondeley impaling Holford for Sir Hugh Cholmondeley of Cholmondeley (1552–1601), who in 1575 married Mary, daughter of Christopher Holford of Holford, Cheshire[1]

H. 6.8 cm (2¹¹⁄₁₆ in.); diam. 49.2 cm (19⅜ in.)

WEIGHT: 2,948 gm (94 oz 15 dwt)

PROVENANCE: by descent to Lord Delamere, sold Christie, Manson & Woods, London, July 16, 1930, lot 63, purchased by Garrard & Co., London, purchased by Richard C. Paine, Boston, Gift of Richard C. Paine, September 12, 1946.

EXHIBITED: London, South Kensington Museum, 1862, no. 5,760 (lent by Lord Delamere); San Francisco, Fine Arts Museums of San Francisco, 1977, p. 37, fig. 48.

PUBLISHED: Hipkiss, 1951, p. 11; Buhler, 1970, p. 73, fig. 9.

DESCRIPTION: The circular dish has a flat rim that is embossed with six ovals enclosing, alternately, clusters of fruit and dolphins. The spaces between the bosses are engraved with flowers and foliage. The rounded well of the basin is similarly engraved, with insects and masks incorporated into the design. The raised center of the dish is filled with three embossed ovals enclosing dolphins and, in between, clusters of fruit against a matted ground. The base of the central boss is stamped with fluting and the middle section with ovolo decoration. The top of the boss is a white silver disk with a coat of arms in *basse-taille* enamels in manganese, green, red, blue, and black.

CONSTRUCTION: The dish was raised from a single sheet, embossed, chased, and engraved. The central boss is composed of five stamped and drawn wires. The silver disk with enameled arms is secured with a serrated bezel. There are some losses to the enamel, particularly the green surrounding the shield. The gilding has been renewed.

According to the catalogue for the 1862 exhibition at the South Kensington Museum, the ewer belonging to this basin was "plundered by the soldiers of the Parliamentary army."[2] Though Cholmondeley Hall was attacked by the Parliamentarians, the loss of plate is not recorded. The ewer matching this basin was most likely vase-shaped.[3] The design of the embossed decoration of alternating medallions enclosing fruit and dolphins is a standard feature of basins made during the first two decades of the seventeenth century; this appears to be among the earliest examples.

The engraved decoration shares characteristics with a group of engraved silver attributed by Charles Oman to Nicaise Roussel (born Bruges, active in England after 1573),[4] particularly in the use of loosely outlined foliate strapwork and stylized flowers filled with broad cross-hatching, best seen on the Mostyn flagons[5] and

18 (Color Plate VII)

on a wine cup of 1587 in the Goldsmiths' Company.[6] Even closer comparison can be made with a standing cup of 1598 in the Armourers' and Braziers' Company,[7] a bowl of 1604 from St. Albans,[8] and a pair of covered cups of 1604,[9] all of which are engraved with flowers that must have been copied from the same source as those on the present example, possibly by the same hand. The complexity and ambition of Roussel's printed grotesque designs, however, exceed by far the decoration on this group of silver, and the attribution of this piece to Roussel would be difficult to justify.

The surviving Cholmondeley records do not shed any light on the history of ownership. Sir Hugh's widow, Dame Mary Cholmondeley, was called "the bold lady of Cheshire" by James I because of her tenacity in a dispute over family lands that lasted forty years. Her will lists several items of plate designated for her daughter Frances and son Thomas, but none can be identified as the present basin.[10] In 1615 she took over the estate of Vale Royal, and in 1624 it was inherited by her son, Thomas Cholmondeley, founder of the family of Cholmondeley of Vale Royal, now the Lords Delamere. The basin is recorded in a Vale Royal plate book of about 1891.[11]

1. The Cholmondeley arms in the Visitation of Cheshire are given with nine quarters, not eleven, as on this dish, numbers four and eleven being omitted. The Holford arms are listed with four quarterings, as on the dish, except that two and three are reversed.
2. London, South Kensington Museum, 1862, no. 5,760, p. 477. On July 8, 1644, the Parliamentary troops entered Cholmondeley House, took sixty-six prisoners, and departed, "leavinge the goods in the howse a praye for the Soldyers, who pillaged the sayme." (Thomas Malbon, *Memorials of the Civil War in Cheshire* [London, 1889], p. 138.)
3. See the example of 1617/8 in the Royal Collection, maker's mark *WC* divided by an arrow, published in Jones, 1911, p. 2, pl. 1. Alternatively, the ewer might have been beaker-shaped with a triangular spout, like the example of 1574 in the Goldsmiths' Company. See Carrington and Hughes, 1926, pp. 31–32, pls. 12–13.
4. Oman, 1978, pp. 47–48.
5. Temple Newsam House, Leeds, (acc. no. 4/78) and Manchester City Art Gallery (acc. no. 1978.1), sold at Christie, Manson & Woods, London, June 29, 1977, lot 137.
6. Carrington and Hughes, 1926, p. 28, pl. 10.

7. Exhibited, London, Goldsmiths' Hall, 1951, cat. no. 61, p. 28.
8. Exhibited, London, Burlington Fine Arts Club, 1901, p. 17, pl. 52.
9. Exhibited, London, St. James's Court, 1903, case M, no. 2, pl. 52, lent by the Earl of Ancaster.
10. Cheshire Record Office; I am grateful to Mr. J. T. Hopkins, Archivist, for his research on my behalf.
11. Cheshire Record Office, DBC 16121/28/1.

• 19 •

FLAGON
Probably London, ca. 1600
Porcelain with underglaze blue decoration (China, Ming dynasty, probably Wan-li period [1573–1619]), with silver-gilt mounts
67.601

Unmarked

H. 34.5 cm (13⁹⁄₁₆ in.); w. 17.8 cm (7 in.); d. 16.4 cm (6⁷⁄₁₆ in.)

PROVENANCE: Landgrave of Hesse (unverified); Sigfried Kramarsky, Amsterdam; purchased from Rosenberg and Stiebel, New York, April 12, 1967, Theodora Wilbour Fund in Memory of Charlotte Beebe Wilbour.

PUBLISHED: Max Sauerlandt, *Edelmetalfassungen in der Keramik* (Berlin, 1929), p. 37, fig. 15; Lunsingh Scheurleer, 1980, p. 188, fig. 33.

DESCRIPTION: The porcelain bottle is in the form of a slightly flattened sphere, with a tall tapered neck. The decoration of a bird on a rock in a clump of bamboo is painted in underglaze cobalt blue. The flagon rests on a spreading foot of silver gilt, stamped with fluted decoration; above is a molding stamped with diamonds. Three straps modeled with caryatid figures are joined to a molded stamped collar at the base of the neck. The ear-shaped handle is in the form of two intertwined serpents with scrolling tails. The rim of the bottle is fitted with a silver collar stamped with a pattern of strapwork. The domed cover is chased with foliage against a matted ground; the finial is baluster shaped. The thumbpiece is X-shaped with molded bars above and below.

CONSTRUCTION: The bottle is wheel thrown of a grayish porcelain paste, decorated in underglaze blue, and glazed with a clear glaze of bluish hue. The silver foot is formed of molded and stamped wires. The three cast straps are pinned to the foot and to the collar, which is composed of molded and stamped wires. The cover is formed and chased; the collar around

19 (Color Plate VIII)

the rim of the bottle is formed of two pieces of sheet, stamped and seamed. The handle is formed of two pieces of twisted wire covered with wriggle-work. The ceramic body has been broken into many pieces and reconstructed.

The market in England for blue and white porcelain flourished in the years around 1600.[1] Converted into a flagon by the addition of a finely finished silver handle and cover, this piece might have had a matching basin as a companion for the sideboard. The crisp quality of the stamped mounts on this piece may be compared to a group of mounted blue and white porcelain bearing the maker's mark of three trefoils slipped. Ranging in date from about 1575 to 1620, these mounts are distinguished by precise molded and stamped decoration and caryatid straps, as on the present flagon. A bowl and a bottle made for William Cecil, Lord Burghley (1520–1598), now in the Metropolitan Museum of Art, are characteristic.[2] The handles of the bottle and several mounted bowls by the same maker, formed of a winged figure with a double twisting tail, are distantly related to the serpent handle of the present flagon. The serpent handle does not seem to have an exact parallel, although the style of the other mounts suggests a date of about 1600.[3]

The unusual pale blue palette of the body and the impurities in the cobalt, which turned dark brown in firing, suggest that the jar may be the product of a provincial kiln rather than the imperial kiln at Jingdezhen.[4]

1. Glanville (1987a, pp. 156–160) surveys the history of Chinese porcelain in English silver mounts. See also Glanville, 1990, pp. 341–351.
2. Acc. no. 44.14.1, Bowl (China, Ming Dynasty, Wan-li period 1573–1619) with English mounts, ca. 1585, diam. 36.5 cm, exhibited New York, Frick Collection, 1986, cat. no. 4, p. 36; acc. no. 44.14.2, Bottle (China, Ming Dynasty, Wan-li period, 1573–1619) with English mounts, ca. 1585, maker's mark three trefoils slipped, h. 34.5 cm, ill. Jones, 1908, p. 9, pl. 7. The present flagon was not among the objects sold by the Marquess of Exeter at Christie, Manson & Woods, June 7–8, 1888.
3. A similar handle may be found on an earlier Antwerp ewer of 1558/9 exhibited Antwerp, Rockoxhuis, 1988, cat. no. 40, p. 93.
4. I am grateful to Robert Mowry and Denise Patry Leidy for their observations regarding the porcelain.

LIVERY BADGE
London?, ca. 1600–1625
Silver, parcel gilt and enameled
1989.145

Unmarked
INSCRIPTIONS: in ink on wood mount, *Robert Dod*

H. 7 cm (2¾ in.); w. 6.8 cm (2¹¹⁄₁₆ in.); d. 1.2 cm (½ in.)

WEIGHT: 19.8 gm (13 dwt)

PROVENANCE: purchased from Asprey, PLC, London, May 22, 1989, Theodora Wilbour Fund in Memory of Charlotte Beebe Wilbour.

DESCRIPTION: The badge is in the form of the crest of Cholmondeley: on a wreath gold and gules a demi griffin sable (armed gold) holding a close helmet silver garnished gold. It is modeled in low relief with gilt and enameled tinctures.

CONSTRUCTION: The badge is formed of a sheet, chased, embossed, cut, pierced, enameled, and gilt. Five loops of twisted round wire are soldered to the reverse. The badge is secured to a contemporary piece of wood with a leather lace.

Though made in prodigious quantity, the badges and tokens worn by a nobleman's retainers on ceremonial occasions are now extremely rare. This badge is one of a pair divided by the British Museum and the Museum of Fine Arts in 1989. Though of a similar design, the two badges differ in several details of craftsmanship, suggesting that, though roughly contemporary, they were not produced simultaneously.[1] Both are mounted on wood plaques that are inscribed in ink with the names of their owners. The British Museum's plaque is inscribed: *Robert Lytler did wear this badge XXV yere batyinge VII weeks from the 7th October 1600 and delivered this up the 25 (Januarie) 1625.* The Boston example bears the name *Robert Dod*.

Robert Dod, yeoman, of Nether Peover, who owned the Boston badge, included in his will (dated 1639) the following reference to Lord Cholmondeley (presumably Robert [1584–1659], who succeeded to his father's estates in 1621): "my eldest sonne William Dodde shall have and inioye that livinges meanes and tenementes which I have in lease from the Rt honble my good Lo. Cholmondleigh." The badge

20

itself is listed in the inventory of his estate, taken January 14, 1639: "The Crest of Cholmley -0 5. -0." The London badge belonged to Robert Lytler of Bradford Wood (Whitegate), whose will (dated 1643) names his "kind and loving maister Thomas Cholmondeley Esq. to be overseer of the same."[2] Thomas Cholmondeley was the fourth son of Sir Hugh Cholmondeley; it appears that Robert Lytler and Robert Dod served two different branches of the Cholmondeley family. The main branch (Cholmondeley of Cholmondeley) was divided after 1615 when Hugh Cholmondeley's widow, Dame Mary Cholmondeley (1563–1626) acquired the former monastery and estate of Vale Royal and turned it over to her younger son Thomas, establishing the cadet branch Cholmondeley of Vale Royal (now the Lords Delamere).

1. The British Museum's example has a different pattern of chasing on the upper edge of the wing and is not pierced in the area where the wing meets the griffin's back. It has retained much more of the black and red pigmentation than the Boston badge.
2. Information provided for Timothy Wilson by Colin Kemp and F. I. Dunn, Cheshire Record Office.

EWER AND BASIN
London, 1604/5
Silver gilt
47.1427–1428

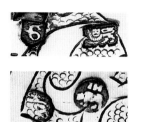

MARKS: on neck of ewer and on rim of basin, date letter *G*; lion passant; leopard's head crowned; maker's mark *IH* over a bear passant in a circle (Jackson, 1921, p. 107; rev. ed. 1989, p. 99) (struck twice on rim of basin)

ARMORIALS: pounced on center of boss of basin, an unidentified coat of arms: Quarterly, 1 and 4, three unicorns' heads couped, two and one; 2 and 3 a lion passant, in pretence, quarterly, 1 and 4, a chief indented, 2 and 3, a saltire between 12 ?

47.1427 (ewer): H. 49.5 cm (19½ in.); W. 21.4 cm (8⁷⁄₁₆ in.); diam. of foot 14 cm (5½ in.). 47.1428 (basin): H. 6 cm (2⅜ in.); diam. of basin 57.5 cm (22⅝ in.)

WEIGHT: 47.1427: 2,849.2 gm (91 oz 12 dwt). 47.1428: 4,323.4 gm (139 oz)

PROVENANCE: J. P. Morgan (1867–1943), sold Parke Bernet, New York, November 1, 1947, lot 468, purchased November 13, 1947, Theodora Wilbour Fund in Memory of Charlotte Beebe Wilbour.

EXHIBITED: Richmond, Virginia Museum of Fine Arts, 1964, cat. no. 74; Minneapolis, Minneapolis Institute of Arts, 1956, cat. no. 16; Birmingham, Alabama, Birmingham Museum of Art, 1991, fig. 20, p. 23; cat. no. 101, p. 111.

PUBLISHED: Hipkiss, 1951, p. 13.

DESCRIPTION: The body of the ewer is ovoid and rests on a high spool-shaped stem on a domed foot. The foot is struck with egg-and-dart and beaded patterns. The dome is chased with dolphins in a wavy sea. The decoration of the body is divided into three registers: acanthus leaves interspersed with round fruits, foliate scrolls enclosing griffins and horses against a matted ground, and oval strapwork enclosing dolphins and swags and clusters of fruit. Reserved at the front of the ewer is a plain shield, the engraving removed. The head of a winged putto is centered on the shoulder of the vessel. The flaring neck of the ewer has a shaped, notched rim; it is decorated with strapwork against a punched ground. A cast head of a grotesque is applied to the center of the neck under the rim, and an identical head is applied to the interior of the vessel below the join of the handle. The handle is in the form of a double scroll, with a grotesque head joining the neck, a female bust at the crest, and fruit clusters and animal masks. The ewer has been repaired at the join of the stem to the main vessel. In several areas, the gilding has flaked off revealing white silver beneath. The matted grounds of the middle and upper registers of the body have probably been reworked.

The round basin has a boss at the center pounced with a coat of arms. Surrounding the boss, three flat-chased oval strapwork panels enclose figures of sea monsters against a wavy ground interspersed with clusters of fruit against a matted ground. The central well of the basin is filled with three similar ovals enclosing sea monsters alternating with circular panels enclosing embossed masks. The interstices are filled with clusters of fruit, griffins, winged sphinxes, and winged horses against a matted ground. The rim of the dish has foliate strapwork broken by oval panels enclosing embossed sea monsters and heads of putti. A long patch has been added to the underside of the rim at the top of the basin.

CONSTRUCTION: The basin is raised with flat-chased, embossed, die-struck, and matted decoration. The chasing and matting in the curved section of the basin appear to have been reinforced. The applied boss at the center is composed of cast, die-struck, and drawn moldings. The central disk is a replacement. A large patch is applied to the underside of the rim and the gilding has been renewed. The foot of the ewer is assembled from three molded, embossed, and die-struck pieces. The spool-shaped section of the stem is formed of two raised pieces. The body of the vessel is raised with embossed, flat-chased, and matted decoration. The neck, joined to the body with a molded and die-struck collar, is also raised, chased, and matted. The handle and applied masks are cast. The gilding has been renewed and is flaking in large areas near the stem.

The ewer and basin are of a design that flourished in the years around 1600. Elements of the design are traceable directly to Italian and German graphic sources, but the division of the surface into strapwork panels filled with geometric scrolls against a matted ground is a distinctly English synthesis of Mannerist motifs. The liberal exchange among goldsmiths of designs and even molds is illustrated by the frequency with which these details appear on wares ranging in date from about 1585 until about 1610. Nürnberg engravers such as Paul Flindt (d. after 1618) composed decorative vessels inspired by antique bronzes. The present ewer has a caryatid handle and applied masks similar to those in an engraving of an oviform ewer by Flindt.[1] The three cast masks on the ewer appear on vessels in the Kremlin collections.[2] The style of the putto heads might be compared to a sheet of designs by Flindt that show the same high foreheads, tight curls, and small features.[3]

21

The alternating panels of clusters of fruit and sea monsters appear on a large group of English ewers and basins.[4] The sea monster in a wavy sea, a reference to the contents of the vessel, is a recurring motif. The present example is distinguished by the winged horses, griffins, and sphinxes in the curved section of the basin, which do not have a parallel on other surviving pieces of English silver. The stiff rendering, particularly evident in the sphinxes, may be attributable to restoration. Other elements of these unusual features are readily found in sixteenth-century printed designs,[5] however, and the notched saddle blankets appear on a livery pot in the Kremlin by the same maker.[6] The Kremlin livery pot also has an unusually high spool-shaped stem section, like the present ewer. The central boss of the basin may originally have been enameled, as on cat. no. 18. The arms must also have been removed from the shield on the front of the ewer, where scratches are visible. The pricked arms on the basin beneath the earl's coronet may have been added when the piece was regilded.

1. Janet S. Byrne, *Renaissance Ornament Prints and Drawings* (New York, 1981), p. 106, fig. 135.
2. See the grotesque mask on the standing cup of 1585/6 (Oman, 1961, pl. 44), the putto heads on a ewer of about 1605 (ibid., pl. 46) and a livery pot of 1604/5 by the same maker as the present example (ibid., pl. 22).
3. Ill. Carsten-Peter Warncke, *Die ornamentale Groteske in Deutschland 1500–1600* (Berlin, 1979), vol. 1, pl. 452.
4. The most closely related examples are: Untermyer Collection, Metropolitan Museum of Art, Ewer and basin, 1610, maker's mark *SO* pellets above and below, h. of ewer 40 cm, ill. Hackenbroch, rev. ed. 1969, no. 25; Eton College, Ewer and basin, 1610/11, maker's mark *SO* a cinquefoil and two pellets below, h. of ewer 38.7 cm, ill. Jones, 1938, p. 3, pl. 2; Sidney Sussex College, Ewer and basin, 1606/7, maker's mark *RW* a pellet below in a shaped shield, h. of ewer 48.9 cm, ill. Jones, 1910, pl. 115; Ewer and basin, 1615, maker's mark a trefoil slipped, h. of ewer 38.7 cm, formerly in the collection of William Randolph Hearst, sold Christie, Manson & Woods, London, December 14, 1938, lot 95; Victoria and Albert Museum, acc. no. M6-1961, Basin, 1607/8, maker's mark *RS* over a device in a plain shield, diam. 58 cm, ill. Glanville, 1990, no. 100, p. 468; Victoria and Albert Museum, acc. no. M13, M13a-1964, Ewer and basin, 1618/19, maker's mark for Thomas Flint, h. of ewer 35 cm, ill. Glanville,

1990, no. 102, pp. 471–472; Lord Petre, Ewer and basin, 1611, ill. Watts, 1924, pl. 31a,b.
5. Inspired by the decoration of the Domus Aurea and other antique monuments, all are common themes in Italian decorative painting of the early sixteenth century; see Nicole Dacos, *La Découverte de la Domus Aurea et la formation des grotesques à la Renaissance* (London, 1969). Winged sphinxes and deer wearing notched saddle blankets like those on the present basin appear in a print by Etienne Delaune (1518–1588); see Eva-Maria Hanebutt-Benz, *Ornament und Entwurf* (Frankfurt, 1983), no. 22, p. 63.
6. Livery pot, 1604/5, maker's mark *IH* over a bear, h. 48.3 cm, ill. Oman, 1961, pl. 22.

• 22 •

COMMUNION CUP AND PATEN COVER
London, 1605/6
Silver
33.63

MARKS: on cup near rim and on inside of paten, date letter *h*; lion passant; leopard's head crowned; maker's mark *IH* over a bear passant in a circle (Jackson, 1921, p. 107; rev. ed. 1989, p. 99)

INSCRIPTIONS: engraved on top of finial, *1606*

H. 22.2 cm (8¾ in.); diam. of rim 8.9 cm (3½ in.)

WEIGHT: 476.3 gm (15 oz 6 dwt)

PROVENANCE: Christie, Manson & Woods, London, April 17, 1928, lot 80; Anonymous Gift in Memory of Charlotte Beebe Wilbour (1833–1914), March 2, 1933.

EXHIBITED: Boston, Museum of Fine Arts, 1933 (no catalogue).

DESCRIPTION: The cup rests on a stepped molded foot with a stamped rim. The domed section of the foot is engraved with a band of sylized foliage. The stem is spool-shaped with a flattened knop. The vessel has high, slightly flaring sides, a flat base, and an everted rim. It is engraved with a band of stylized foliage. The cover is slightly domed and engraved with a band of foliage; it has a spool-shaped finial with a broad flat top.

CONSTRUCTION: The domed foot of the vessel is raised with applied cast and stamped wire moldings. The stem is formed from two raised pieces joined to a formed knop with molded wires at each end. The body of the vessel is raised and engraved. The cover is formed from a single disk, with an applied wire forming the interior bezel; the finial is composed of a raised spool-shaped base surmounted by a flat disk.

22

• 23 •

FLAGON
Probably John Acton
London, 1607/8
Silver gilt
56.1184

MARKS: on cover near finial and repeated on underside of base, date letter *K;* lion passant; leopard's head crowned; maker's mark *IA* a pellet below in a shaped shield (Jackson, 1921, p. 114; rev. ed. 1989, p. 103)

INSCRIPTIONS: scratched on base, *39 00; XXXIX oz half . . .*

H. 30.4 cm (12 in.); w. 20.1 cm (7¹¹⁄₁₆ in.); diam. of foot 13.5 cm (5⁵⁄₁₆ in.)

WEIGHT: 1219.1 gm (39 oz 4 dwt)

PROVENANCE: Christie, Manson & Woods, London, May 18, 1898, lot 138; Earl of Kilmorey, sold Christie, Manson & Woods, London, July 13, 1926, lot 95, purchased by Walter H. Willson, Ltd., London; Mrs. F. H. Cook, sold Sotheby & Co., London, June 14, 1934, lot 151; William Randolph Hearst, sold Christie, Manson & Woods, London, December 14, 1938, lot 96; James Robinson, New York; purchased from Thomas Lumley, Ltd., London, December 13, 1956, Theodora Wilbour Fund in Memory of Charlotte Beebe Wilbour.

EXHIBITED: Birmingham, Alabama, Birmingham Museum of Art, 1991, cat. no. 102, pp. 24, 112, fig. 24.

PUBLISHED: *Connoisseur* 117, no. 500 (1946), p. 111 (James Robinson advertisement); Clayton, 1971, p. 136, no. 284, rev. ed. 1985, p. 188, fig. 284.

DESCRIPTION: The foot of the flagon is molded and stamped with egg-and-dart decoration. A flared border above is flat-chased in a fluted pattern. The tall body of the flagon has slightly tapering sides. The decoration is flat-chased in three horizontal registers with a pattern of intertwining foliage, flowers, grapes, and greyhounds against a punched ground. At the center of the decoration is an asymmetrical blank shield. The bun-shaped cover has a flaring rim and molding stamped with ovolo and fluted decoration. It is flat-chased with a pattern of foliage and greyhounds. The thumbpiece is in the shape of a cartouche enclosing the head of a putto. The spool-shaped finial is surmounted by a cast collar and a baluster finial. The handle is ear shaped and is engraved along the spine with a foliate pattern and on the terminus with a hatched pattern.

CONSTRUCTION: The body of the flagon is raised. The foot rim is formed from four pieces, chased, die-punched, and soldered. The cover is raised; the molded, die-struck rim is attached.

The handle is formed from two pieces. The thumbpiece and finial are cast. The gilding has been renewed.

Tall straight-sided vessels such as this were described in contemporary inventories as livery pots. Intended as serving jugs, they were made for both domestic and liturgical use; many domestic examples were later presented to churches for use in the service of communion wine.[1]

The maker's mark *IA* a pellet below has recently been attributed to John Acton, who was apprenticed to Hugh Kayle.[2] He became free in 1595, and from his shop in Lombard Street, supplied plate to the King. Of the twenty-four pieces by Acton recorded, the best known are the pair of flagons of 1601/2 with engraving attributed to Nicaise Roussel known as "The Mostyn Flagons."[3] They are similar in design to the present flagon, with identical stamping of the moldings of the foot, rim, and cover. The precise, geometric style of the flat chasing and the punched background on this flagon are found on several pieces of about the same date by different makers, most notably a pair of small tankards of 1608/9 and 1619/20 at Gonville and Caius College, Cambridge, that have flat-chased scrolling foliage enclosing animal figures.[4] Other examples of the style appear on a bell salt of 1603 and on a flagon of 1619 from St. Mary Abbots Church.[5] On the salt, the foliage scrolls enclose bunches of grapes, whereas on the flagon, a stylized flower is centered on the branch. The punched backgrounds of these pieces are not as precisely ordered as that on the present example, which is exceptional. The asymmetrical outline of the shield on the front of the flagon is unusual, but may also be seen on a salt in the Schroder Collection.[6]

1. Glanville, 1990, pp. 266–267.
2. Taylor, 1984, p. 99. For Hugh Kayle (active 1569, d. 1604) see cat. no. 7.
3. Temple Newsam House, Leeds, (acc. no. 4/78) and Manchester City Art Gallery, (acc. no. 1978.1), sold Christie, Manson & Woods, London, June 29, 1977, lot 137.
4. One of the pair has the date letter for 1608/9 and the maker's mark *IH* over a bear passant; the other is marked for 1619/20 and bears the maker's mark *TE* in monogram. See Jones, 1910, pp. 28–29, pl. 32. Oman tentatively attributes this decoration to the engraver Nicaise Roussel. Oman, 1978a, pp. 4–8. The motif of the animals emerging from a blossom also ap-

23

pears on an engraved flagon in Moscow (Jones, 1909, p. 10, pl. 5, no. 1). Roussel's engraved designs, however, are much more complex and mannered. See also cat. nos. 17 and 18.
5. For the salt, see London, Seaford House, 1929, cat. no. 91, pl. 29; for the flagon, see Oman, 1957, pl. 108b.
6. Maker's mark *ER,* ca. 1600, ill. Schroder, 1983, cat. no. 34, pp. 110–111.

· 24 ·

EWER
Probably London, ca. 1610
Porcelain (China, Ming Dynasty, probably Wan-li period [1573–1619]) with silver mounts
55.471

Unmarked
H. 22.1 cm (8¹¹⁄₁₆ in.); w. 19.6 cm (7¾ in.); d. 13.3 cm (5¼ in.)

PROVENANCE: purchased from Nicolas Landau, Paris, September 15, 1955, Theodora Wilbour Fund in Memory of Charlotte Beebe Wilbour.

EXHIBITED: New York, China House Gallery, 1980–1981, cat. no. 27, p. 51; New York, Frick Collection, 1986–1987, cat. no. 2, p. 32.

PUBLISHED: Fontein, 1982, cat. no. 273.

DESCRIPTION: The porcelain vessel has a bulbous body with shallow vertical lobes and a tall flaring neck cut in to a narrow straight-sided rim. A bulbous lobe on the shoulder forms the base of the spout. The porcelain is decorated in underglaze blue with birds and flowers. The silver mounts consist of a stamped foot rim, three vertical stamped and molded straps with undulating outline, and a circular collar with stamped decoration at the base of the neck, to which the straps and the handle are attached. The ear-shaped handle is formed of flat sheet, scrolled at both ends and engraved; a thin, molded wire decorates the spine. A collar encircles the top of the neck, anchoring the hinge and cover. The thumbpiece is in the form of a winged mermaid. The cover is domed, with a stamped molded rim and a small flange, and is chased with vertical lobes. The finial is pagoda shaped. The silver spout is in the form of the neck and head of a dragon or griffin, with pointed ears and wattles.

CONSTRUCTION: The foot ring is composed of molded and stamped wires. The other elements are formed, with the exception of the spout and the thumbpiece, which are cast. The vertical straps are joined to the foot and collar

with hinges; the collar around the neck of the bottle is formed in two pieces and pinned.

A surprisingly large number of Wan-li *kendis* with European mounts have survived. The *kendi* was produced throughout south Asia, and was originally designed as a drinking vessel that would not touch the lips.[1] In the Near East, the form was adopted for use as a water-pipe or hookah. *Kendis* were also made in the shapes of animals,[2] but the exported examples with metal mounts are invariably of a form similar to the present piece.

The broad popularity of blue and white porcelain jugs with silver mounts is recorded in numerous Dutch still-life paintings,[3] which show that the ewers were appreciated for the rich and luminous quality of the porcelain. Among the examples related to this are *kendis* and jugs with German and Dutch mounts. A ewer in the Kunstgewerbemuseum, Berlin, with German silver-gilt mounts has a similar smeary cobalt decoration under a thick glassy glaze.[4] The present ewer has coarse clay, thick glaze, and imperfections in the cobalt that suggest that it was produced in a provincial kiln, not at Jingdezhen.[5] A large proportion of these blue and white wares were brought to Europe by Portuguese traders who established a trading center in Macao in 1557.[6]

The precise dating of the silver mounts is difficult, since few are marked. The distinctive spout in the form of a dragon's head on the present piece is found on several other ewers, most notably on a silver flagon from Tong Church, Shropshire, marked in London 1606.[7] The similarity in the modeling of the heads suggests that they may be from the same mold. A ewer with a similar spout and cover, but more complex mounts incorporating a cast bracket in the form of a lion, was recorded in a still life by P. van Roestraten.[8] Other details of the mounts are less English in character, particularly the stamped crosses on the foot ring, which are more commonly found on Dutch or German work. The 1649 inventory of the Upper Jewel House includes a "Cheynye large pott with an eagle Beake and serpent handle with a Cover richly garnisht," but the high price of fifty pounds placed on the piece suggests that it was larger in scale and more lavishly mounted than the present example.[9]

84

1. See Chicago, David and Alfred Smart Gallery, University of Chicago, *Blue and White Porcelain and Its Impact on the Western World* (1985) catalogue by John Carswell, cat. no. 54, p. 112.

2. John Alexander Pope, *Chinese Porcelains from the Ardebil Shrine* (Washington, D.C., 1956), pl. 97.

3. Lunsingh Scheurleer, 1980, pp. 187–220.

4. Berlin, Kunstgewerbemuseum, *Kunst der Welt in den Berliner Museen* (Stuttgart, 1980), p. 78, no. 32.

5. I am grateful to Robert Mowry and to Denise Patry Leidy for their observations about the Chinese porcelain.

6. For a survey of the importation of Chinese porcelain to England, see Glanville, 1987a, pp. 156–160.

7. Clayton, rev. ed. 1985, p. 188, fig. 283. Another of similar design, dated 1606, is part of the church plate of Monken Hadley, Middlesex, ill. Glanville, 1990, p. 296, fig. 175.

8. See Lunsingh Scheurleer, 1980, p. 187, fig. 31; an apparantly identical ewer is also illustrated (fig. 32), then in the collection of Nicolas Landau, also the former owner of the present object.

9. Oliver Millar, "The Inventories and Valuations of the King's Goods, 1649–1651," *Walpole Society* 43 (1972), p. 30.

· 25 ·

ARCHITECTURAL SALT
London, ca. 1610
Silver
61.654

MARKS: on dome of cover, base near central column, and under top section near center column, maker's mark a ship in a plain shield (Jackson, 1921, p. 111; rev. ed. 1989, p. 107)

H. 29.8 cm (11¾ in.); W. 11.4 cm (4½ in.)

WEIGHT: 737.1 gm (23 oz 14 dwt)

PROVENANCE: R. W. M. Walker, Esq., London, sold Christie, Manson & Woods, London, July 11, 1945, lot 222, purchased by Thomas Lumley, Ltd., London, sold to Colonel Howard Bury, Ireland; sold Sotheby & Co., London, November 17, 1960, lot 100, purchased by Thomas Lumley, Ltd., London, purchased September 20, 1961, Theodora Wilbour Fund in Memory of Charlotte Beebe Wilbour.

EXHIBITED: London, Park Lane, 1929, cat. no. 539, pl. 6; Victoria and Albert Museum, 1929–1945.

PUBLISHED: Watts, 1924, p. 42, pl. 21; Smith, 1968, p. 216.

DESCRIPTION: The square base of the salt rests on four ball feet, each surmounted by a pinnacle. The flange and side of the base are stamped with an ovolo pattern. The base is domed and supports five columns; one at each corner resting on a square base with a molded wire at the top and bottom edge, and a fifth at the center with a stamped molding at the top and the bottom. The larger receptacle for salt forms the entablature. The removable cover is composed of two tiers: the lower level has a molded flange and a border stamped with an ovolo pattern, four pinnacles at the corners, and a domed center. The upper section of the cover rests on four scroll brackets with circular moldings stamped with ovolo decoration above and below. A second, smaller container for salt surmounts this fitting; it has a domed cover, ovolo stamping on the rim, and a finial in the form of a standing warrior holding in his right hand a shield and in his left a spear.

CONSTRUCTION: The spherical feet are formed in two halves. They are surmounted by cast pinnacles. The square base of the salt is raised. The columns are seamed and attached to the base and entablature with threaded silver rods. The base of the entablature is raised with an applied, stamped flange and a complex molding of three pieces. The removable receptacle for the salt is raised. The square cover for the large salt is raised with applied wire edges and cast pinnacles at the corners. The smaller salt is supported on two molded, stamped rings attached by cast brackets and a threaded post. The cover is formed and stamped; the finial is cast. The surface of the salt is extensively rubbed and worn. The feet and the pinnacles on the cover have been reattached. The mechanism which attaches the small salt to the cover of the large salt is a modern addition.

Though considerably altered in appearance, this salt is a late example of a form that was established by the 1570s. Perhaps the grandest surviving of the architectural salts, that is, standing salts in the form of a classical temple incorporating columns, is the Gibbon salt in the Goldsmiths' Company,[1] in which the columns are arranged at the center of each side rather than at the corners. The Gibbon Salt and the Affabel Partridge salt of 1577/8 in the Museum's collection[2] have rich cast and chased ornament, and a central cylinder of rock crystal enclosing a gilt figure.

The relatively austere appearance of this example may be attributed in part to a later date, but is largely due to its condition. The best comparison is found in the Butleigh Salt, now in the Barber Institute of Fine Arts, Birmingham.[3] It is fully marked for 1606, and, though similar in scale to the present example, is nearly twice as heavy. Philippa Glanville has observed that the weight of a great salt is frequently deceptively low, and does not reflect the scale of the object or its importance on the table.[4] The Butleigh Salt is much more highly decorated than the present example. It rests on feet in the form of griffins, the bases and capitals of the columns are modeled and chased, and the central column is covered overall with a scale pattern.[5]

It is difficult to speculate how the present salt may have been altered. It was almost certainly gilt like all other surviving architectural salts; the worn surface suggests that some chasing and engraving may have been removed. The pinnacles surmounting the ball feet do not have an architectural reference, and may be additions. The plain column in the center may replace a more complex figure group or an ornamented column. The maker's mark, which is rather large for an English mark, is recorded by Jackson on a bell salt of 1608/9.

1. Worshipful Company of Goldsmiths, The Gibbon Salt, 1576, silver gilt, h. 30.5 cm, ill. Carrington and Hughes, 1926, pl. 17, pp. 37–39.
2. See cat. no. 10.
3. Barber Institute of Fine Arts, Birmingham, The Butleigh Salt, London, 1606, maker's mark *M,* h. 31.8 cm, sold Sotheby & Co., London, January 31, 1946, lot 146. See also Glanville, 1990, p. 289, fig. 170.
4. Ibid., p. 282.
5. The only available comparison for the plain columns and bases on the present salt is a copper-gilt Spanish monstrance of about 1620; the pinnacled canopy is supported by eight columns that are similar in profile to the present salt. Victoria and Albert Museum, acc. no. M.196–1956, Monstrance, Spanish, copper-gilt, h. 74.6 cm. See Charles Oman, *The Golden Age of Hispanic Silver 1400–1665* (London, 1968), cat. no. 133, p. 47, fig. 231.

25

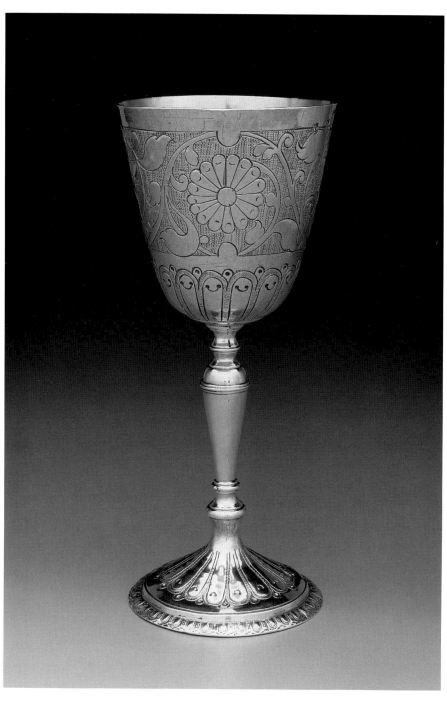

26

WINE CUP
London, 1612/13
Silver, parcel gilt
62.167

MARKS: on rim, date letter *p*; lion passant; leopard's head crowned; maker's mark *HB* conjoined a star below (Jackson, 1921, p. 113; rev. ed. 1989, p. 109)

INSCRIPTIONS: engraved on underside of foot, *.I.W. .I.F.*

H. 17.3 cm (6¹³⁄₁₆ in.); diam. of rim 7.9 cm (3⅛ in.)

WEIGHT: 186.2 gm (5 oz 18 dwt)

PROVENANCE: purchased from Firestone & Parson, Boston, February 14, 1962, Theodora Wilbour Fund in Memory of Charlotte Beebe Wilbour.

PUBLISHED: Gruber, 1982, p. 69, fig. 58.

DESCRIPTION: The cup rests on a slightly conical foot that has a stamped fluted border and flat-chased decoration in a rayed pattern emanating from the juncture of the stem. The U-shaped cup is supported on a tall baluster stem. A flat-chased pattern on the underside of the cup echos the decoration on the foot. The sides of the cup have flat-chased flowers in scrolling foliage against a matted ground.

CONSTRUCTION: The foot and body of the cup are raised. The stem is cast in two pieces with a vertical seam. The foot is strengthened by an applied stamped wire.

This is one of a large number of similarly decorated wine cups to have survived from the first two decades of the seventeenth century. The chased fluted decoration on the foot and underside of the cup is a standard formula; on many examples the scrolling foliage encloses a bunch of grapes,[1] a reference to the use of the vessel as a wine cup. Such domestic wine cups were probably produced in sets.

1. Compare the following related examples: Cup, 1605, maker's mark *AB* conjoined, h. 17.8 cm, sold Sotheby & Co., London, February 1, 1973, lot 140; Victoria and Albert Museum, Cup, 1609/10, maker's mark *EW* in a shaped shield, h. 15.1 cm, ill. Glanville, 1990, cat. no. 17, p. 404; Cup, 1609, h. 16.5 cm, ill. Wenham, 1931, pl. 36.

BELL SALT
London, 1614/5
Silver gilt
35.1556

27

MARKS: on side of lower and middle sections, date letter *p;* lion passant; leopard's head crowned; maker's mark *HM* conjoined a mullet and two pellets below and a pellet above in a shaped shield (Jackson, 1921, p. 113; rev. ed. 1989, p. 106) (repeated on inside of cover)

INSCRIPTIONS: on side of middle section, pounced, *DPC*

H. 21.6 cm (8½ in.), W. 10.1 cm (4 in.)

WEIGHT: 260.5 gm (8 oz 7 dwt)

PROVENANCE: Davies Gilbert, Trelissick (unverified); William Bruford & Sons, Exeter; William E. Godfrey, New York, purchased by Frank Brewer Bemis, 1925, Gift of Frank Brewer Bemis, November 7, 1935.

PUBLISHED: Hipkiss, 1929, p. 38; Buhler, 1952, p. 228, no. 6; Gruber, 1982, p. 160, fig. 217.

DESCRIPTION: The salt rests on three ball feet and is composed of three separate sections. The middle and lower sections are spool-shaped; each is fitted with a well for salt at the top. The sides are decorated with strapwork and geometric ornament against a matted ground. The lower borders are chased with a bead-and-reel pattern, and the molded rims have a stamped bead pattern. The removable cover is domed and surmounted by a threaded sleeve and a removable pierced finial. The dome is chased with acanthus leaves and has a stamped beaded rim.

CONSTRUCTION: The three sections of the salt are raised, with applied rims of molded or stamped wire. The finial is cast and fabricated in three sections. The hollow ball feet are formed in two sections. The surface of the salt has a grainy texture that may be attributable to regilding.

Approximately thirty salts of a similar design are known, ranging in date from 1591 to 1620. The origin of the form has been discussed at some length, but remains uncertain.[1] Philippa Glanville has recently shown that single and double bell salts were produced in sets.[2] There is almost no variation in the form in the thirty years during which it was popular; each example has similar proportions and ball feet, sometimes cursorily chased with claws, and a threaded pierced finial to be used for casting pepper or spice. The flat-chased ornament consists of flowers within scrollwork, scales, or most often, foliage within strapwork, as on this example. The Stoke Prior Bell Salt is a single-tier example that represents a category of more modest undecorated domestic plate that has not survived in any quantity.[3]

1. Penzer lists twenty-five bell salts, and discusses inventory references from the mid-sixteenth century to "bell salts." See N. M. Penzer, "Christ's Hospital Plate, I," *Apollo* 72, no. 425 (1960), pp. 16–18; see also Schroder, 1983, pp. 109–111. The present salt was not included on Penzer's list.
2. Glanville, 1990, p. 284.
3. Victoria and Albert Museum, acc. no. 284-1893, the Stoke Prior Bell Salt, 1596/7, maker's mark a bird's claw, h. 9.7 cm, ill. Glanville, 1990, cat. no. 93, p. 461.

· 28 ·

PORTRAIT MEDALLION DEPICTING JAMES I, ANNE OF DENMARK, AND CHARLES, PRINCE OF WALES
Attributed to Simon de Passe (ca. 1595–1647)
London, ca. 1619
Silver
1972.986

Unmarked
INSCRIPTIONS: engraved around edge of reverse, *IACOBUS D.G MAG: BRITT: ET. HIB. REX. ET SERENISS. ANNA D:G. MAG. BRITT REGINA UNA CUM ILL.P. CAROLI. M. BRIT. PRINCIP*[is] *-OTENTISS:*

ARMORIALS: engraved on the reverse, the royal arms of James I and Anne of Denmark

H. 6.3 cm (2½ in.); W. 5.1 cm (2 in.)

WEIGHT: 17.1 gm (11 dwt)

PROVENANCE: Sotheby & Co., London, June 22, 1972, lot 129; purchased from Cyril Humphris, Ltd., London, December 13, 1972, Theodora Wilbour Fund in Memory of Charlotte Beebe Wilbour.

EXHIBITED: Sarasota, Florida, The John and Mable Ringling Museum of Art, *Dutch Seventeenth Century Portraiture*, 1980, catalogue by William H. Wilson, cat. no. 120.

PUBLISHED: Brett, 1986, p. 102, fig. 284.

DESCRIPTION: The oval medallion is finely engraved on the obverse with the portrait busts of James I, Anne of Denmark, and Charles, Prince of Wales. The reverse depicts the royal arms of James and Anne of Denmark supported by a lion and a wild man and surmounted by a helmet, coronet, and mantling. Below are the feathers and motto of the Prince of Wales and the mottoes of the King and Queen.

CONSTRUCTION: The medallion is formed from a thin sheet of silver and engraved.

This medallion is one of a large number attributed to Simon de Passe (ca. 1595–1647). Trained in his father's Utrecht studio, Simon de Passe arrived in London in about 1616, where he executed a series of portrait medallions of the royal family, including a gold medallion of Elizabeth I, and single portraits of James I, Anne of Denmark, and the Prince of Wales.[1] The series must have been commissioned by James I, who would have been following a Tudor tradition of presenting painted portrait miniatures to a small circle of admirers.[2]

There are at least four examples of this design known.[3] Though they have been published as bearing de Passe's monogram, it is difficult to be certain if they are indeed signed. On the present example there appears to be the monogram *SP* on the reverse near the lower left edge of the oval containing the feathers of the Prince of Wales, but it is difficult to interpret and does not match any of de Passe's recorded monograms, nor is it in keeping with the inscriptions on any other medallions.[4]

There has been considerable debate about the method of manufacture of this group. Similarities on a minute scale between certain medals have led to the suggestion that they were struck; alternate hypotheses include the possibility that they were struck from an etched plate, or that an inked sheet from an engraved original was used to transfer the design to a fresh

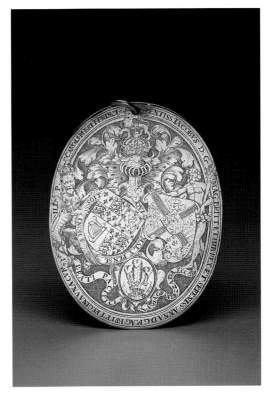

28

blank.[5] It has been proposed more recently that some were cast.[6] The present example is almost certainly engraved. In spite of the surface wear, the variation in the weight and depth of the lines is quite consistent with engraved work.[7] It does appear, however, that the similarities between some of these medals can only be attributable to mechanical reproduction.

1. D. Franken, *L'Oeuvre Gravé des van de Passe* (Amsterdam, 1881); K. G. Boon, ed., *Hollstein's Dutch and Flemish Etchings, Engravings and Woodcuts,* vol. 16 (Amsterdam, 1974).
2. See London, Victoria and Albert Museum, *Artists of the Tudor Court,* 1983, catalogue by Roy Strong, pp. 9–10.
3. Victoria and Albert Museum, acc. no. 962–1904, Glanville, 1990, cat. no. 128, pp. 484–485; British Museum, see British Museum, *Medallic Illustrations of the History of Great Britain and Ireland* (London, 1911), pl. 16, no. 6; Sotheby & Co., July 19, 1979, lot 198.
4. See G. K. Nagler, *Die Monogrammisten,* vol. 4 (Munich, 1909), p. 959. Variations on de Passe's inscription on other medals include: *Si.Pas.fe* on a medal of Elizabeth I in the Queen's collection (exhibited New York, *Britain Salutes New York,* 1983, pp. 52–55); *SP fe* in the borders of a medal of Anne of Denmark in the Victoria and Albert (acc. no. 259–1906, ill. Glanville, 1990, cat. no. 127, p. 484); and *Simon Passaeus sculp.* on a medallion of Charles, Prince of Wales, in the British Museum (see Frederiks, 1958, cat. no. 74, p. 24).
5. G. F. Hill, "The Technique of Simon de Passe," *Numismatic Chronicle,* 4th series, 15 (1915), pp. 230–242.
6. Mark Jones, "The Technique of Simon van de Passe Reconsidered," *Numismatic Chronicle* 143 (1983), pp. 227–230.
7. I am grateful to Roy Perkinson for his observations about this piece.

FOOTED DISH
London, 1619/20
Silver
61.184

MARKS: on rim, maker's mark *CB* in monogram in a plain shield (Jackson, 1921, p. 107; rev. ed. 1989, p. 103); leopard's head crowned; lion passant; date letter *b*

ARMORIALS: engraved in center, the arms of Langworthy of Bath, Somerset, differenced with a crescent for a second son, and the motto *Vetuste Digne*

H. 7.4 cm (2¹⁵⁄₁₆ in.); diam. 23 cm (9¹⁄₁₆ in.)

WEIGHT: 361.2 gm (11 oz 12 dwt)

PROVENANCE: Christie, Manson & Woods, London, April 4, 1922, lot 106; Christie, Manson & Woods, London, May 5, 1937, lot 105; Mrs. R. Makower, sold Sotheby & Co., London, March 16, 1961, lot 133, purchased April 12, 1961, Theodora Wilbour Fund in Memory of Charlotte Beebe Wilbour.

PUBLISHED: Came, 1961, p. 47, fig. 34; Clayton, 1971, p. 108, fig. 222, rev. ed., 1985, p. 150, fig. 222; Brett, 1986, p. 123, fig. 407.

DESCRIPTION: The dish rests on a spool-shaped foot that is stamped around the rim with an ovolo pattern. The foot has alternating oval panels of piercing and flat-chasing. The circular dish has a slightly domed center, curved sides, and a broad flat rim. It is pierced and chased overall with panels of fruit and foliage enclosing putto heads. The rim is similarly chased and pierced with a band of foliage.

CONSTRUCTION: The dish is raised, embossed, chased, and pierced. The rim has been strengthened by the addition of a thin band to the underside. The foot is raised, pierced, and chased.

This is one of a small group of footed dishes with pierced and embossed decoration that has long been associated with a Portuguese prototype. The English and Portuguese examples have a slightly curved bowl with geometric decoration divided into three concentric registers.[1] In 1950 Charles Oman proposed that the designs were inspired by imported Portuguese dishes, but the resemblance had been observed as early as 1896 when a dish was catalogued as Portuguese, with London hallmarks for 1621.[2] Ruling out the possibility of a community of Portuguese-trained craftsmen in London or a series of printed designs, Oman determined that the

English makers were copying imported silver. He pointed to James I's 1604 treaty with Spain that opened avenues of trade for English merchants in Lisbon, as evidenced by Portuguese silver sold by Charles I in 1626 and by documented examples in English churches. If his theory about the source of this English form is correct, it echos a similar pattern in the production of lobed bowls in Boston following a Portuguese model.[3]

Philippa Glanville points out that the function of these dishes is not clear in inventory references and suggests that they were probably used in the service of dessert.[4] There are at least three other dishes similar to the present one.[5] One of identical design in the Gilbert Collection bears hallmarks for 1652. It has been suggested that it was unmarked at the time of manufacture and submitted for assay only when it changed hands some thirty years later. An unpierced dish of 1631 by the same maker as the present example shows a more restrained use of similar motifs; it is divided into five lobes and has a border incorporating the heads of winged putti and lozenges.[6]

1. It should be added that the formula also appears in other metals; a silvered copper example in the Victoria and Albert Museum has a pierced border and incorporates the heads of winged putti similar to those on the present example. Victoria and Albert Museum, M6-1981.
2. Oman and Rosas, 1950, pp. 162–164; Charles Oman, "Portuguese Silver in the Possession of English Churches," *Apollo* 54, no. 317 (1951), pp. 14–16; Christie, Manson & Woods, London, April 12, 1896, lot 161.
3. A bowl by Jeremiah Dummer in the Yale University Art Gallery follows a Portuguese design; see Kathryn C. Buhler and Graham Hood, *American Silver* (New Haven, 1970) cat. no. 10, p. 19.
4. Glanville, 1990, p. 449.
5. Fitzwilliam Museum, Cambridge, M.26.1938, Dish, 1616/17, maker's mark *TC*, diam. 28 cm, see exh. cat. Cambridge, Fitzwilliam Museum, 1975, cat. no. S1, p. 36; Gilbert Collection, Los Angeles, Dish, marked 1652/3, maker's mark *IF*, diam. 24.5 cm, see Schroder, 1988, cat. no. 20, p. 96; Honorable Society of the Middle Temple, Dish, 1619, maker's mark probably *BS*, diam. 31.7 cm, see Clayton, rev. ed. 1985, p. 151, fig. 225.
6. Footed dish, 1631, maker's mark *CB* in monogram, diam. 29.9 cm, see Sotheby & Co., London, January 31, 1963, lot 152.

29

STEEPLE CUP
London, 1619/20
Silver gilt
46.1126

MARKS: on rim, date letter *b*; lion passant (repeated on underside of foot); leopard's head crowned; maker's mark *FW* in monogram in a shaped shield (Jackson, 1921, p. 112; rev. ed. 1989, p. 108)

INSCRIPTIONS: engraved on underside of foot, *Elizabeth Montagu Duchess Dow* of Buccleuch & Queensberry 1817*

H. 47.5 cm (18¹¹⁄₁₆ in.); diam. 12.8 cm (5¹⁄₁₆ in.)

WEIGHT: 776.8 gm (25 oz)

PROVENANCE: Elizabeth, Duchess of Buccleuch and Queensberry (m. 1767, d. 1827); Lord Montagu of Beaulieu, sold Christie, Manson & Woods, London, May 26, 1905, lot 63; Sydney Loder, Esq.; sold Sotheby & Co., London, April 10, 1930, lot 127, purchased by Crichton Brothers, London; Richard C. Paine, Boston, Gift of Richard C. Paine, October 10, 1946.

EXHIBITED: London, Seaford House, 1929, cat. no. 105 (lent by Sidney Loder, Esq.); Minneapolis, Minneapolis Institute of Arts, 1956, cat. no. 17; New York, Cooper-Hewitt Museum, 1985 (not in catalogue).

PUBLISHED: Hipkiss, 1951, p. 13; N. M. Penzer, "The Steeple Cup—Part IV," *Apollo* 72, no. 428 (1960), p. 109; N. M. Penzer, "An Index of English Silver Steeple Cups," *Proceedings of the Society of Silver Collectors,* no. 6, n.d., p. 19.

DESCRIPTION: The cup stands on a high waisted foot that is chased and embossed with stylized acanthus leaves and melons. The rim is stamped with flutes alternating with flowers. The baluster stem has a cast collar above and below, with three brackets joining the center of the baluster to the upper collar. The lower section of the cup is chased with a pattern of acanthus and melons. A flat-chased pattern of semicircles and leaves surrounds the rim. The domed cover has a flat flange and is embossed with acanthus leaves and melons in a manner similar to that on the body of the cup and on the foot. The finial is supported on a raised disk surrounded by a stamped border. Three cast caryatid figures serve as the base to the finial, which is pyramidal and is pierced on each side with a strapwork pattern.

CONSTRUCTION: The body of the vessel, the cover, and the foot are raised, with embossed and flat-chased decoration. The stem is cast in several pieces. The brackets, two rayed collars on the stem, and the finial are cast. The top of the stem is fitted to receive a threaded mount soldered onto the base of the body.

The steeple cup, a standing cup with a finial in the shape of a spire, has survived in large quantity from about the last decade of the sixteenth century through the middle of the seventeenth century, though inventory records indicate that they were in use from at least the 1560s.[1] Though made initially for domestic use, many were later presented to churches for use as communion cups, further explaining the large number of surviving examples.

Penzer recorded 148 steeple cups,[2] categorizing the common pattern on the present example as "standard."[3] The stylized embossing around the base of the bowl represents acanthus leaves interspersed with melons. The earliest appearance of this pattern on a steeple cup is in 1614, though a similar motif was used on other wares at a slightly earlier date.[4]

Lady Elizabeth Montagu, for whom the cup was inscribed in 1817, inherited the personal estate, plate, and jewels of her father, George Brudenell, Duke of Montagu and fourth Earl of Cardigan (1712–1790). She may have purchased the cup from Robert Garrard who supplied his clients with newly fashionable antique silver.

1. Glanville, 1990, p. 252.
2. N. M. Penzer, "An Index of English Silver Steeple Cups," *Proceedings of the Society of Silver Collectors,* no. 6, n.d., pp. 1–23. He lists two other cups that bear the same maker's mark as the present example: one in the church of Barford St. Martin, Wiltshire, of 1611, illustrated in Nightingale, 1891, p. 45, and another from St. Alban's, described in Charles Henry Ashdown, *Notes on the Corporation Plate and Insignia of the City of St. Albans* (London, 1903), p. 7.
3. See N. M. Penzer, "The Steeple Cup—I," *Apollo* 70, no. 418 (1959), pp. 161–166; idem, "The Steeple Cup—II," *Apollo* 71, no. 422 (1960), pp. 103–109; idem, "The Steeple Cup—III," *Apollo* 71, no. 424 (1960), pp. 165–170; idem, "The Steeple Cup—IV," *Apollo* 72, no. 428 (1960), pp. 105–110; idem, "The Steeple Cup—V," *Apollo* 72, no. 430 (1960), pp. 173–178.
4. See, for example, the ewer of 1605 (cat. no 21) and the standing cup of the same year in the Kremlin, ill. Jones, 1909, no. 2, pl. 11.

30

31

· 3 1 ·

TANKARD
German or English, ca. 1620
Serpentine with silver mounts
59.718

Unmarked

ARMORIALS: engraved on cover, the arms of
Sebastian Harvey (ca. 1552–1620/1) of London
and Walton in Stone, Staffordshire.

INSCRIPTIONS: engraved on underside of
foot rim, *Sir Sebastian Harvey, came to be Lord
Maior 1618*

H. 13.5 cm (5⁵⁄₁₆ in.); w. 12.4 cm (4⅞ in.);
diam. of foot 8.3 cm (3¼ in.)

PROVENANCE: purchased from John Hunt,
Dublin, November 12, 1959, Theodora Wilbour
Fund in Memory of Charlotte Beebe Wilbour.

DESCRIPTION: The black serpentine body of
the tankard is bombé in shape, with two registers of horizontal molding at the mid-section
and below the rim. The base is mounted with a
silver foot rim with a serrated bezel. The mid-
section and rim of the vessel are encircled with
molded silver bands to which the ear-shaped
handle is attached. The silver cover is stepped
and slightly domed. The thumbpiece is in the
form of an elongated scroll.

CONSTRUCTION: The stone vessel is lathe
turned. The silver foot ring, moldings, and
handle are fabricated. The cover is raised.

Ranging in color from rich green to red and black, the stone known as serpentine was valued for its fine texture and polish as well as for the antidotal power attributed to it. Vessels, including ewers, beakers, bowls, and tankards, were mounted with pewter and silver—usually gilt—from the late sixteenth century through the seventeenth century. The stone itself was probably finished in Saxony, and many examples were exported to the Netherlands and to England for mounting.[1]

The stone body of this tankard has fine molded ribbing consistent with those produced in Saxony.[2] The heavy gauge of the silver mounts, the simple construction of the handle, and the thumbpiece are best compared with German mounted examples, but it is impossible to be certain if the mounts are German or English.

The arms and inscription refer to Sebastian Harvey, son of Sir James Harvey, Ironmonger, by Anne or Agnes, daughter of Count Sebastian Gens or Gent of Antwerp, who was born about 1552 at Walton in Stone, Staffordshire. He served as Sheriff of London from 1609–1610 and as Lord Mayor from 1618–1619; he was knighted July 17, 1616. He died without surviving male issue February 21, 1620/1, when his estate was estimated at £30,000.[3]

1. Klaus Pechstein, *Goldschmiedewerke der Renaissance, Kataloge des Kunstgewerbemuseums Berlin 5* (Berlin 1971), cat. nos. 81–84; Cologne, Kunstegewerbemuseum der Stadt Köln, Overstolzenhaus, *Ein rheinischer Silberschatz,* 1980, pp. 302–307; A. C. A. W. van der Feltz, "Serpentijnstenen kannen met Zutphense en Utrechtse monturen," *Antiek* 9, no. 8 (1975), pp. 809–814; J. Verbeek, "Vaatwerk van Serpentijnsteen in openbare verzamelingen in de Nederlanden," *Antiek* 5, no. 1 (1970), pp. 9–25. For an English-mounted example, see Victoria and Albert Museum, M.92–1914, Tankard, serpentine with silver mounts, ca. 1630, maker's mark *WR* with an arch, h. 22.2 cm, ill. Oman, 1965, pl. 48.
2. Compare with an example sold by Christie, Manson & Woods, New York, April 18, 1989, lot 279. A tankard in the Victoria and Albert Museum is nearly identical in profile: acc. no. M31–1953, Tankard, serpentine with silver mounts, Swedish or German, 1643, unmarked, ill. Lightbown, 1975, cat. no. 77.
3. George Edward Cokayne, *Some Account of the Lord Mayors and Sheriffs of the City of London* (London, 1897), pp. 81–82. His arms are recorded as or, a chevron between three leopard faces, gules. The crescent for difference is recorded by J. Nicholl, *Some Account of the Worshipful Company of Ironmongers,* 2d ed. (London, 1866), p. 259. I am grateful to Mr. R. M. Harvey of the Guildhall Library for his assistance.

· 32 ·

FLAGON
London, ca. 1620
Tin-glazed earthernware (possibly Germany or Low Countries) with silver mounts
67.1018

MARKS: on neck and cover, *R* (unrecorded)

INSCRIPTIONS: engraved on underside of foot, *8oz 2 dwt 12 gr*

H. 28.6 cm (11¼ in.); w. 17.8 cm (7 in.); d. 13.2 cm (5³⁄₁₆ in.)

PROVENANCE: purchased from John Hunt, Dublin, December 13, 1967,[1] Theodora Wilbour Fund in Memory of Charlotte Beebe Wilbour.

PUBLISHED: Glanville, 1990, p. 338, fig. 197.

DESCRIPTION: The pottery flagon has a flat base, a molded foot, tall tapering sides, and an ear-shaped handle with scrolling terminus. The interior and exterior are glazed with a bright turquoise tin glaze; the foot has been wiped clean. The silver mount on the foot is attached with a serrated bezel. The neck is mounted in silver stamped with panels of rosettes and ovolos. The domed cover has a molded rim and is engraved with scrolling foliage enclosing flowers. At the center is a finial in the form of a cockerel. The plain box hinge is secured to the handle with a foliate edge. The thumbpiece is in the form of a double-headed eagle.

CONSTRUCTION: The flagon was wheel thrown from a fine buff-colored earthenware. The silver foot rim and neck mount are fabricated and seamed; the pattern on the neck is die struck. The cover is formed from three pieces: the molded wire rim is attached to a second plain wire that forms the flat step of the cover, and the domed section is applied. The thumbpiece and finial are cast. The pottery shows few signs of wear. The engraving of the cover appears to have been renewed.

This flagon belongs to a small group of bright turquoise tin-glazed vessels with silver mounts. They include examples in the Ashmolean Museum,[2] the Bristol Museum,[3] Agecroft Hall,[4] and the Victoria

and Albert Museum.[5] These jugs are all bulbous in form, with a straight neck, and have a brilliant turquoise glaze inside and out; only the present example is of a flagon shape. Though traditionally categorized with the so-called "Malling jugs," and considered to be English, they are now thought to be of Continental, and possibly German, manufacture.[6]

The die-stamped decoration of the mounts suggests a date of about 1620; it is identical to that on a mother-of-pearl box with silver mounts in the Victoria and Albert Museum.[7] The box bears the unidentified mark *R,* which is larger in scale and unrelated to the mark on the present flagon. The unusual construction of the cover of the flagon in three pieces, its heavy engraving, and blank shield all suggest that the cover may be a later addition to the piece. The scratch weight on the foot rim does not match the current weight of the object (21 oz), and it is unlikely that the mounts alone weigh as much as eight ounces.

1. The flagon was sold with the information that it had been in the Hollingsworth Magniac collection. It is not listed in the Christie, Manson & Woods sale catalogues of that collection of July 2, 4–8, 11–15, 1892.
2. Ashmolean Museum, acc. no. M.146, Jug with English silver mounts, tentatively labeled German, ca. 1560, unmarked.
3. Bristol Museum, Jug, possibly Greenwich, ca. 1580, h. 17.6 cm, ill. Frank Britton, *English Delftware in the Bristol Collection* (London, 1982), p. 45, no. 1.1.
4. Agecroft Hall, Richmond, acc. no. 1985.12, Jug, tin-glazed earthenware with silver mounts, ca. 1590, h. 19 cm, sold Christie, Manson & Woods, London, November 27, 1985, lot 224.
5. Victoria and Albert Museum, acc. no. 144.1894, Jug, tin-glazed earthenware with silver-gilt mounts, ca. 1600–1620, h. 16 cm, ill. Glanville, 1990, cat. no. 50, p. 431.
6. For a summary, see cat. no. 3. I am grateful to Michael Archer for his observations on the date and origin of the ceramic body.
7. Acc. no. M245-1924, Casket, mother-of-pearl with silver-gilt mounts, ca. 1600, h. 8.5 cm, ill. Glanville, 1990, cat. no. 109, p. 477.

32

· 33 ·

COMMUNION CUP, PATEN COVER, AND WAFER BOX
London, 1622–39
Silver
1984.164–166

MARKS: on rim of cup, maker's mark *RB* a mullet below in a shaped shield (Jackson, 1921, p. 117; rev. ed. 1989, p. 111) (repeated on rim of paten and on interior base of box)

ARMORIALS: engraved on the cup and the cover of the box, the arms of Stuart impaling Howard for Ludovic Stuart, second Duke of Lennox and first Duke of Richmond (1574–1624), and his wife Frances, daughter of Viscount Howard of Bindon; engraved on the paten and the cup, the crest of Stuart

INSCRIPTIONS: pounced on the side of the cup, *FLR* below a ducal coronet

1984.164 (Cup): H. 21.3 cm (8⅜ in.); diam. of rim 10.8 cm (4¼ in.). 1984.165 (Paten): H. 3.5 cm (1⅜ in.); diam. of rim 13.5 cm (5⁵⁄₁₆ in.). 1984.166 (Box): H. 2.9 cm (1⅛ in.); diam. 7 cm (2¾ in.)

WEIGHT: 1984.164–165: 713 gm (22 oz 18 dwt). 1984.166: 91.4 gm (2 oz 19 dwt)

PROVENANCE: by 1924 the cup belonged to St. Mary's Convent, Wantage, Berkshire (ill. E. A. Jones, "The Old Plate at the Church Congress," *Country Life* 56 [1924], p. 779); it was sold by John Kennedy, Esq., at Sotheby & Co., London, May 9, 1957, lot 142, bought by H. R. Jessop, Ltd., London, sold to John Bell, Aberdeen, bought by H. R. Jessop, Ltd., London, 1982; the cup and the wafer box were reunited by Mrs. G. E. P. How (How [of Edinburgh], London) and purchased by the Museum May 9, 1984, Theodora Wilbour Fund in Memory of Charlotte Beebe Wilbour, Gift of Mrs. Robert Hamlin by exchange, and Gift of Mrs. Stuart C. Welch.

PUBLISHED: Glanville, 1987, p. 213, fig. 80.

DESCRIPTION: The cup rests on a molded stepped base that rises to a spool-shaped stem with a flattened central knop. The body of the cup has a flat base and slightly flaring sides. The engraved coat of arms is enclosed within a wreath. On the opposite side the crest is engraved within a wreath. The cover is slightly domed with a broad flange and a spool-shaped finial with a circular flat top. The low round box has a flat base and a flat removable cover with a plain bezel that fits over the rim of the base. The arms on the cover are contained within an engraved circle and a cartouche.

CONSTRUCTION: The dome of the foot is raised, with applied wire moldings. The stem is composed of two raised spool-shaped pieces, joined by the knop, which is fabricated. The body of the vessel is raised, as is the cover. The finial is constructed of two pieces. The top and bottom of the box are formed of flat sheets; the sides are seamed.

The cup and box are pricked with the initials of Frances, Duchess of Richmond and Lennox (1577–1639), and engraved with her arms and those of her husband, Ludovic Stuart, second Duke of Lennox and first Duke of Richmond (1574–1624). She was the daughter of Thomas Howard, Viscount Howard of Bindon, and had married first Henry Prannel, Esq. (d. 1599), and then Edward Seymour, Earl of Hartford (d. 1621). Her marriage to the Duke of Lennox must have taken place shortly after her second husband's death. Ludovic Stuart was a cousin of James VI of Scotland (later James I of England) and as next in succession he was a favorite of the King from a young age. After the accession of James to the throne, Lennox served as a gentleman of the bedchamber and a privy councillor; in 1613 he was created Baron Settrington of York and Earl of Richmond. He was sent as an ambassador to Paris and in 1607 he was named high commissioner of the King to the Scottish Parliament. In 1623 he was created Earl of Newcastle-upon-Tyne and Duke of Richmond; he died February 16, 1623/4. His widow was described as so desolate in her sorrow that she cut off her hair, and the King delayed the opening of Parliament in honor of his death.[1]

The pricked monogram on the cup and cover suggest that the set was made for the Duchess's personal use. She died in 1639, and her will, which is lengthy and explicit, suggests the lavish generosity for which she was renowned during her lifetime. She made numerous bequests of plate, not from her own possessions, but specifying a sum of money for a piece to made up and engraved with "my Lords arms and myne." To Sir William Seymour, third Earl of Hartford, she bequeathed "a cupp of gold of twoe hundred poundes price . . . of the fashon of a Comunion Cup, and if he like that fashon not of what fashon of what piece of plate he most desireth." A gold communion cup worth fifty

pounds was also bequeathed to the Dean of Durham.[2]

This communion set is distinguished by the quality of the engraving and by the the wafer box, the survival of which appears to be unique. The shape of the cup is conservative in design, but the paten is a form that evolved in the first decades of the seventeenth century. It is designed to serve as cover in an upright position, with the foot inside the bowl, rather than inverted over the cup, as had been standard design for Elizabethan communion cups.[3] The wafer box was presumably used to store the unconsecrated wafer, more necessary, perhaps, in a private chapel than in a parish church. Though other similar boxes have survived separated from their communion cups, they have generally been identified as secular objects, for example from a toilet service.[4]

1. "Wills Relating to Cobham Hall," *Archaelogia Cantiana* 11 (1877), pp. 225–231.
2. Ibid., pp. 235, 241.
3. See Oman, 1957, p. 216; see also cat. no. 22.
4. See for example the box from the Noble Collection, sold Christie, Manson & Woods, London, March 28, 1962, lot 120.

34

· 34 ·

SEAL
Probably London, ca. 1630
Silver
1982.619

Unmarked
ARMORIALS: on the face of the seal, the arms of Browne, for Viscount Montague, quartering fifteen others

H. (hinge open) 3.4 cm (1⁵⁄₁₆ in.); diam. 5.6 cm (2³⁄₁₆ in.)

WEIGHT: 128.3 gm (4 oz 2 dwt)

PROVENANCE: purchased from Brand Inglis, Ltd., London, December 8, 1982, Anna Augusta Chapin Fund and Gift of Mrs. Stuart C. Welch.

DESCRIPTION: The face of the circular seal depicts the arms of Browne quartering fifteen others surmounted by a coronet, helm, crest, and mantling with the motto, *Veritate Duce*. The supporters, two lynxes, are shown with a plain collar and a line. The seal has a hinged semicircular handle on the reverse.

CONSTRUCTION: The seal is carved; the handle and hinge are fabricated and applied.

It is impossible to date this seal precisely, but it may have been made for Francis Browne, third Viscount Montague, on the occasion of his succession to the title on the death of his father in 1629. Born July 2, 1610, Frances Browne was probably educated at Eton. The Montagues were among the most prominent Catholic families, and like his father, the third Viscount was indicted as a recusant. In 1637 he married Elizabeth, daughter of the first Marquess of Worcester. In 1644 he fled to France, and his Royalist sympathies were eventually rewarded when he served as the Cup Bearer at the Coronation of Charles II.

Keeping the seal and restricting its use may have been the responsibility of the Secretary, a position described by the second Viscount in his *Book of Household Rules* of 1595 in which the organization and management of Cowdray House is laid out in some detail. The secretary must be "a man of a good, grave discretion, and especially very secrett." He must keep "letters of weight fyled upp together in good order" and answer those to which Lord Montague had not time to reply himself. "He shall nott, butt att verye special tymes, weare his lyverye, and that att my speciall appoyntemente. His upper garment in the howse I wish to be a comely black cloake."[1]

1. Mrs. Charles Roundell, *Cowdray: the History of a Great House* (London, 1884), pp. 61, 79.

35

WINE CUP
London, 1630/1
Silver
33.64

MARKS: on rim, date letter *n*; lion passant (repeated on underside of foot); leopard's head crowned; maker's mark *RC* a pheon below in a heart-shaped shield (Jackson, 1921, p. 116; rev. ed. 1989, p. 110)

INSCRIPTIONS: engraved around underside of foot, *The Guift of Jane Quinbye Grandmother and Richard Porter Uncle to Jane Porter:1614:*[1]

H. 17.9 cm (7 1/16 in.); diam. of rim. 9.2 cm (3 5/8 in.)

WEIGHT: 315.7 gm (10 oz 2 dwt)

PROVENANCE: Anonymous Gift in Memory of Charlotte Beebe Wilbour (1833–1914), March 2, 1933.

EXHIBITED: Boston, Museum of Fine Arts, 1933 (no catalogue).

DESCRIPTION: The cup rests on a plain, trumpet-shaped foot which rises to a molded baluster stem. The body of the cup has a rounded base and flaring sides.

CONSTRUCTION: The body of the vessel is raised. The foot is raised and the stem is cast in two pieces. The lower join and the foot have been repaired. The surface has been mechanically buffed.

1. The discrepancy in date between the hallmarks and the inscription suggests that the cup was made in 1630 to replace a cup that had been given in 1614 and broken or damaged, or that Jane Porter was only able to have the cup made in 1630, though she had been given or bequeathed the money for its purchase in 1614.

STANDISH
London, 1630/1
Silver
54.87

MARKS: on base inside large compartment, date letter *n*; lion passant; leopard's head crowned; maker's mark *WR* an arch above a pellet below in a plain shield (Jackson, 1921, p. 118; rev. ed. 1989, p. 115) (repeated on cover)

ARMORIALS: engraved on cover of large compartment, the arms of Tracy in a lozenge, for a spinster member of the Tracy family

H. 8.4 cm (3⁵⁄₁₆ in.); w. 8.9 cm (3½ in.); d. 11 cm (4⁵⁄₁₆ in.)

WEIGHT: 188.2 gm (6 oz 1 dwt)

PROVENANCE: Christie, Manson & Woods, London, June 6, 1909, lot 65, purchased by Crichton Brothers, London; Sir John Noble, by descent to Michael Noble, sold Christie, Manson & Woods, London, December 13, 1944, lot 78, purchased by The Goldsmiths' & Silversmiths' Co.; purchased from Garrard & Co., London, March 11, 1954, Theodora Wilbour Fund in Memory of Charlotte Beebe Wilbour.

EXHIBITED: London, Lansdowne House, *Loan Exhibition of English Decorative Art* (1929), cat. no. 93, p. 18, pl. 27 (lent by Sir John Noble); London, Seaford House, 1929, cat. no. 151, p. 19; Minneapolis, Minneapolis Institute of Arts, 1956, cat. no. 90, p. 33, fig. 15.

PUBLISHED: Jackson, 1911, vol. 2, pp. 902–903, figs. 1178–1179; Edward Wenham, "Silver Standishes and Inkstands," *The Antique Collector* 26, no. 2 (1955), p. 76, fig. 1; Clayton, 1971, p. 157, fig. 304, rev. ed. 1985, p. 213, fig. 306; Clayton, 1985a, p. 61, fig. 15; Gruber, 1982, p. 274, fig. 401; Finlay, 1990, p. 152, fig. 221; Glanville, 1990, pp. 359–360, fig. 211.

DESCRIPTION: The standish rests on a flat base of geometric outline with notched edges. At the front is a straight-sided, shield-shaped box with a flat hinged cover. Behind it is a smaller rectangular box of similar construction. Two tall cylindrical quill rests support a D-shaped ridged handle with a quatrefoil finial. On the horizontal bar joining the cylinders is a figure of a putto holding a book and a torch; below is a pierced apron with a scalloped edge. Two cylindrical containers are fitted into molded rims at the back; one is pierced for sprinkling sand, the other has a removable cover to serve as an inkwell.

CONSTRUCTION: The base and the various boxes are fabricated of sheet that is seamed and soldered; the two covered boxes share the same hinge. The moldings are made of drawn wire, and the ridged handle is formed of wire wrapped around a round core. The finial and the putto are cast.

Jackson cited this standish as the earliest known[1]; Michael Clayton illustrates a rectangular box-shaped example marked 1610, but allows for the possibility that it may have been altered.[2] Though the objects have not survived, there are numerous inventory references for silver standishes from the sixteenth century on. As a New Year's gift in 1577, the Queen was presented with a "Standishe of siluer guilt with boxes for Inke Dust and Counters all of siluer guilt."[3] In addition to the inkwell,

36

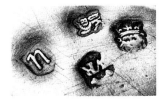

the other components of the standish included a pierced caster for sprinkling pounce, a powder of gum sandarac used to fix the ink. The boxes would have contained wafers and knives for trimming the quills, and the tubular stands flanking the handle would have held quills and sealing wax. The design of the present standish seems to be a unique survival, but a similar example is recorded in a portrait of a Salisbury merchant William Windover, dated 1633. He is shown with a document in one hand and a pen in the other, seated in front of a standish with cylindrical compartments for pounce, ink, and a seal, and two tall containers for pens joined by an arched handle.[4]

1. Jackson, 1911, vol. 2, pp. 902–903.
2. Clayton, rev. ed. 1985, pp. 213–219. Two other standishes predating this example are also recorded. One, sold Christie, Manson & Woods, London, June 22, 1937, was described as a "miniature inkstand, the base of shaped oblong form on three pear-shaped feet with an oblong box along one side, the lid engraved with formal foliage, a silver-gilt ink bottle, cylindrical pounce box, and another pen holder in the center, 3½ in. long, 1627, maker's mark *IC* in a heart-shaped shield." The second, sold Christie, Manson & Woods, London, July 17, 1909, lot 40, is a rectangular stand on cast bracket feet with overall decoration of embossed scrolling stylized foliage. Though marked for 1615, it appears to have been altered.
3. Collins, 1955, p. 557.
4. The collection of the Salisbury and South Wiltshire Museum, acc. no. 47/54, *Portrait of William Windover,* artist unknown, oil on panel, 1633, ill. Glanville, 1990, fig. 213, p. 361.

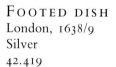

· 37 ·

FOOTED DISH
London, 1638/9
Silver
42.419

MARKS: on rim of dish, maker's mark *CR* in monogram in a plain shield (Jackson, 1921, p. 120; rev. ed. 1989, p. 117); leopard's head crowned; lion passant (repeated on underside of foot); date letter *a*

INSCRIPTIONS: engraved on underside of foot, *B* over *M*M*

H. 6.4 cm (2½ in.); diam. of rim 24.6 cm (9¹¹⁄₁₆ in.)

WEIGHT: 354.4 gm (11 oz 8 dwt)

PROVENANCE: J. Dunn-Gardner,[1] sold Christie, Manson & Woods, London, April 30, 1902, lot 268; Samuel Montagu (Lord Swaythling), sold Christie, Manson & Woods, London, May 6, 1924, lot 92, purchased by Spink & Son, London; W. H. Woodward, London, sold Sotheby & Co., London, April 23, 1931, lot 160; Walter H. Willson, Ltd., London, purchased by Theodora Wilbour, 1942, Anonymous Gift in Memory of Charlotte Beebe Wilbour, September 11, 1942.

PUBLISHED: Cyril G. E. Bunt, "Some Seventeenth-Century Silver," *Antiques* 22 (1932), p. 210, fig. 3.

DESCRIPTION: The dish rests on a low trumpet-shaped foot. The center of the dish is slightly domed, with flaring sides and a broad rim with a fluted edge. A pattern of embossed rays spreads from a floret in the center of the dish.

CONSTRUCTION: The dish is raised from a single sheet and embossed with a two-pronged tool. The foot is also raised.

Low footed dishes such as this, and the smaller oval dishes without feet, often with two handles, are generally called fruit dishes, or sweetmeat dishes, though it is not clear how specialized their function was. Philippa Glanville has shown that these pieces served the same purpose as Elizabethan spice plates. Supplied individually, rather than in sets, these dishes are referred to in inventories as fruit or spice plates.[2]

Charles Oman and José Rosas first proposed that the simple decoration on these light gauge wares reflects the influence of Portuguese silver that was available in London after the renewal of trading relations with Lisbon in 1604.[3] Variations in the decoration of these dishes include a punched spiral incorporating lozenges and an eight-pointed star enclosed in a punched circle.[4] A late appearance of this style is found in two bowls of 1690 and 1694 with scalloped edges and punched with a rayed pattern similar to that on the present example.[5]

1. Lent by J. Dunn-Gardner to the Victoria and Albert Museum from 1871 to 1901.
2. Glanville, 1987, p. 58.
3. Oman and Rosas, 1950, p. 162. See also cat. no. 29.
4. See a dish of 1638, maker's mark *TM* in monogram, sold Christie, Manson & Woods, London, June 27, 1979, lot 142.
5. Dish, 1694, diam. 21 cm, sold Sotheby & Co., London, March 16, 1961, lot 134; see also Jackson, 1911, vol. 1, p. 260, figs. 275–276.

37

38

TANKARD
London, 1639/40
Silver
1978.226

MARKS: on cover and repeated under base, maker's mark *TI* three annulets and a bird with a branch in its beak above (unrecorded); date letter *b*; lion passant; leopard's head crowned

ARMORIALS: engraved on front, the arms of Newdigate impaling Leigh for Sir Richard Newdigate (1602–1678) first Baronet, and second son of Sir John Newdigate, who married Juliana, daughter of Sir Francis Leigh in 1630

INSCRIPTIONS: scratched on base, *The Gift of Mrs. Katherine Newdigate to her Brother Thomas Newdigate* (partially defaced); engraved on handle, *C*T*M*

H. 19.1 cm (7½ in.); w. 19.4 cm (7⅝ in.); diam. of base 15.7 cm (6³⁄₁₆ in.)

WEIGHT: 918.6 gm (29 oz 11 dwt)

PROVENANCE: Brigadier R. H. Keenlyside, sold Sotheby Parke Bernet, London, February 26, 1976, lot 187; purchased from Brand Inglis, Ltd., London, September 13, 1978, Theodora Wilbour Fund in Memory of Charlotte Beebe Wilbour.

PUBLISHED: Gale Glynn, "Heraldry on English Silver," *Proceedings of the Silver Society* 3 (1983), pp. 6–7.

DESCRIPTION: The tankard rests on a broad flaring foot. It has tapering sides and a matted surface decoration overall with a reserved oval at the center containing the engraved coat of arms. The ear-shaped handle has a bifurcated, scrolling thumbpiece. The cover has a broad rim and a bun-shaped finial, and is decorated with concentric matted and plain circles.

CONSTRUCTION: The body of the tankard is raised from a single sheet, as is the cover. The rim is thickened and has an incised molding. The foot is seamed and formed. It has a heavy wire rim and a molded wire applied to the juncture with the body. The handle is assembled from three formed pieces. There are traces of two engraved lines on the edge of the spine of the handle. The cast finial, riveted to the cover, may have been reattached. The inscription on the base of the tankard is crudely engraved and defaced.

The design of this tankard exhibits two features that are unusually early for the 1639 date of the hallmark—the matted surface and the skirt foot. The broad spreading foot of Commonwealth tankards is probably a survival of the flaring foot that appeared on earlier flagons. This is among the earliest of the skirt-footed tankards, a

form that survived virtually without change through the 1650s.[1] The matted decoration of the body became a standard decoration for Charles II tankards; in this early application it must have been inspired by the treatment of standing cups, which were often matted in bands.[2] It has been suggested that the armorials and matted decoration may have been a slightly later addition to an otherwise plain tankard. As Gale Glynn has shown, however, the arms of Sir Richard Newdigate (second son of Sir John Newdigate) are differenced with a crescent, which he would not have used after 1642, when his older brother died, thus confirming the early date of the engraving.[3] Sir Richard Newdigate of Arbury, Warwickshire, had a distinguished career as a lawyer, serving as Serjeant at Law (1653/4 and again in 1660), Judge and Chief Justice of the Upper Bench and Member of Parliament for Tamworth (1660). He presided at the trials for high treason of the Earls of Bellasis and Dumfries, incurring Cromwell's displeasure when he established that there was no law making it treason to levy war against a Lord Protector. He was removed from his position, but was reinstated by 1657, and advanced to the chief justiceship of the Upper Bench in 1659. He was created a Baronet by Charles II in 1677 without payment of the usual fees. He died in 1678 and was succeeded by his son, Richard.

1. Other early tankards include: Skirt-footed tankard, 1638, maker's mark *DI* with escallop between and a mullet above, h. 14 cm, collection of Lord Rothemere, sold Christie, Manson & Woods, December 3, 1941, lot 63 (the truncated thumbpiece appears to have been damaged). A similar skirt-footed tankard with matted decoration is illustrated in *Christie's Pictorial Archive,* fiche 62; it is recorded as having the maker's mark *TB* in monogram a bird below, and hallmarks for 1636. An example characteristic of the mid-century skirt-footed tankards was sold at Christie, Manson & Woods, London, March 20, 1963, lot 109; it is dated 1654, bears the maker's mark *AF,* and differs from the present example in having a protruding rim at the front of the cover and no finial. Finials on mid-century tankards are rare; see the covered alepot of 1646 in the Museum of London, ill. Glanville, 1987, fig. 23.
2. See, for example, the two standing cups of 1632 (Winchester College, maker's mark *PG* above a rose, h. 36 cm) and 1635 (Goldsborough Church, maker's mark *RC* between six pellets, h. 43.5 cm), ill. Oman, 1970, pls. 1A, 1B.
3. Gale Glynn, "Heraldry on English Silver," *Proceedings of the Silver Society* 3 (1983), pp. 6–7.

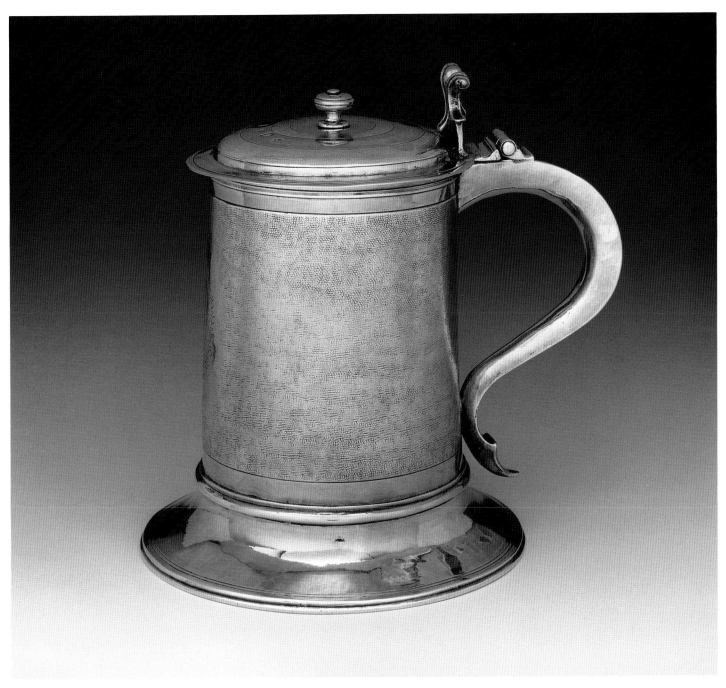

38 (Color Plate IX)

39

BOOK COVER
(John Downame, *A Briefe Concordance to the Bible*, London, 1631, bound with the Apocrypha and engravings depicting scenes from the New Testament published by Robert Peake)
London, ca. 1640–1655
Silver
63.1253

Unmarked
H. 15.6 cm (6⅛ in.); w. 9.2 cm (3⅝ in.); d. 2.9 cm (1⅛ in.)

PROVENANCE: Mrs. Scott Murray, Hampshire; Christie, Manson & Woods, London, 1962–1963; purchased from How (of Edinburgh), London, September 18, 1963, Theodora Wilbour Fund in Memory of Charlotte Beebe Wilbour.

EXHIBITED: Victoria and Albert Museum, 1937–1939 (lent by Mrs. Scott Murray).

PUBLISHED: Christie, Manson & Woods, *Christie's Review of the Year, October, 1962–August, 1963* (London, 1963), p. 110.

DESCRIPTION: The bookbinding is covered with red velvet; each cover is mounted with a pierced silver rectangular plaque. At the center is an oval medallion with a beaded border enclosing a profile bust—on the front Charles I and on the back Henrietta Maria. The surrounding foliate cartouche is enclosed in a lozenge with a guilloche outline. At each corner is an oval medallion with a beaded border containing engraved figures of the Virtues. On the front cover, clockwise from the upper left, are represented Fortitude, Fidelity, Justice, and Prudence; on the back cover are Charity, Temperence, Hope, and Patience. The openwork interstices are filled with grotesques and scrolling foliage, with standing winged female figures, each holding a wreath at the top and bottom. The entire rectangle is framed with a guilloche border. The two hinged silver clasps are decorated with the profile bust of Henrietta Maria.

CONSTRUCTION: Each book cover is constructed from a single flat sheet that is pierced and engraved. The medallions at the corners are applied and engraved. The bust at the center and the cartouche surrounding it is a separate piece; the cast ovals are let into the pierced cartouches. The clasps are cast and hinged to the back cover. The silver mounts are nailed to the book cover. The lower section of the front cover has been broken in several places, and the velvet is extensively worn.

The design of this finely pierced and engraved book cover has traditionally been associated with Théodore de Bry (1528–1598) and his son J. Théodore de Bry (1561–1623).[1] It was the father who seems to have specialized in decorative pierced panels for goldsmiths; an inkstand attributed to him in the Victoria and Albert Museum shows his sophisticated use of intertwining foliate scrolls inhabited by grotesques and naturalistic fauna.[2] The book mounts are plainer than de Bry's designs, and the flowing scrolls are interrupted by the medallions and borders, but the ultimate source of both designs was probably a late Mannerist engraving. The similarity of these mounts to a group of Antwerp book covers[3] raises the possibility that they were imported to England and fitted later with the royal portraits for English customers.

Identical portraits of Charles I and Henrietta Maria appear on a large number of small objects including boxes, jewelry, and books. Few are marked, and the pieces have usually been dated about 1640. Recently Timothy Schroder has suggested that many were more likely made after the King's death, when there was a demand for tokens of Royalism.[4] The stylistic range of these objects would indicate that they were produced in several workshops, probably over a number of years.

At least three other books are mounted with similar pierced silver plaques. The most closely related is a book in the Huntington Art Gallery with mounts of identical design, varying only in the decoration of the clasps, which have engraved medallions of Moses and another prophet.[5] The Huntington binding encases a *Book of Common Prayer* of 1635, Speed's *Genealogies* of 1638, and Sternhold and Hopkin's *Psalmes* of 1635. These mounts were made from the same design as the present example, presumably in the same workshop. On a more modest scale, but certainly from the same workshop, are the oval plaques adorning a Scottish publication of 1633 in the Abbey Collection; they are engraved with biblical scenes bordered with guilloche in the same style as the figures of the Virtues on the present book.[6] A third binding, which houses a 1643 edition of the New Testament was described by Cyril Davenport in 1896.[7] A group of counter boxes is similarly decorated, with pierced panels enclosing winged grotesque figures and with portraits of Charles I and Henrietta Maria set into the ends.[8]

A third group of objects is related in design and, though not necessarily from the same workshop, must be contemporary with the book covers. This includes a box of weights in the British Museum covered with velvet and mounted with pierced plaques and a jewel box mounted with silver plaques in a private collection.[9] The interior of the jewel box is fitted with a mirror flanked by cast busts of Charles I and Henrietta Maria, as on the book covers. The plaques are pierced and engraved with lush flowers and scrolling foliage emanating from a vase in the center.

Schroder, in discussing a gold tobacco box in the Gilbert Collection related to the last group of objects, proposed a date of 1670–1680, based on the iconography and comparison to an identical box that bears a maker's mark.[10] The Gilbert box has a bead and reel border, lush flowers, and a pair of putti—baroque features that do not appear on the bookbindings. The strictly Mannerist design on the book covers would indicate an earlier date, though perhaps later than the death of the King.

1. See D. Guilmard, *Les Maîtres Ornemanistes* (Paris, 1880), pp. 367–369.
2. Hayward, 1976, p. 400, figs. 642–643.
3. Exhibited Antwerp, Rockoxhuis, 1988, cat. nos. 98–100, pp. 137–138.
4. Schroder, 1988, p. 106.
5. Wark, 1978, cat. no. 371, pp. 163–166.
6. John Forrest Hayward, "Silver Bindings from the Abbey Collection," *Connoisseur* 130 (1952), p. 100, fig. 3.
7. Cyril Davenport, *Royal English Bookbindings* (London, 1896), p. 65. A similarly mounted book, lacking the pierced surround, is illustrated on pl. 66.
8. See cat. no. 40.
9. Jewel box (private collection), ca. 1640–1650, L. 17.5 cm, ill. Clayton, 1971, p. 35, fig. 50; Box of weights, ca. 1640–1650, British Museum.
10. Schroder, 1988, p. 104, cat. no. 23. The box bears the maker's mark *BB* a crescent below, which appears on silver of about 1675–1685. See Sotheby Parke Bernet, London, March 3, 1983, lot 79.

40

· 40 ·

COUNTER BOX
Probably London, ca. 1640–1655
Gold
1977.497

Unmarked
H. 3.2 cm (1¼ in.); diam. 4.5 cm (1¾ in.)

WEIGHT: 45.5 gm (1 oz 9 dwt)

PROVENANCE: Sotheby Parke Bernet, New York, February 10, 1977, lot 598; purchased from S. J. Shrubsole, New York, Theodora Wilbour Fund in Memory of Charlotte Beebe Wilbour, June 9, 1977.

DESCRIPTION: The sides of the cylindrical box are divided into three openwork panels filled with caryatids against a background of foliage. The removable top is composed of a central oval with the profile bust in low relief of Charles I, facing left, surrounded by a band of pierced foliage and caryatids. The base of the box is similarly designed, with the bust of Henrietta Maria enclosed within the oval.

CONSTRUCTION: The sides of the box are formed of a seamed sheet, pierced and engraved. The base is a flat disk, pierced and engraved, with the cast bust of Henrietta Maria let in. The cover is similarly constructed, with an applied wire bezel that fits over the sides of the box.

A large number of silver counter boxes is known, many retaining their counters, which were used both as markers for games and for accounting.[1] The portrait heads of Charles I and Henrietta Maria on this gold box and on a large group of similar objects appear to be cut directly from badges and medals.[2] Similar portrait heads appear on book covers,[3] boxes,[4] and pendants,[5] almost invariably unmarked. The date of some of these objects is difficult to ascertain. In discussing an oval gold box in the Gilbert Collection, Timothy Schroder suggested that some were made as commemorative pieces and should be dated to the period of the Restoration rather than to the Commonwealth.[6] The strictly Mannerist style of the openwork sides of this box, however, is quite different from the more baroque treatment of the Gilbert box. The Boston box may be from the same workshop as a book cover in the Museum's collection (cat. no. 39). The engraved decoration on many of the counters belonging to these boxes is after a portrait series issued before 1640,[7] and there is no tradition of such engraving in England after the Restoration. The objects with pierced and engraved plaques and portraits of Charles I should perhaps be divided into two groups, those made during the lifetime or immediately after the death of the King, and those made as commemorative pieces later in the century.

1. For examples of similar counter boxes in silver, see several in the Victoria and Albert Museum, ill. Glanville, 1990, cat. nos. 116–119; Sotheby & Co., London, September 18, 1975, lot 93; Sotheby's, London, February 10, 1987, lot 25; Sotheby's, London, November 19, 1987, lot 25. See Glanville, 1990, p. 365, for a discussion of the sixteenth-century records of counters.
2. See the numerous entries for such medals in Edward Hawkins, *Medallic Illustrations of the History of Great Britain and Ireland* (London, 1885), cat. nos. 186–288. Many of these are recorded as memorial medals issued at the death of the King. Cat. no. 265 appears to be the same model as the present example; it is attributed to Thomas Rawlins (ca. 1620–1670) and is described as a pattern for a shilling.
3. See cat. no. 39.
4. See a gold box in the Gilbert Collection, ill. Schroder, 1988, cat. no. 23, pp. 104–106.
5. There is a gold pendant in the Museum of Fine Arts, Boston, acc. no. 69.1149, and a gilt-bronze example at Agecroft Hall, Richmond, acc. no. 1983.1.
6. Schroder, 1988, cat. no. 23, pp. 104–106.
7. Helen Farquhar, "Silver Counters of the Seventeenth Century," *Numismatic Chronicle* 4th series, 16 (1916), pp. 133–193.

· 41 ·

COMMUNION CUP
Patrick Borthwick (free 1642, d. 1685)
Edinburgh, 1645
Silver
1973.172

MARKS: on rim of bowl and on base of stem, maker's mark *PB* a crown above a heart below in a shaped shield (Jackson, 1921, p. 499; rev. ed. 1989, p. 542); Edinburgh town mark; deacon's mark of Adam Lamb *AL* conjoined (Jackson, 1921, p. 498; rev. ed. 1989, p. 542)

INSCRIPTIONS: engraved around rim, FOR THE KIRKE OF HADINGTOVNE* 1645

H. 23.1 cm (9⅛ in.); diam. of rim 21.1 cm (8⁵⁄₁₆ in.)

WEIGHT: 975.3 gm (31 oz 7 dwt)

PROVENANCE: Kirk Session, St. Mary Haddington, sold Sotheby & Co., London, November 30, 1972, lot 113–114, purchased from S. J. Shrubsole, New York, April 11, 1973, Theodora Wilbour Fund in Memory of Charlotte Beebe Wilbour.

PUBLISHED: Thomas Burns, *Old Scottish Communion Plate* (Edinburgh, 1892), p. 234; "The Sale Room," *Apollo* 97, no. 133 (1973), fig. 2, p. 321; Clayton, rev. ed., 1985, p. 102, pl. 16; Brett, 1986, p. 124, fig. 412.

DESCRIPTION: The cup rests on a molded base that has a stamped foliate pattern on the domed section and an ovolo pattern above. The stem is hexagonal in section and spool shaped in profile and has a central knop with a scroll pattern in low relief. The low bowl has gently sloping sides and hit-and-miss engraving around the rim. The inscription is engraved just below the rim.

CONSTRUCTION: The bowl of the cup is raised and is screwed to the stem. The domed foot of the stem is raised and die-struck with a strengthening wire applied to the rim. Two molded and die-struck wires join the foot to the hexagonal stem, which is raised in two sections joined by a seamed, fabricated knop with molded wires above and below. At the top of the stem are two molded and die-struck wires. A plain disk is set into the opening at the top and fitted with a threaded collar for the screw mount.

This cup is one of a set of four made for St. Mary's, Haddington (East Lothian). The set was sold in 1972; one cup is now in the Glasgow Museum and Art Gallery,[1] another was returned to the church by an anonymous donor, and the location of the remaining cup is unknown. The distinctive

41

and varied forms of Scottish communion plate reflect the turmoil surrounding the Reformed service in the second quarter of the seventeenth century. One of the most hotly debated issues was whether to receive communion while seated or kneeling. Communion was celebrated infrequently, usually twice a year, and tradition allowed the seated communicant to drink deeply of the wine. The congregation was accommodated at several tables, and cups were usually made in sets to furnish the tables.[2] In his study of Scottish church plate, Thomas Burns categorized the predominate types of communion cups, pointing to the deep bowl and hexagonal stem of this example as distinctive features.[3] Though rare, several related examples from the period 1640 to 1650 are known. In addition to the Haddington cups there are a set of four from Tollbooth, Edinburgh, two of which are by Patrick Borthwick, and a set of four from St. Giles, Edinburgh, made by Jon Scott.

1. Glasgow Museum and Art Gallery, acc. no. E 73-6. I am grateful to Brian J. R. Blench for his assistance.
2. Thomas Burns, *Old Scottish Communion Plate* (Edinburgh, 1892), pp. 19–64.
3. Ibid., p. 234.

· 42 ·

SEAL OF GOVERNOR JOHN LEVERETT (1616–1679)
Probably London, ca. 1650
Silver
36.150

Unmarked
ARMORIALS: the face of the seal depicts the arms of Leverett

L. 5.9 cm (2⁵⁄₁₆ in.); w. 4.3 cm (1¹¹⁄₁₆ in.)

WEIGHT: 39.7 gm (1 oz 6 dwt)

PROVENANCE: Gift of Mrs. Charles H. Taylor, February 6, 1936.

DESCRIPTION: The seal is oval in shape. Within a double border is a coat of arms surmounted by a helmet and mantling.

CONSTRUCTION: The seal is carved. A wire loop has been applied to the upper rim. On the reverse is evidence that a handle has been removed.

42

This seal bears the Leverett arms and is presumed to have belonged to John Leverett (1616–1679), who served as Deputy Governor of the Massachusetts Bay Colony from 1671 to 1673 and as Governor from 1673 to 1679. Since it is unmarked, there remains the possibility that it was made in the Colonies, but it is more likely that Leverett acquired it, as well as a gold signet ring now in the Essex Institute, Salem, during one of two long sojourns in England. He served in the Parliamentary army between 1644 and 1648, and from 1655 to 1662 he was agent in England for the Massachusetts Bay Colony.[1] The seal is lacking the tab handle on the reverse used to hold it while impressing wax and has been mounted later as a pendant.

While spectographic analysis might shed light on the question of whether it is English or American, such analysis requires removal of a sample. The object was examined by energy dispersive x-ray fluorescence to determine its alloy composition. The results indicated an average silver content of 94.4 percent, well above sterling, with copper and gold readings of 5.3 and .07 percent. Comparison with other mid-seventeenth-century English pieces showed that the standard often exceeds sterling.[2] American examples of the first half of the eighteenth century tend to show an alloy composition well below sterling.[3] A broad scientific survey of the wares of the seventeenth century, however, has not yet been published. An accurate identification of the place of manufacture would require more complete data on trace elements than can be shown by x-ray fluorescence.

1. The ring was exhibited, Boston, Museum of Fine Arts, 1982, vol. 3, cat. no. 408, p. 402.
2. The objects were examined in January, 1991, in the Museum's Research Laboratory. Three English pieces were also analyzed with the following results: 35.1559 (Two-handled cup, London, 1567/8, cat. no. 49), Cu 5.8, Ag 93.85; 35.1561 (Two-handled cup, London, 1665/6, cat. no. 60), Cu 4.35, Ag 95.2; 40.617 (Cup, London, 1675/6, cat. no. 73), Cu 4.6, Ag 95.25.
3. Victor F. Hanson, "The Curator's Dream Instrument," in *Application of Science in Examination of Works of Art,* ed. William Young (Boston, 1973), pp. 18–30.

· 43 ·

TWO-HANDLED CUP AND COVER
London, ca. 1650
Silver gilt
58.718a,b

MARKS: on rim (struck three times) and on inside of cover, maker's mark a hound sejant in a shaped shield (Jackson, 1921, p. 123; rev. ed. 1989, p. 120)

ARMORIALS: engraved in center panel on front and back of cup, the arms of Berkeley and Cotheridge, Worcester, possibly for Rowland Berkeley, Esq., of Cotheridge, High Sheriff of Worcester in 1764 and Member of Parliament for Droitwich in 1774; engraved in center panels on front and back of cover, the crest of Berkeley

INSCRIPTIONS: inside cover and under foot, scratched, *47 00/3846*

H. 20.3 cm (8 in.); w. 23.5 cm (9¼ in.); diam. of foot 13.9 cm (5⅛ in.)

WEIGHT: 1,459.6 gm (46 oz 18 dwt)

PROVENANCE: R. B. Berkeley, Esq., Cotheridge Court, Worcester, sold Christie, Manson & Woods, London, June 13, 1929, lot 35, purchased by the Goldsmiths' and Silversmiths' Co., London; Richard C. Paine, Boston, sold Parke Bernet, New York, April 15, 1950, lot 57; purchased from Thomas Lumley, Ltd., London, September 18, 1958, Theodora Wilbour Fund in Memory of Charlotte Beebe Wilbour.

PUBLISHED: Kathryn C. Buhler, "Some Recent Accessions," *Bulletin of the Museum of Fine Arts* 56 (1958), p. 101.

DESCRIPTION: The cup rests on a low trumpet-shaped foot. The body of the cup has slightly flaring sides and is lobed in six sections. The ear-shaped handles are modeled with an abstract organic motif, incorporating a serpent's head. The domed cover is also hexagonally lobed. The finial is urn shaped. The body of the cup and the cover are decorated with panels of matting within engraved outlines. The coat of arms is engraved in an oval reserve in the center panel of each side; a similar reserve on each side of the cover contains the engraved crest.

CONSTRUCTION: The foot, body, and cover are raised. The rim of the cup is thickened. The handles and finial are cast; the finial has been reattached with a modern screw. The gilding has been renewed.

This cup is one of a group of two-handled cups by the so-called Hound Sejant maker, one of the most skilled and prolific makers of the Commonwealth period.[1] His mark appears on objects made between about 1646 and 1666, though many of the more ambitious pieces were not submitted for assay, presumably because they were special commissions. He produced ecclesiastical plate and large-scale domestic pieces for aristocratic clients; both reflect his knowledge of contemporary Continental ornament. This cup and a closely related example in the Kimball Art Museum are representative.[2] Philippa Glanville has proposed that his mark, possibly derived from a family crest, suggests that he may have been a junior member of a landed Flemish family.[3] That he worked for the wealthiest of patrons is evidenced by the survival of two gold cups bearing the mark.[4] The first is similar in form to the present example; it has a lobed body and cover with a low flaring foot. The second gold cup is embossed with a "grape" pattern, each lobe enclosing auricular or floral ornament. A silver cup fully marked for 1666 with handles identical to those on the present example and covered entirely with embossed auricular decoration is in the collection of Wadham College, Oxford.[5]

1. For an overview of his work, see Oman, 1970, pp. 27–28.
2. Kimball Art Museum, Fort Worth, Two-handled cup and cover, ca. 1650, maker's mark a hound sejant, h. 22.9 cm, formerly in the Makower Collection, sold Sotheby & Co., London, March 16, 1961, lot 147.
3. Glanville, 1990, pp. 95, 434.
4. Two-handled cup and cover, gold, ca. 1650, maker's mark a hound sejant, h. 17.8 cm, ill. Grimwade, 1951, pp. 76–78; Exeter College, Oxford, Two-handled cup and cover, gold, ca. 1665, maker's mark a hound sejant, h. 15.2 cm, ill. Jones, 1907a, pl. 7, no. 2.
5. Moffatt, 1906, p. 184, pl. 90.

43

· 44 ·

RECUSANT CHALICE
London, ca. 1650–70
Silver, parcel gilt
62.673

MARKS: on rim and on underside of foot, maker's mark *IH* in a heart-shaped shield (Jackson, 1921, p. 135; rev. ed. 1989, p. 133)

H. 13.7 cm (5⅜ in.); diam. of base 7.9 cm (3⅛ in.)

WEIGHT: 176.5 gm (5 oz 13 dwt)

PROVENANCE: purchased from Thomas Lumley, Ltd., London, September 19, 1962, Theo-

dora Wilbour Fund in Memory of Charlotte Beebe Wilbour.

DESCRIPTION: The cup rests on a flaring hexafoil base with molded lower rim. One face of the base is engraved with the crucifixion. The baluster stem has three angels' heads applied to the central knop. The cup has a flat base, slightly flaring sides, and a gilt interior.

CONSTRUCTION: The cup is composed of three pieces which are screwed together: a foot, knop, and bowl. The foot is formed from a single piece with an applied molded wire rim and a formed disk below the threaded post. The knop is cast in two pieces, with applied cast putti's heads. There are traces of gilding on the knop. The bowl is raised. The surface of the bowl and marks are worn.

Recusant chalices of the seventeenth century are generally designed to be dismantled into three pieces, and it has been assumed that this was to enable the itinerant priest to discreetly store them away from agents seeking to accuse and fine papists.[1] For the same reasons, recusant plate is rarely hallmarked or inscribed with an owner's arms or name; thus, dating of these stylistically conservative objects is difficult. Charles Oman identified a group of chalices similar to this one that share the distinctive feature of a cast putto's head decorating the knop.[2] While the motif appears on an earlier group of recusant chalices, this design incorporates wings that curve above the head, almost touching. He considered them to be the work of a single shop, since they share not only the identical cast heads, but similar engraved decoration and construction features. This chalice is among the smallest of those in the group; the largest is 20 cm high. None is hallmarked, and one, a chalice in Gosforth, Cumberland, is inscribed with the date 1690. The maker's mark *AM* in monogram appears on an Anglican chalice with the same features in St. George's Chapel, Windsor. Since this mark, attributed to Arthur Manwaring, appears on silver between about 1650 and 1667, the group has been dated accordingly. The mark on the present chalice, *IH* in a heart-shaped shield, was recorded by Jackson on a tumbler of 1675/6 and on a tankard of 1681/2.[3]

1. For recusant plate see Oman, 1957, part 4; John Webb, "English Recusant Base-Metal Chalices," *Archeological Journal* 143 (1986), pp. 352–362.
2. Oman, 1957, pp. 270–271, note 2.
3. Jackson, 1921, p. 135; rev. ed. 1989, p. 133.

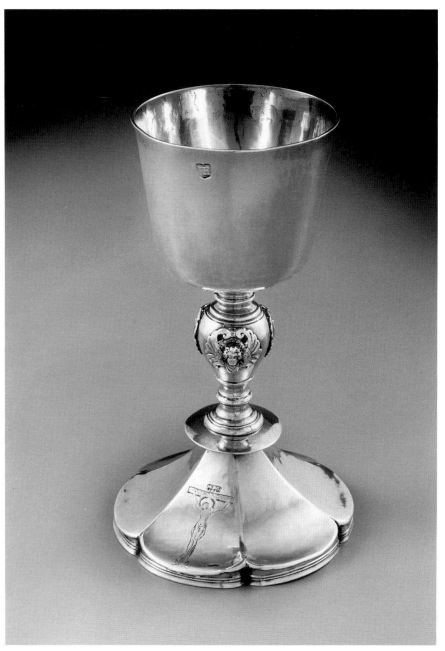

44

45 (Color Plate x)

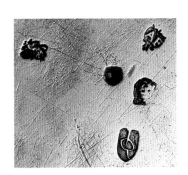

· 45 ·

TWO-HANDLED CUP AND COVER
London, 1653/4
Silver
1976.2a,b

MARKS: on base and on top of cover, maker's mark *AF* in a shaped shield (Jackson, 1921, p. 124; rev. ed. 1989, p. 121); leopard's head crowned; date letter *q;* lion passant (on base only)

ARMORIALS: engraved in center panel on side of cup, the arms and crest of Smith for John Smith of St. Giles, Cripplegate, younger son of John Smith, Esq. of Stoke Prior

H. 15.1 cm (5¹⁵/₁₆ in.); w. 20.3 cm (8 in.); diam. of base 13 cm (5⅛ in.)

WEIGHT: 954.4 gm (30 oz 13 dwt)

PROVENANCE: Philip Argenti, Esq.; purchased from Sotheby Parke Bernet, Monaco, December 1, 1975, lot 335 [S. J. Shrubsole, New York], purchased January 14, 1976, Theodora Wilbour Fund in Memory of Charlotte Beebe Wilbour.

EXHIBITED: London, Seaford House, 1929, cat. no. 153, p. 19, pl. 40b, lent by Philip Argenti, Esq.

PUBLISHED: *Connoisseur* 190 (1975), p. 68 (announcement of Sotheby Parke Bernet, Monaco, sale); Glanville, 1990, p. 127, fig. 55.

DESCRIPTION: The cup has a flat base and straight sides that are slightly tapered. The C-shaped handles are rectangular in section. The flat stepped cover has a plain rim and a central finial of a flattened bun shape. The surface of the cup and cover is decorated with open rounded arches enclosing symmetrical stylized foliage against a matted ground. The engraved coat of arms is enclosed in an oval reserve in the center panel and surrounded by mantling.

CONSTRUCTION: The body of the cup is raised and the rim is thickened; the handles are cast and applied. The cover is raised, with an applied interior bezel; the finial is cast. The surface is flat chased against a matted background.

This cup and three others to which it is closely related are evidence that silver of the highest quality was commissioned during the Commonwealth.[1] With the group attributed to the Hound Sejant maker (see cat. no. 43), these cups constitute some of the finest silver of the mid-century to have survived. Of a similar austere outline and heavy gauge, a two-handled cup and cover from the Rothermere Collection at Middle Temple, marked 1651/2 and probably by the same maker, has identical handles and a matted surface overall.[2] Another cup in the collection of Colonial Williamsburg also has matted decoration but varies in the design of the handles, which are in the form of caryatids, and the base, which is embellished by a skirt foot.[3] The third related example, in the collection of Peterhouse College, Cambridge, shares the caryatid handles and skirt foot of the Williamsburg cup, but its surface is decorated with flat-chased foliage and scrolls.[4]

The bold geometric flat-chased decoration on this cup appears on other drinking vessels of the period. A small round tankard and a skirt-footed tankard of 1646/7 and 1655/6 show a similar stylized floral design against a matted ground.[5] The convention of geometric ornament against a matted ground was well established; see for example the standing cup in the Museum's collection, cat. no. 26, and the pair of sixteenth-century two-handled cups at Corpus Christi College, Cambridge.[6] A more direct stylistic comparison might be made with the low-relief carving on contemporary oak furniture, in which classical arcades are used to confine simplified and robust foliage.[7] Both are an interpretation of late Mannerist motifs.

1. Glanville (1987, pp. 50–53) discusses the destruction and subsequent replacement of plate during the Civil War.
2. Middle Temple, Two-handled cup and cover, 1651, maker's mark AF in a shaped shield (?), h. 12.7 cm, ill. Clowes, 1957, p. 32.

3. Colonial Williamsburg Foundation, Two-handled cup and cover, 1655/6, maker's mark AF in a shaped shield, h. 18.4 cm, ill. Davis, 1976, pp. 56–57, no. 45.
4. Peterhouse College, Cambridge, Two-handled cup and cover, 1657/8, maker's mark AF in a shaped shield, h. 17.8 cm, ill. Jones, 1910, p. 4. pl. 3. The same maker was responsible for a skirt-footed tankard of traditional design, hallmarked 1653/4, ill. Taylor, 1956, pl. 18b.
5. See Oman, 1970, pl. 26A-B. Another small tankard is in the Gilbert Collection, Los Angeles; see Schroder, 1988, pp. 93–95.
6. Corpus Christi College, Cambridge, Pair of two-handled cups, 1555/6 maker's mark TL linked in a plain shield, and 1570/1, maker's mark IP in a shaped shield, h. 15.2 cm, presented to the college by Archbishop Parker, ill. Jones, 1910, p. 43, pl. 52.
7. See, for example, the chests illustrated by John Kirk, *American Furniture and the British Tradition to 1830* (New York, 1982), pp. 168–169.

· 46 ·

PAIR OF CANDLESTICKS
Arthur Manwaring (free 1642/3, d. ca. 1669[1])
London, 1653/4(?)
Silver with traces of gilding
67.602–603

MARKS: on each, around rim of socket, maker's mark AM in monogram (Jackson, 1921, p. 124; rev. ed. 1989, p. 121); leopard's head crowned; lion passant; date letter q(?)

67.602: H. 16.2 cm (6⅜ in.); diam. 14.5 cm (5¹¹⁄₁₆ in.). 67.603: H. 16.1 cm (6⁵⁄₁₆ in.); diam. 14.6 cm (5¾ in.)

WEIGHT: 67.602: 292 gm (9 oz 8 dwt). 67.603: 309 gm (9 oz 19 dwt)

PROVENANCE: W. T. Dobson, Milnethrop, Westmorland, sold Christie, Manson & Woods, London, July 30, 1952, lot 188; Christie, Manson & Woods, London, June 30, 1954, lot 157, purchased by Viscount Furness; purchased from S. J. Phillips, London, April 12, 1967, Theodora Wilbour Fund in Memory of Charlotte Beebe Wilbour.

EXHIBITED: Toronto, Royal Ontario Museum, 1958, no. C22, fig. 23, p. 21; Boston, Museum of Fine Arts, 1982, cat. no. 236, p. 251.

PUBLISHED: Oman, 1970, p. 30, pl. 59A; Clayton, 1971, p. 39, fig. 67, rev. ed. 1985, p. 55, fig. 67; Clayton, 1985a, p. 61, fig. 12; Müller, 1986, p. 40; Schroder, 1988, p. 107.

46

DESCRIPTION: The candlesticks are in the form of an inverted trumpet bell, with a smooth spreading base rising to a straight cylindrical nozzle. At the middle of the stem is a drip pan in the shape of a plain disk with an incised line around the edge. A simple molded band and a small rim around the socket are the only other decorative details.

CONSTRUCTION: The flaring base of the candlestick is raised with a wire applied to the rim for strength. The stem and nozzle are formed of two seamed sections with drawn molded wire applied to the juncture of the base, top rim, and mid-section. The drip pan is formed of a single sheet. There are traces of gilding near the edges of the nozzle.

Only a few pre-Restoration candlesticks have survived, the earliest of which is an elaborately worked example in the Kremlin Armory Museum by the Trefoil Slipped maker.[2] The absence of similarly grand examples from the first half of the seventeenth century has been taken to indicate that the form was only executed in austere or strictly functional designs. Philippa Glanville has pointed out that this is an accident of survival and provides the inventories of the Earl of Pembroke (1560s) and Hatfield House (1620s) as evidence that richly ornamented silver candlesticks were produced in large sets from the sixteenth century on.[3] A set of four candlesticks of 1637/8 with high domed bases, straight nozzles, and plain drip pans are more similar in character to the present pair.[4] The so-called "trumpet-base" candlestick is quite common in brass, but this pair and another pair in the Kremlin are the only examples in silver known. The Kremlin candlesticks are related only superficially to the present

examples. Presented to Tsar Alexei by Charles II's ambassador, the Earl of Carlisle, they are monumental pieces, embossed overall with naturalistic flowers and foliage.[5]

Arthur Manwaring mastered several distinctive styles during his long career. These candlesticks, the sugar box in the Museum's collection (cat. no. 54), and a dish in the Thyssen collection,[6] represent his domestic wares of the Commonwealth period, but he was also a skilled chaser, as evidenced by the standing cup made for the Goldsmiths' Company in the auricular style.[7]

1. Arthur Manwaring completed his apprenticeship under William Tyler and was free January 20, 1642/3. His mark occurs on wares after 1650, and he is presumed to have died by 1669, the year his son Andrew gained his freedom. I am grateful to Gerald Taylor for having provided this information.
2. Kremlin Armory Museum, Candlestick, 1619/20 or 1624/5; maker's mark a trefoil slipped, h. 23 cm; exhibited London, Sotheby's, 1991, cat. no. 105, p. 174.
3. Glanville, 1990, p. 353.
4. Pair of candlesticks, 1637/8, maker's mark WG in a heart, h. 14 cm, sold Sotheby's New York, October 28, 1987, lot 209.
5. Kremlin Armory Museum, Pair of candlesticks, 1663/4, maker's mark an escallop with a mullet above, h. 47.3 cm, ill. Oman, 1961, pl. 30.
6. Thyssen-Bornemisza Collection, Dish, 1650/1, maker's mark of Arthur Manwaring, diam. 34 cm, ill. Müller, 1986, cat. no. 2, pp. 40–41.
7. Standing cup, 1663/5, maker's mark of Arthur Manwaring, h. 50.5 cm, ill. Oman, 1970, pl. 3A.

47

· 47 ·

FOOTED DISH
London, 1655/6
Silver
33.65

MARKS: on rim of bowl, leopard's head crowned; maker's mark *RN* a mullet between pellets above (Jackson, 1921, p. 125; rev. ed. 1989, p. 122); lion passant (repeated on underside of foot); date letter *S*

H. 6.7 cm (2⅝ in.); diam. of bowl 20.6 cm (8⅛ in.)

WEIGHT: 391.2 gm (12 oz 12 dwt)

PROVENANCE: sold Christie, Manson & Woods, London, May 1, 1918, lot 27; Goldsmiths' and Silversmiths' Co., by 1922; Anonymous Gift in Memory of Charlotte Beebe Wilbour (1833–1914), March 2, 1933.

EXHIBITED: Boston, Museum of Fine Arts, 1933 (no catalogue).

PUBLISHED: *Connoisseur* 64 (1922), p. 65 (Goldsmiths' and Silversmiths' Co.).

DESCRIPTION: The bowl rests on a low trumpet-shaped foot divided into eight lobes with vertically chased lines. The curved sides of the bowl are divided into nine lobed panels, each enclosing a chased line. The center is slightly domed.

CONSTRUCTION: The bowl is raised and chased; the raised foot is applied.

Like two other footed dishes in the collection (cat. nos. 29 and 37), this piece was probably used as a fruit or sweetmeat dish. There are several other examples by the same maker, notably a pair of the same year given by Lord Rothermere to the Middle Temple.[1] A more ambitious version of the style may be seen in a large sideboard dish, also by the *RN* maker at St. John's College, Cambridge.[2]

1. Clowes, 1957, p. 30.
2. St. John's College, Cambridge, Dish, 1655/6, maker's mark *RN* a mullet below, diam. 38.7 cm, ill. Jones, 1910, p. 78, pl. 39.

48

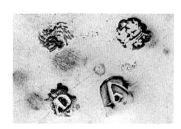

PUBLISHED: Wenham, 1931, pl. 26; N. M. Penzer, "Scroll Salts," *Apollo Annual 1949* (London, 1949), (mentioned).

DESCRIPTION: The body of the salt is spool shaped; the diameter of the upper section is slightly smaller than that of the lower section. The receptacle for salt is a rounded well set into the top of the spool. On the edge of the rim are three brackets with scrolling volutes.

CONSTRUCTION: The body of the salt was formed from a single sheet, seamed vertically into a cylinder, and hammered into the spool shape. The rim of the base is strengthened by the addition of a wire. The top of the salt is formed from a single sheet. The scrolls are cast.

Penzer reviewed the varying terminology applied to salts of this form and identified the earliest examples of this undecorated, waisted shape as the Dethick Salt at the Mercers' Company (1638), and the Reeve Salt at the Innholders' Company (1639).[1] Harvard University's example, the marks of which are worn, was given to the college in 1644 by Richard Harris. It is engraved with the initials of Elizabeth and Jose Glover, who brought it to America in 1638, and it was bequeathed by Elizabeth to her brother Richard Harris.[2] The present salt, and another slightly larger example of the same year at Eton College, are the only known Commonwealth examples of the form.[3] The form survived with little variation, as shown by a large salt of 1664 at Winchester College, and an example of 1661 in the Saddlers' Company.[4] Earlier English variations include a small straight-sided example at Colonial Williamsburg.[5] Post-Restoration salts maintain the waisted shape, but are often square or octagonal in profile, with four, rather than three, scrolls.[6] In other media such as delftware, however, the plain round form persisted until the third quarter of the century.[7] Though it has often been stated that a napkin was draped over the three scrolls to cover the salt, the evidence of numerous Dutch pictures confirms that the scrolls were used to support a plate, sometimes bearing fruit.[8] The pulley-shaped salt appears to have been first made in the Netherlands, where it is often lobed, with ball feet and balls instead of scrolls used around the top.[9] In an engraving of a banquet at Fontainebleau in 1663 by Abraham Bosse, the table is set with scroll salts and casters or cruets at regular intervals between every third diner.[10]

· 48 ·

SCROLL SALT
London, 1656/7
Silver
39.19

MARKS: in center of well, lion passant (repeated on underside of base and on each scroll); leopard's head crowned; date letter *t*; maker's mark *AD* conjoined a pellet above a crescent below in a shaped shield (Jackson, 1921, p. 125; rev. ed. 1989, p. 123)

INSCRIPTIONS: pounced on flange between scrolls, *MK*

H. 12.7 cm (5 in.); diam. of base 15.7 cm (6³⁄₁₆ in.)

WEIGHT: 431 gm (13 oz 17 dwt)

PROVENANCE: Samuel Montagu (Lord Swaythling), sold Christie, Manson & Woods, London, May 6, 1924, lot 87, purchased by Crichton Brothers, London; Walter H. Willson, Ltd., purchased by Theodora Wilbour, 1938, Anonymous Gift in Memory of Charlotte Beebe Wilbour, January 12, 1939.

1. N. M. Penzer, "Scroll Salts," *Apollo Annual 1949* (London, 1949), p. 48. Both salts were exhibited in London, Goldsmiths' Hall, 1951, cat. nos. 94–95.

2. See Frederic B. Robinson, "Harvard's 'Great Salt,'" *Bulletin of the Fogg Art Museum, Harvard University* 5 (1935), pp. 6–9.

3. Eton College, Salt, 1656/7, maker's mark *AD* conjoined a crescent below, h. 17.2 cm, ill. Jones, 1938, p. 6, pl. 4. Jones describes the shield as plain.

4. For the former, see Oman, 1962a, p. 30, fig. 13; for the latter, see Edward Alfred Jones, *Old Silver of Europe and America* (Philadelphia, 1928), no. 12, pl. 30.

5. Colonial Williamsburg Foundation, Scroll salt, 1635/6, h. 5.9 cm, see Davis, 1976, cat. no. 145, p. 142.

6. See Oman, 1970, pls. 47a, 47b.

7. See, for example, the London example of about 1675, exhibited, Atlanta, High Museum of Art, *Fair as China Dishes, English Delftware from the Collection of Mrs. Marion Morgan and Brian Morgan* (1977), catalogue by Brian Morgan, cat. no. 18, p. 39. Morgan refers to an eighteenth-century example in the Glaischer Collection.

8. See a still life by Pieter Claesz (1597/8–1660) in the Rijksmuseum, Amsterdam, ill. Christopher Wright, *The Dutch Painters* (Woodbury, 1978), p. 75. Davis (1976, pp. 142–143) discusses the use of the brackets.

9. See the Leiden example of 1655 ill. Hernmark, 1977, vol. 2, p. 149, pl. 387.

10. Gruber, 1982, p. 202, fig. 290.

• 49 •

TWO-HANDLED CUP
London, 1657/8
Silver
35.1559

MARKS: on rim, maker's mark *IG* a mullet below in a heart-shaped shield (Jackson, 1921, p. 127; rev. ed. 1989, p. 123); leopard's head crowned; lion passant; date letter *v*

INSCRIPTIONS: pounced on side of cup, *MS/MK/1662*

H. 9 cm (3⁹⁄₁₆ in.); w. 20 cm (7⅞ in.); d. 11.6 cm (4⁹⁄₁₆ in.)

WEIGHT: 263.6 gm (8 oz 9 dwt)

PROVENANCE: Estabrook & Co., Boston, given to Frank Brewer Bemis, 1924, Bequest of Frank Brewer Bemis, November 7, 1935.

PUBLISHED: Buhler, 1952, p. 229 (mentioned).

DESCRIPTION: The cup rests on a low spreading foot. It has slightly flaring sides and a plain everted rim. The surface of the body is chased with a stylized pattern of flowers inside an arcade of pointed arches against a matted ground. In the center panel of the cup is an oval containing pounced initials and a date. On the inside base of the cup is a chased flower within a double dotted hexafoil and a circle. The S-shaped handles are modeled with scrolls.

CONSTRUCTION: The body of the cup is raised and chased. The formed foot and cast handles are applied.

49

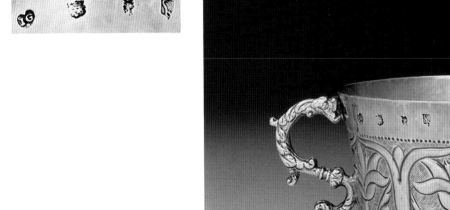

50

DESCRIPTION: The cup rests on a low flaring foot ring. The shape of the cup is that of a flattened sphere. The body of the vessel is chased on the lower third with a stylized pattern of leaves against a matted ground. The two cast handles are C-shaped, with caryatid figures and scrolls. The cover fits tightly over the rim of the cup. It is chased with a pattern of leaves similar to that on the body of the cup. The finial rests on a spool-shaped stem; it has a broad flat top.

CONSTRUCTION: The body of the cup is raised, embossed, and matted. The formed foot and cast handles are applied. The cover is raised, embossed, and matted. The raised finial is applied. The foot, formed of a previously marked piece of plate, is a replacement.

• 50 •

TWO-HANDLED CUP AND COVER
London, 1657/8
Silver
35.1558

MARKS: on base of cup and on outside rim of cover, maker's mark *WC* in a clipped rectangle (Jackson, 1921, p. 128; rev. ed. 1989, p. 124); leopard's head crowned; date letter *v*; lion passant (repeated on knop of cover); on foot rim, maker's mark *-R* (indecipherable); leopard's head crowned; lion passant; date letter *q* for 1633

INSCRIPTIONS: pounced on side of cup, *W* over *IE*

H. 12.7 cm (5 in.); w. 19.7 cm (7¾ in.); diam. of rim 13 cm (5⅛ in.)

WEIGHT: 636.5 gm (20 oz 8 dwt)

PROVENANCE: St. Andrew's Castle, Bury St. Edmunds (unverified); William E. Godfrey, New York, purchased by Frank Brewer Bemis, 1928, Bequest of Frank Brewer Bemis, November 7, 1935.

PUBLISHED: Hipkiss, 1929, p. 37; Buhler, 1952, p. 228, no. 7.

• 51 •

SPOUT CUP
Norfolk, possibly Norwich, ca. 1660
Silver
62.672

MARKS: on cover, leopard's head (?); maker's mark *TS* in monogram in a shaped shield (Jackson, 1921, p. 444; rev. ed. 1989, p. 337); date letter (?) *G* in a shaped shield; fleur-de-lys

H. 12 cm (4¾ in.); w. 11 cm (4⁵⁄₁₆ in.); d. 9.7 cm (3¹³⁄₁₆ in.)

WEIGHT: 268.7 gm (8 oz 11 dwt)

PROVENANCE: G. J. Levine, Norwich; J. H. Barnes, Esq., sold Christie, Manson & Woods, London, November 29, 1961, lot 117; purchased from Thomas Lumley, Ltd., London, September 19, 1962, Theodora Wilbour Fund in Memory of Charlotte Beebe Wilbour.

PUBLISHED: Margaret Holland, *English Provincial Silver* (New York, 1971), p. 113, ill. p. 103; Glanville, 1990, p. 438 (mentioned).

DESCRIPTION: The cup rests on a plain flat base with a straight-sided foot. The bulbous body of the jug narrows at the neck and has a wide straight rim incised with four lines. The plain cover is slightly domed. The strap handle is ear shaped with a serrated terminus; the thumbpiece is in the form of a lion's mask. The curving tubular spout rises from the base of the cup at a right angle to the handle.

CONSTRUCTION: The body of the pot is formed of three pieces: the raised main section, a seamed, straight-sided foot, and a let-in base. The seamed spout is applied to the base of the foot. The cover and strap handle are formed and the thumbpiece is cast.

The marks on this rare spout cup have been the subject of some debate. The maker's mark *TS* in monogram was used by the Norwich maker Timothy Skottowe, who served as warden of the Norwich Company of Goldsmiths in 1624 and died in 1645.[1] A spout cup by Skottowe in the Victoria and Albert Museum bears Norwich marks and the date letter *T* for 1642/3.[2] Proposing that the fleur-de-lys might represent the town mark of Lincoln,[3] Jackson suggested that Skottowe worked in both Lincoln and Norwich. Skottowe, however, is not known to have had any connection with Lincoln. The situation is further complicated by the fact that the maker's mark appears on a group of silver known to have been made after Skottowe's death. In addition to the present cup, the mark appears on trefid spoons of the 1660s and on a tankard that is pricked with the date 1678.[4] More recently,

G. N. Barrett has recorded the mark on a group of church plate from six parishes in Norfolk, several of which bear pricked dates of the 1660s.[5] Though it has been suggested that the *TS* in monogram mark might have been used by Timothy Skottowe's son, there is no record of Skottowe's son being admitted to the freedom of Norwich or succeeding him in business. It seems likely that the maker of the Boston spout cup and the Norfolk church silver of the 1660s was based in Norwich, but the association with Skottowe should be relinquished.

The form of this spout cup, which echos that of a pewter measure, appears to be unique.[6] Spout cups, which were more common in America than in England, were used for serving posset and syllabub; the ale or sack which separated from the mixture could be drunk from the bottom of the vessel through the spout.[7]

1. See the remarks by Commander G. E. P. How in the catalogue of the Ellis Collection, sold Christie, Manson, & Woods, London, November 13, 1935, pp. 62–63.
2. Acc. no. M84-1920, Spout cup, Norwich, 1642/3, maker's mark of Timothy Skottowe, h. 11.1 cm, ill. Glanville, 1990, cat. no. 59, p. 438.
3. Jackson, 1921, pp. 442–443. Bury St. Edmunds has also been proposed. See Margaret Holland, *English Provincial Silver* (New York, 1971), p. 113.
4. Tankard, ca. 1660–1680, maker's mark *TS* in monogram, h. 14.3 cm, sold Sotheby's, New York, December 13, 1984, lot 171.
5. G. N. Barrett, "A 'Norwich Silver' Problem Solved?," *Norfolk Archaelogy* 39 (1986) pp. 313–314. I am grateful to Tim Kent for bringing this to my attention.
6. See the pewter example illustrated in Schroder, 1988a, p. 39.
7. Glanville, 1990, p. 269.

51

• 52 •

TWO-HANDLED CUP AND COVER
Probably London, ca. 1660
Silver
63.1254a,b

Unmarked

ARMORIALS: engraved on the rim, the arms and crest of Evelyn impaling another

H. 20 cm (7⅞ in); W. 19.1 cm (7½ in.); D. 14.3 cm (5⅝ in.)

WEIGHT: 855.4 gm (27 oz 10 dwt)

PROVENANCE: purchased from John Hunt, Dublin, September 18, 1963, Theodora Wilbour Fund in Memory of Charlotte Beebe Wilbour.

PUBLISHED: Moeller, 1974, p. 16, pl. 11; Gruber, 1982, p. 153, fig. 203; ter Molen, 1984, vol. 2, p. 114, no. 628.

DESCRIPTION: The cup is of bombé shape and rests on a low modeled foot. The two high ear-shaped handles are in the form of intertwined serpents. The body of the cup is embossed overall with abstract auricular patterns incorporating grotesque masks and faces. The removable cover has an irregular outline and rises to a high finial in the form of a hooded, squatting grotesque figure. The cover is embossed with abstract auricular patterns.

CONSTRUCTION: The body of the cup is raised, embossed, and chased. The foot is cast and applied; the handles are formed of two heavy tapered wires, twisted, with the cast serpent's heads applied. The cover and finial are raised from a single sheet, embossed, and chased. Two short wires are soldered to the front and back interior of the cover to act as stops.

Though traditionally attributed to Christian van Vianen (ca. 1600–1667), this cup has more recently been published as the work of an English craftsman influenced by van Vianen's designs.[1] Stylistically, it is difficult to categorize. The virtuosity of the craftsmanship evident in the cover, which is formed from a single thin sheet, suggests the hand of a silversmith specializing in the auricular style.

Christian van Vianen was the son of the Utrecht silversmith and designer Adam van Vianen (ca. 1568–1627), and nephew of Paulus van Vianen (d. 1613), goldsmith to Rudolph II of Prague.[2] Christian is pre-

sumed to have been trained by his father. He received his first commission from Charles I in 1630, and moved to London in 1632. Few works have survived that can be firmly attributed to his English period. He remained in London until about 1643, when he moved back to Utrecht; he returned to England after the Restoration. In 1663 he was appointed "Silversmyth in Ordinary to his Maᵗⁱᵉ for Chastwork within his Maᵗⁱᵉ Closett and Bed Chamber & alsoe the Closett & Bed Chambʳ of the Queene." In Utrecht in about 1650 he published a book of his father's designs under the title *Constighe Modellen, Van verscheijden Silvere Vaten.* The present cup and cover share several characteristics with a design on plate 20, in particular the high ear-shaped handles terminating in serpents' tails, the division of the body into six lobes, and the crouching figure that serves as a finial on the cover.

The auricular elements of both Adam and Christian van Vianen's work are generally conceived as an integral part of the object rather than a surface treatment. The silver-gilt ewer signed by Adam in 1614 and Christian's Dolphin Dish of 1635 are characteristic.[3] The forms are defined by the assembled organic shapes, and there is no recognizable substructure. The Boston cup, by contrast, is readily identified as a bombé form with ear-shaped handles and a domed cover to which an auricular surface pattern has been applied. Ter Molen cites the recognizably English shape as convincing evidence that the cup was made by an English follower of Christian van Vianen.[4]

Several two-handled cups and covers with auricular decoration bearing the marks of English goldsmiths are known. A cup of 1666 at Wadham College, Oxford, by the Hound Sejant maker, and another of 1668 with the maker's mark *GC* in monogram show the application of lobate motifs to the English form.[5] The cartilagenous modeling of the Boston cup is more fluid and more thoroughly integrated into the form than either of these English examples, however. A closer stylistic comparison might be made with a low covered two-handled cup bequeathed by the widow of the tenth Earl of Northumberland to the Duke and Duchess of Somerset. Probably

52 (Color Plate XI)

made about 1636–1642, it has been attributed to Christian van Vianen.[6] The Boston cup and the Northumberland cup have similar handles terminating in serpents' heads, a similar lobed foot, hexafoil outline, and irregularly shaped cover that hangs over the body of the vessel. Other features of the Boston cup that are uncharacteristic of English design and construction are the pinched corners of the rim of the body, the absence of an interior bezel to secure the cover, and most importantly, the modeling of the grotesque figure. The monkeylike face and ribs visible though the drapery are best compared to the supporting figure at the base of the ewer by Adam van Vianen at the Rijksmuseum.[7]

While the form of the cup does not seem to be Dutch, the design and construction do not seem to be English[8]; therefore, the cup might tentatively be attributed to one of several Continental-trained craftsmen working in England. Among them, John Cooqus and Michiel de Bruyn van Berendrecht might be considered. John Cooqus, Christian van Vianen's son-in-law, is known only from documents, although it has been suggested that his mark might have been *GC* in monogram.[9] Michiel de Bruyn van Berendrecht was Christian van Vianen's partner in London after 1660; a small two-handled cup and cover made while he was active in Utrecht shows his interpretation of the van Vianen style.[10] Perhaps the most likely candidate is the Zurich-born maker Wolfgang Howzer. A silver-gilt cup bearing Howzer's mark has the same distinctive foot as the present cup.[11] Though the chasing on Howzer's cup is in the form of conventional baroque foliage, other examples of his work, such as the chapel plate at Auckland Palace, show a mastery of the auricular style.[12]

The engraved coat of arms has traditionally been identified as that of John Evelyn (1620–1706), the writer and diarist, and Mary, daughter of Sir Richard Browne, whom he married in 1646. The representation of tinctures on engraved silver were not standardized by the third quarter of the seventeenth century, however, so the sinister arms should not necessarily be blazoned as argent, a chief gules. The style of the engraving suggests that the arms may be a later addition.

1. Moeller, 1974, p. 16, pl. 11, attributed the cup to van Vianen; ter Molen, 1984, vol. 2, p. 114, no. 628 proposes that the cup is English.
2. The most thorough summary of documentary material regarding the van Vianen family is ter Molen, 1984.
3. Ibid., vol. 1, pls. 23, 34. Detailed photographs of the ewer are found in Christie, Manson & Woods, Amsterdam, October 19, 1976.
4. Ter Molen, 1984, vol. 2, p. 114, no. 628.
5. Both are illustrated in Oman, 1970, pls. 9B, 11B.
6. Lightbown, 1968, p. 436.
7. Rijksmuseum, Amsterdam, acc. no. TM 409, exhibited Utrecht, Centraal Museum, *Zeldzaam Zilver uit de Gouden Eeuw: De Utrechtse edelsmeden Van Vianen* (Utrecht, 1985), cat. no. 61, p. 75. Details of the grotesque figure are illustrated in Christie, Manson & Woods, Amsterdam, October 19, 1976, lot 544.
8. The cup was examined by energy dispersive x-ray fluorescence. The average weight percentage of silver in the body and cover is 94.9. While higher than sterling, this is not inconsistent with contemporary objects of English manufacture. Copper, gold, and lead measured 4.6, 1.1, and .3 percent, respectively. Localization of the source of the metal would require analysis of the trace elements by spectographic analysis, a destructive technique.
9. I am grateful to Philippa Glanville for her suggestions regarding this maker. In 1679 Cooqus petitioned the Goldsmiths' Company for touch and assay.
10. Two-handled bowl and cover with crouching figure as finial, Utrecht, 1646, w. 22.2 cm, ill. Sotheby's, Geneva, May 14, 1985, lot 149.
11. Partridge Fine Arts, London, Two-handled cup and cover, silver gilt, ca. 1670, maker's mark *WH* probably for Wolfgang Howzer, h. 17.8 cm, sold Christie's, New York, October 30, 1991, lot 306.
12. Ill. Oman, 1970, pls. 43a,b.

53

· 53 ·

Pair of Salts
London, 1661/2
Silver
1975.16–17

MARKS: on inside of bowl, maker's mark *PD* three pellets above a cinquefoil below (Jackson, 1921, p. 129; rev. ed. 1989, p. 125) (struck twice on 1975.16); leopard's head crowned; lion passant; date letter *D*

1975.16: H. 2.4 cm (15/16 in.); diam. 7.2 cm (2 13/16 in.). 1975.17: H. 2.2 cm (7/8 in.); diam. 7 cm (2 3/4 in.)

WEIGHT: 1975.16: 33 gm (1 oz 1 dwt). 1975.17: 33 gm (1 oz 1 dwt)

PROVENANCE: purchased from How (of Edinburgh), London, February 12, 1975, Theodora Wilbour Fund in Memory of Charlotte Beebe Wilbour.

EXHIBITED: Boston, Museum of Fine Arts, 1982, vol. 2, cat. no. 231.

PUBLISHED: Clayton, 1985a, p. 77, fig. 12.

DESCRIPTION: The fluted salts are octafoil in section with sides tapering to a flat rim surrounding the circular depression for the salt.

CONSTRUCTION: The sides of the salts are formed of a single raised and crimped sheet. The tops are formed separately and soldered at the rim.

Small salts intended for daily use are recorded in sixteenth-century inventories, though the earliest to have survived is early seventeenth century in date. Philippa Glanville has examined the distinctions made between the great salt and the more modest trencher salt; the latter was more likely ungilded, often made as part of a set, and weighed as little as two ounces.[1] Private examples of the mid-seventeenth century are extremely rare, but several from livery companies have survived. A set of six in the Untermyer Collection at the Metropolitan Museum of Art bears the arms of the Painter Stainers' Company and an inscription indicating that they were presented by James Heames, Warden.[2] These are in the shape of a quatrefoil and are constructed in the same manner as the present salts. The predilection for geometric shapes was established early in the century; a triangular pair of about 1640 reflects the origin of the term trencher salt in the slice of trencher bread spread with salt and cut crosswise into four pieces, one piece distributed to each diner.[3]

1. Glanville, 1990, p. 281.
2. Metropolitan Museum of Art, Set of six salts, 1662, maker's mark *CS*, l. 10.2 cm, see Hackenbroch, 1963, cat. no. 78, p. 47, pl. 90. See also a set in the Wax Chandlers' Company, ill. Oman, 1970, pl. 50B.
3. See Glanville, 1990, p. 282. The triangular salts, part of the Borough of East Retford corporation plate, are illustrated in Oman, 1970, pl. 50A.

54

· 54 ·

SUGAR BOX

Probably Arthur Manwaring (free 1642/3, d. ca. 1669)
London, 1661/2
Silver
33.66

MARKS: on base of interior, repeated on inside edge of cover (partially obliterated), maker's mark *AM* in monogram (Jackson, 1921, p. 124; rev. ed. 1989, p. 121); leopard's head crowned; lion passant; date letter *D*

ARMORIALS: engraved on cover, the crest of Harward, Surrey, Webb, Wilde, or Wylde

H. 9.7 cm (3¹³⁄₁₆ in.); W. 19 cm (7½ in.); D. 16 cm (6⁵⁄₁₆ in.)

WEIGHT: 584 gm (18 oz 15 dwt)

PROVENANCE: Anonymous Gift in Memory of Charlotte Beebe Wilbour (1833–1914), March 2, 1933.

EXHIBITED: Boston, Museum of Fine Arts, 1933 (no catalogue).

DESCRIPTION: The oval box rests on four flattened bun-shaped feet. It has a flat base, straight sides, and a slightly domed hinged cover with a broad rim. The cover is secured by means of a hinged tab that is pierced to fit over a post on the side of the box.

CONSTRUCTION: The body of the box is raised and has a thickened rim. The feet are constructed of two formed hemispheres, soldered at the center. The cover is raised and engraved; the hinges are fabricated.

Like the pair of candlesticks also in the Museum's collection (cat. no. 46), this sugar box is an example of the austere domestic wares produced by Manwaring during the Commonwealth.[1] Though unembellished, the thickened rim and substantial weight distinguish this box from much of the more modestly constructed plate of the period. Philippa Glanville has pointed out that the tradition of sweetening wine with sugar and the importance of sweetmeats in the service of dessert played a role in establishing the form of the sugar box in the sixteenth century.[2] Large plain oval boxes like the present example were made with several variations including scroll feet or no feet.[3]

1. For references to other works by Manwaring, see cat. no. 46.
2. Glanville, 1990, pp. 366–367.
3. Christ Church College, Oxford, Sugar-box, 1670/1, maker's mark *RP* above a mullet, w. 21 cm, ill. Oman, 1970, pl. 51B; Goldsmiths' Company, Sugar box, 1651/2, maker's mark *AF,* w. 19 cm, ill. Oman, 1970, pl. 51A.

55

· 55 ·

TWO-HANDLED CUP AND COVER
London, 1663/4
Silver
33.68

MARKS: on base of cup, repeated on outside edge of cover, maker's mark *PD*, three pellets above, a cinquefoil below in a plain shield (Jackson, 1921, p. 129; rev. ed. 1989, p. 125); date letter *f*; lion passant; leopard's head crowned

ARMORIALS: engraved on front of cup, repeated on the cover, the arms and crest of Yong of Medhurst, Sussex[1]

INSCRIPTIONS: pounced on side of cup (very worn), *YAM;* scratched on base, *RBJ, IY* (repeated), *1663*

H. 13.3 cm (5¼ in.); w. 17.5 cm (6⅞ in.); diam. of rim 10. 5 cm (4⅛ in.)

WEIGHT: 441.3 gm (14 oz 3 dwt)

PROVENANCE: Lord Wavertree by 1929; Anonymous Gift in Memory of Charlotte Beebe Wilbour (1833–1914), March 2, 1933.

EXHIBITED: London, Park Lane, 1929, cat. no. 672, pl. 10 (lent by Lord Wavertree); Boston, Museum of Fine Arts, 1933 (no catalogue); Boston, Museum of Fine Arts, 1982, vol. 2, cat. no. 260.

DESCRIPTION: The cup is bombé in shape and rests on a plain flat base. The domed cover fits over the rim of the cup, resting on two applied strips at the top of the scroll-shaped handles. The spool-shaped finial has a broad flat top engraved with a crest in mantling.

CONSTRUCTION: The body of the vessel is raised from a single sheet; the cast handles are applied. The cover is raised. The finial is constructed of two pieces.

1. The engraving of the arms on the cover differs in style from that on the body of the vessel and may be a later addition.

TANKARD

Jacob Bodendick (born Limburg, active in
London after 1661, free by redemption
1673, not recorded after 1688)
London, 1664/5
Birch with silver gilt mounts
1974.563

MARKS: on inside of cover, maker's mark *IB*
above a crescent and two pellets (similar to
Jackson, 1921, p. 130; rev. ed. 1989, p. 128);
leopard's head crowned; lion passant; date
letter *G*

ARMORIALS: chased on the cover, the arms of
Crawford of Auchinames and of Drumsoy

H. 20.6 cm (8⅛ in.); W. 22.9 cm (9 in.); diam.
of base 16.5 cm (6½ in.)

PROVENANCE: sold Sotheby Parke Bernet,
London, December 12, 1974, lot 151 [How
(of Edinburgh), London], purchased January 8,
1975, Theodora Wilbour Fund in Memory of
Charlotte Beebe Wilbour.

PUBLISHED: Clayton, rev. ed., 1985, p. 397,
fig. 600A; Brett, 1986, p. 130, fig. 448.

DESCRIPTION: The cylindrical tankard has a
domed and stepped foot with bands of twisted
wire decoration above and below an embossed
thistle pattern. The body of the vessel is made
of birch, carved with three roundels enclosing
figural scenes: a mermaid holding in her left
hand a lute, in her right, a flower with a scroll
above inscribed, *FORMOSSA SUPERNE*; a putto
tying a blindfold on a lion with a scroll above
inscribed, *CAPTIS OCULIS CAPITUR*; a spider hanging on a web over a knotted snake, with a scroll
above inscribed, *AFFLUIT INCAUTIS*. Between
each large roundel is a pair of smaller roundels,
similarly wreathed in laurel and enclosing a
bird. The domed cover has a twisted wire
around the rim; the dome is embossed with an
acanthus and floral pattern. At the center is an
applied embossed coat of arms, a nineteenth-
century addition. The handle is molded with
grotesque ornament, and the thumbpiece is in
the form of a bearded face with an acanthus
headdress.

CONSTRUCTION: The body of the vessel is
hollowed from a single piece of wood. The interior is lined with a silver-gilt sleeve mounted
at the base with a threaded pin that fits through
a hole in the wood base and is bolted to the
silver foot mount. The mount is composed of a
flat sheet soldered to the top of the embossed
molding, with drawn and twisted wire borders
above and below. The handle is cast in two
pieces and bolted to the foot and rim. The
cover is raised and embossed, with an applied
flange and a twisted wire around the rim. The

embossed and chased plaque bearing the armorials is bolted to the center. The hinge is fabricated; the thumbpiece is cast. The gilding has
been renewed.

Bodendick seems to have favored the design of the sleeve tankard, originally a
north German type. Most often the tankard is composed of an embossed silver
sleeve with a continuous scene, probably
imitating ivory tankards of a similar design.[1] A closely related example marked by
Bodendick in 1674 has similar proportions,
an identical handle, and an embossed scene
of the Judgment of Paris.[2]

The auricular design of this handle was
used, with small variations, on a large
number of sleeve tankards and mounted
exotica, particularly those of Hamburg
manufacture.[3] The handle of this tankard
corresponds closely to that on another tankard by Bodendick in this collection (see
cat. no. 59), though the scale and fineness
of the chasing differ.

The thumbpiece in the form of a mask
with a foliate headdress is unusual in the
context of both German and English baroque silver. It was used on another tankard by Bodendick with a pierced sleeve
exhibited in 1901 at the Burlington Fine
Arts Club and now in the Museum of Fine
Arts, Houston.[4]

The carved body of the tankard was
probably made by the Norwegian carver
Samuel Halvorsen, also known as Halvor
Fanden, who was active in the mid-1660s.
A tankard in the Nationalmuseet, Copenhagen, signed *S.H.S.* and dated 1663, is
carved with three roundels framed with
laurel wreaths against a ground of fruit and
foliage.[5] One of the roundels contains a
scene of a putto blindfolding a lion, identical in composition and style to that on the
present example.[6] The motif, which represents a lion made blind and docile by love,
is taken from Jacob Cats's *Proteus,* a book
of emblems published in Amsterdam in
1658. The roundel on the Museum's tankard depicting the spider suspended over
the sleeping snake is also based on an em-
blem from Cats's *Proteus.*[7] It suggests, like
the previous image, the power of love over
the strong, and that even the serpent, if
caught unaware, can be overcome by the
meek spider. The composition of these two
scenes is quite closely based on Cats's
prints, though the tree from which the spider hangs is rendered with large fruit or

56

cones similar in style to ornament on other tankards carved by Halvorsen. The third roundel on the Museum's tankard is taken from a book of emblems by Diego de Saavedra Fajardo published in 1659.[8]

It is unclear whether the wood section of the Museum's tankard was cut down from a fully finished wood tankard or if it was made as a plain cylinder to be mounted as a sleeve tankard. On other Norwegian tankards in this group the wood handles are attached to the main section of the body; there is no indication on the present example that a handle was removed, and it is possible that it was made to be mounted in silver.

The cover and foot of the tankard appear to have been modified, presumably in the mid-nineteenth century when the arms were added. Though the construction is consistent with other sleeve tankards by Bodendick, the style of the embossed floral borders around the foot is stiff and tight. The floral garlands around the cover are more typical of Bodendick's flowing designs, but the coarseness of the chasing suggests that it has been reworked.

1. See, for example, a pair of Hamburg tankards in the Gilbert Collection, ill. Schroder, 1988, cat. no. 149, pp. 550–553. For other works by Bodendick, see cat. nos. 59, 64, 66, 75, and 82.
2. Thyssen-Bornemisza Collection, ill. Müller, 1986, cat. no. 3, pp. 42–45.
3. See a Hamburg tankard in the Hermitage Museum, St. Petersburg, exhibited Lugano, Villa Favorita, *Ori e argenti dall'Ermitage,* 1986, cat. no. 23, p. 241. The mounted ostrich egg in the Museum of Fine Arts (cat. no. 70) also has a comparable handle.
4. Museum of Fine Arts, Houston, acc. no. 88.31; see London, Burlington Fine Arts Club, 1901, no. 38, p. 17, pl. III.
5. See Guthorm Kavli, "Fanden og Olkannene, Barokk Treskjaerekunst i Norge," *Arbock* (Bulletin of the Kunstindustrimuseet i Oslo) (1950–1958), pp. 31–77. I am grateful to Christian Theuerkauff, Jorgen Hein, and Fritze Lindahl for their assistance.
6. Ibid., p. 37, fig. 6. See also F. J. Billeskov Jansen, "Hollandske Emblemer og Norske Valbirkkander," *Danske Studier* (1956), pp. 13–17.
7. Jacob Cats, *Alle de Wercken, So Ouden als Nieuwen, Book I: Proteus Ofte Minne-beelden Verandt in Sinne-beelden* (Amsterdam, 1658), p. 20.
8. Diego de Saavedra Fajardo, *Idea de un principe politoco Christiano* (Amsterdam, 1659), p. 651, pl. 78.

· 57 ·

STANDING CUP
London, 1664/5
Silver gilt
1971.266

MARKS: on rim, maker's mark *PD* a cinquefoil below (similar to Jackson, 1921, p. 129; rev. ed. 1989, p. 125); leopard's head crowned; lion passant (repeated on underside of foot rim); date letter G

ARMORIALS: engraved on rim, under an earl's coronet, the arms of Sackville, Earls of Dorset; beneath an earl's coronet, the crest of Leeson, Earls of Milltown, both probably a later addition

H. 16.1 cm (6⅜ in.); diam. of rim 10.1 cm (4 in.)

WEIGHT: 337.4 gm (10 oz 17 dwt)

PROVENANCE: Countess of Milltown, Russborough, Ireland, by descent to Colonel R. W. Chandos-Pole, Radburne Hall near Derby, sold Christie, Manson & Woods, London, July 1, 1914, lot 48; Major J. W. Chandos-Pole, sold Christie, Manson & Woods, London, March 31, 1971, lot 125 [S. J. Phillips, Ltd., London], purchased September 15, 1971, Theodora Wilbour Fund in Memory of Charlotte Beebe Wilbour.

DESCRIPTION: The cup rests on a trumpet-shaped stem with a stepped foot. The lower section of the foot is flat-chased with a pattern of lobes containing stylized flowers against a matted ground. The bucket-shaped cup has a slightly flaring rim. The sides of the cup are chased with stylized flowers (poppy heads?) and bunches of grapes within an arcade against a matted ground. The inside base of the cup is decorated with a chased star against a matted ground.

CONSTRUCTION: The body of the vessel is raised, chased, and matted. The stem is raised and similarly decorated. The gilding has been renewed and covers the interior of the foot. In a large area near the engraved coat of arms the gilding has been removed; the shadow of earlier engraving is still visible.

This wine cup is representative of a group of simply constructed cups that appear between about 1650 and 1665. It is distinguished, however, by its size and weight; it is twice the size and five times the weight of a similarly decorated example in the collection of the Goldsmiths' Company.[1] The two cups have in common coarsely chased geometric flowers (pomegranates or poppy heads) with matting enclosed in punched

57

borders. The division of the cup into vertical panels and the spreading trumpet-shaped stem also appear on other cups of this type.[2]

1. Wine cup, 1657, maker's mark *GS* with two dots above and a crozier between in a shaped shield, h. 8.9 cm, ill. Carrington and Hughes, 1926, pp. 67–68, pl. 35.
2. For example, see Wine cup, 1662, maker's mark *SR* with a cinquefoil below, h. 4.5 cm, sold Christie, Manson & Woods, New York, February 5, 1981, lot 172; Wine cup, 1653, maker's mark *ET* a crescent below, h. 8.6 cm, Hackenbroch, 1963, cat. no. 28, p. 21, pl. 34.

58 (Color Plate XII)

· 58 ·

TWO-HANDLED CUP AND COVER
London, ca. 1665
Gold
60.534a,b

Unmarked

H. 8.7 cm (3⁷⁄₁₆ in.); w. 11.6 cm (4⁹⁄₁₆ in.); diam. of rim 7.9 cm (3⅛ in.)

WEIGHT: 271 gm (8 oz 13 dwt)

PROVENANCE: Thomas Lumley, Ltd., London; Sotheby & Co., London, March 24, 1960, lot 41 [Thomas Lumley, Ltd., London], purchased May 11, 1960, Theodora Wilbour Fund in Memory of Charlotte Beebe Wilbour.

PUBLISHED: Grimwade, 1951, p. 77, pl. 4; Came, 1960, p. 76, fig. 4; Moeller, 1974, p. 16, fig 12; Gruber, 1982, p. 152, fig. 202; Brett, 1986, pp. 17, 130, fig. 445.

DESCRIPTION: The cup rests on a low spreading foot that is chased with acanthus leaves. The body of the cup is of a slightly flared shape with a flat bottom. It is chased and embossed overall with lobate ornament suggesting masks and foliage. Each S-shaped handle has a scrolled terminus and is surmounted by the head of a bird. The cover is slightly domed, with a plain rim and a circular handle in the form of a coiled serpent and an applied inner bezel. It is chased and embossed with lobate and foliate decoration similar to that on the body.

CONSTRUCTION: The cup, cover, and foot are raised, embossed, and chased. The handles are cast, and the finial is formed of a piece of coiled engraved wire. The tip of one handle is a repair of base metal, cast after the original handle.

The genesis of the enthusiasm in England for the auricular style is traditionally ascribed to the arrival in 1630 of the Utrecht goldsmith Christian van Vianen. Relying primarily upon the designs of his father, Adam, Christian executed commissions for the King and his circle for the duration of his residence in England, probably between 1632–1643 and 1660–1667.[1] Auricular designs were also popularized by other Continental goldsmiths active in England such as Jacob Bodendick (see cat. nos. 56, 59, 64) and Wolfgang Howzer; see also cat. no. 52.

A small number of English silversmiths adopted the style, and it is found on pieces hallmarked as late as 1668.[2] Arthur Grimwade suggested the possibility that this unmarked gold cup may have been made by the Hound Sejant maker, who produced some of the most ambitious plate of the Commonwealth period.[3] Two gold cups bearing his mark have survived, one with a handle in the form of a coiled serpent similar to the present cup.[4] The two-handled cup and cover by the Hound Sejant maker at Wadham College, Oxford, to which he compared it, shows a similar tentative application of the lobate style to an essentially English form.[5] Other English makers, such as Arthur Manwaring and Henry Greenway, made similar use of these Dutch-inspired motifs.[6] The handles are best compared to the cast brackets used on Renaissance standing cups, rather than to those caryatid or auricular handles commonly found on post-Restoration cups.[7]

In general, the English interpretation of the style is characterized by the application of more superficial chased lobate forms to a familiar English shape. The perfume burner presented to Tsar Alexei by the Earl of Carlisle on behalf of Charles II shows the English treatment of the auricular style.[8] While the present cup is more sculptural than the perfume burner, the acanthus chasing around the foot, the caryatid handles, and the chased naturalistic flower in the center of the base suggest that it is the work of an English-trained maker.

1. The most thorough study of the documents regarding the van Vianen family is ter Molen, 1984; for Christian van Vianen's history, see vol. 1, pp. 35–40.
2. See, for example, the two-handled cup and cover with the maker's mark *GC* in monogram, ill. Oman, 1970, pl. 11A. See also cat. no. 52.

3. Grimwade, 1951, p. 80. For a further discussion of the Hound Sejant maker, see cat. no. 43.
4. Two-handled cup and cover, gold, ca. 1650, maker's mark a hound sejant, h. 17.8 cm, ill. Grimwade, 1951, pp. 76–78; Exeter College, Oxford, Two-handled cup and cover, gold, ca. 1665, maker's mark a hound sejant, h. 15.2 cm, ill. Jones, 1907a, pl. 7, no. 2.
5. Wadham College, Oxford, Two-handled cup and cover, silver gilt, 1666, maker's mark a hound sejant, h. 18.5 cm., ill. Moffatt, 1906, pl. 90.
6. Oman (1970, p. 36) discussed the maker who used the mark *HG* between two mullets and four pellets, tentatively identified as Henry Greenway.
7. For example, see the brackets on a standing cup of 1617/18 in the Kremlin Armory Museum, ill. Oman, 1961, pl. 18.
8. Kremlin Armory Museum, Perfume burner, 1663, maker's mark of John Noye, h. 45 cm, exhibited London, Sotheby's, 1991, p. 184, cat. no. 108.

· 59 ·

TANKARD

Jacob Bodendick (born Limburg, active in London after 1661, free by redemption 1673, not recorded after 1688)
London, ca. 1665
Silver and silver gilt
55.461

MARKS: on rim near handle, *IB* a pellet between a crescent and two pellets below in a plain shield (Jackson, 1921, p. 130; rev. ed. 1989, p. 128) (repeated on underside of base and on cover)

H. 17 cm (6¹¹⁄₁₆ in.); w. 20.8 cm (8³⁄₁₆ in.); d. 15.1 cm (5¹⁵⁄₁₆ in.)

WEIGHT: 1,513.9 gm (48 oz 13 dwt)

PROVENANCE: Sotheby & Co., London, May 19, 1955, lot 82 [Garrard & Co., London]; purchased September 15, 1955, Theodora Wilbour Fund in Memory of Charlotte Beebe Wilbour.

EXHIBITED: University Park, Pennsylvania, Pennsylvania State University Museum of Art, 1982, cat. no. 91.

PUBLISHED: Gruber, 1982, p. 80; Brett, 1986, p. 130, fig. 447.

59 (Color Plate XIII)

DESCRIPTION: The cylindrical tankard rests on a molded foot. Plain gilt bands around the rim and foot of the body enclose a white sleeve that is pierced and chased with naturalistic birds and foliage; the gilt lining shows through the piercing. The slightly domed cover consists of a white sleeve, pierced and chased with flowers, over a gilt substructure. The S-shaped handle is modeled with auricular motifs incorporating a claw. The thumbpiece is in the form of a tripartite scroll.

CONSTRUCTION: The tankard and cover are assembled from six pieces. The body of the vessel is a straight-sided cup. Two wire moldings are applied to the upper border. The pierced and embossed sleeve covering the body is formed from two sheets, seamed under the handle and at the front, slipped over the cylindrical body, and secured by the foot. The foot is a separate raised disk bolted to the body. The gilt cover is raised; the embossed and pierced sleeve is bolted through the center. Five small holes around the edge of the cover may originally have served to align and secure the sleeve. The sleeve has been extensively repaired; patches strengthen the underside of each thin join. The rim is formed by a wire soldered to the underside of the edges of the flowers. The handle is cast in two pieces and bolted to the body.

While the high quality of the numerous objects bearing the mark *IB* a crescent and two pellets below had long been recognized, it was not until 1970 that Charles Oman proposed Jacob Bodendick as the maker.[1] Bodendick was born in Limburg and granted denization in 1661. In 1664, Charles II addressed the Goldsmiths' Company requesting that Bodendick and the Swiss goldsmith Wolfgang Howzer be permitted to have their work assayed and marked, and in 1673 Bodendick was granted the freedom of the Company by redemption.[2]

Bodendick specialized in lavishly embossed and pierced floral decoration, a taste that had flourished in northern Germany and the Netherlands and was in great demand in England after the Restoration. Two-handled cups and covers constructed of a gilt lining and a pierced white sleeve must have been made in large quantity since about thirty examples survive.[3] The design of the embossed sleeve of most of these cups is similar to that of the tankard—a naturalistically rendered bird in the center of each side against a dense floral background. Only one other tankard with a pierced sleeve is known. It is also marked by Bodendick, and has a handle identical to the present tankard.[4] The extreme naturalism and softness of the flowers depicted on the present tankard is shared by only some of the cups: a cup of 1669 in the Victoria and Albert Museum, another unmarked example in the Metropolitan Museum of Art, and a third in the Portland Art Museum are comparable.[5]

The cover of the Boston tankard seems to have been completely finished around the rim and cut away later in order to fit over the thumbpiece. It is possible that Bodendick purchased the sleeve and cover from a shop specializing in their production and adapted the cover for its unusual application on a tankard. Yvonne Hackenbroch has proposed that the pierced and embossed sleeves were manufactured by a single workshop,[6] but the wide range in quality suggests that there may have been several centers of production. This tankard is among the finest in this style.

1. Oman, 1970, pp. 34–35.
2. Ibid., pp. 33–35.
3. See cat. no. 79.
4. Tankard, ca. 1670, parcel gilt, maker's mark only, exhibited London, Burlington Fine Arts Club, 1901, case B, no. 38, p. 17, pl. 111, fig. 4.
5. Victoria and Albert Museum, acc. no. 290–1854, Two-handled cup and cover, silver and silver gilt, 1669–1670, maker's mark *GC* in monogram, h. 17.8 cm, ill. Oman, 1965, pl. 65; Metropolitan Museum of Art, Two-handled cup and cover, silver and silver gilt, unmarked, ca. 1680, h. 19 cm, ill. Hackenbroch, rev. ed. 1969, pl. 61; Portland Art Museum, Portland, Oregon, Two-handled cup and cover, silver and silver gilt, ca. 1670, maker's mark of Jacob Bodendick, h. 19.4 cm, published G. E. P. How, *Notes on Antique Silver* 4 (1945), p. 8, pl. 4.
6. Hackenbroch, rev. ed. 1969, p. 36.

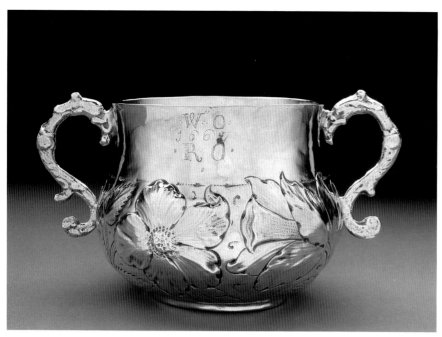

60

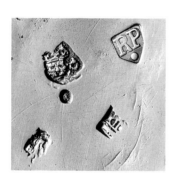

• 60 •

TWO-HANDLED CUP
London, 1665/6
Silver
35.1561

MARKS: on underside of base, maker's mark *RP* a pellet below in a plain shield (Jackson, 1921, p. 131; rev. ed. 1989, p. 128) (struck twice); date letter *h;* lion passant; leopard's head crowned

INSCRIPTIONS: pricked near rim, *WO/1667/ RO*

H. 7.9 cm (3⅛ in.); w. 13.7 cm (5⅜ in.); diam. of rim 7.9 cm (3⅛ in.)

WEIGHT: 141.7 gm (4 oz 11 dwt)

PROVENANCE: William E. Godfrey, New York, purchased by Frank Brewer Bemis, 1927, Bequest of Frank Brewer Bemis, November 7, 1935.

DESCRIPTION: The bombé cup rests on a flat base. The lower half of the cup is chased with naturalistic flowers and leaves. The S-shaped handles are modeled with dolphins and foliage.

CONSTRUCTION: The body of the cup is raised from a single sheet, embossed, and chased. The handles are cast and have been reattached.

• 61 •

COVERED CUP
London, 1666/7
Silver
61.655a,b

MARKS: on rim of cup and on underside of flange of cover, maker's mark *WW* a fleur-de-lys and two pellets below in a shaped shield (Jackson, 1921, p. 131; rev. ed. 1989, p. 128); leopard's head crowned; lion passant (repeated on rim of foot); date letter *I*

INSCRIPTIONS: engraved around flange of cover, *Regi, Patriae, Amico Fidelis, in praelio navali adverus Batavos, strenui Ducis opera fungens, fortissimam animam exhalavit 3 Junii [sic] 1665* (Faithful to his king, his country and his friends, he breathed out his last soul on June 3rd, 1665, performing the duty of a zealous leader in a naval battle against the Dutch)

ARMORIALS: engraved on cup and cover, the arms and crest of Ley surmounted by an earl's coronet for James Ley, third Earl of Marlborough, who was born January 28, 1617/18 and succeeded his father in 1638. He died June 2, 1665.

H. 24.1 cm (9½ in.); w. 14 cm (5½ in.); diam. of foot 10.8 cm (4¼ in.)

WEIGHT: 718.9 gm (23 oz 2 dwt)

PROVENANCE: Lady Horner (unverified); sold Christie, Manson & Woods, London, May 5, 1937, lot 121; Ernest Makower; Mrs. R. Makower, sold Sotheby & Co., London, March 16, 1961, lot 143; purchased September 20, 1961, from Thomas Lumley, Ltd., London, Theodora Wilbour Fund in Memory of Charlotte Beebe Wilbour.

PUBLISHED: Clayton 1971, p. 93, fig. 189, rev. ed. 1985, p. 132, fig. 189.

DESCRIPTION: The urn-shaped cup rests on a domed foot with a plain rim. The domed cover has a wide flange of shaped outline and rises to a finial in the shape of a two-handled urn surmounted by a flame. The surface is chased overall with a pattern of lobes with auricular chasing on their upper edges.

CONSTRUCTION: The cup, foot, and cover are raised and chased. The foot is strengthened by an applied drawn wire. The soldered join of the foot to the body of the cup is covered by a heavy molded wire. The cover has an interior wire bezel. The cast finial rests on a formed disc with a molded wire border.

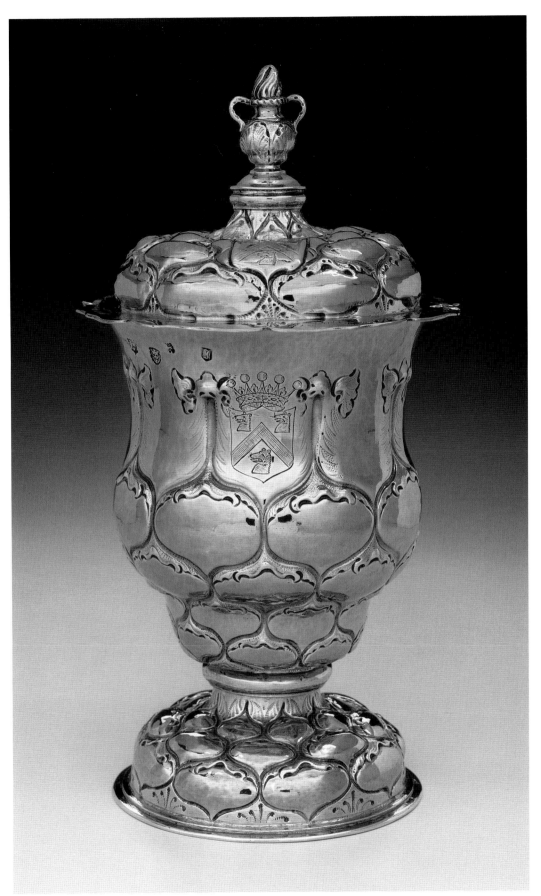

61

James Ley, in whose memory this cup was made, succeeded his father as Earl of Marlborough in 1638. The inscription refers to his loyalty and staunchness as a naval commander; he was General of Ordnance in the West, Admiral in command at Dartmouth in 1643; he established a colony at Santa Cruz in the West Indies, and was nominated Governor of Jamaica in 1664. He never assumed the post, however, as he was killed while commanding the *Old James* in the battle of Solebay, off Lowestoft, as related in the inscription. The Dutch were subsequently defeated. He was buried in Westminster Abbey on June 14, 1665. His will named Sir George Carteret, Vice Chamberlain of the Household and Treasurer of the Navy, as executor. Carteret's son George was to receive "the plate, lynen and bedding . . . as shall be aboard the ship I depart in." Others named in the will were his uncle William Ley, who succeeded him, John Bland, merchant of London, and the poor of the parish of Westbury, who were to receive twenty pounds to be distributed by "the old wife of Coll: Wanklin."[1] The cup must have been commissioned by one of these beneficiaries.

The form of this cup appears to be unique; made in the form of an urn, which is echoed in the finial, it is probably a reference to its commemorative function. Late seventeenth-century standing cups almost invariably have a baluster stem and straight-sided bowl.[2] The lobed, chased decoration is also unusual. It may be related to the German form known as a "traubenpokal" after the embossing in the form of a bunch of grapes, several examples of which bear London hallmarks.[3] Another similar use of such a pattern is on a salt made in The Hague in 1653.[4] Other seventeenth-century English vessels with overall lobed decoration include a gold two-handled cup and cover by Jacob Bodendick that is divided into ogee-shaped lobed panels interspersed with acanthus leaves and naturalistic foliage.[5] A second gold cup at Exeter College, Oxford,

marked with a hound sejant, has the most closely related decoration, combining ogee-shaped lobes with auricular borders similar to the present example, and foliate embossing.[6]

In discussing an embossed dish by *WW* in the collection of the Cleveland Museum of Art, Henry Hawley tentatively proposes that the mark may have been used by William Wheeler, Jr.[7] In the absence of the registers for the years of this maker's activity (1666–1676) it is impossible to assign a name to the mark with any certainty. Hawley also points out a stylistic similarity between this maker's work and that of the Limburg-born maker Jacob Bodendick, suggesting that *WW* may have marked pieces made in Bodendick's shop.[8] The form and decoration on this covered cup, while not characteristically English, are also unique within the context of Continental goldsmiths' work and unfortunately do not shed any light on the identity or training of the maker.

---

1. Public Record Office Prob. 3/7/64. The third Earl's mother, Mary, Countess of Marlborough later married Colonel Wanklin; their names are inscribed on the Westbury Cup, given to the church in 1671. See cat. no. 14.
2. See, for example, the cups illustrated by Clayton, rev. ed. 1985, pp. 132–133.
3. See the Nürnberg example of about 1610 illustrated in Hayward, 1976, pp. 383–384, pl. 480. In his catalogue of the Gilbert Collection, Schroder (1988, pp. 79–80) proposes that those cups bearing London marks are more likely of German manufacture, but were imported into England in considerable quantity.
4. Salt, The Hague, 1653, maker's mark of Pieter Groen, h. 14.5 cm, ill. Frederiks, 1961, p. 49, pl. 98.
5. Countess of Yarborough, Gold cup and cover, 1675/6, maker's mark of Jacob Bodendick, h. 21.6 cm, ill. Jones, 1907a, p. 7, pl. 9. See also the covered bowl in the Museum's collection by Thomas Jenkins, cat. no 68.
6. Jones, 1907a, p. 4, pl. 7, no. 2.
7. Hawley, 1984, pp. 338–340.
8. For a further discussion of Bodendick, see cat. nos. 56, 59, 64, 66, 75, 82.

62

crowned (repeated inside cover); lion passant (repeated on flange of cover); date letter *K*

H. 32 cm (12⅝ in.); diam. 19.2 cm (7⁹⁄₁₆ in.)

WEIGHT: 1,204 gm (41 oz 18 dwt)

PROVENANCE: Walter H. Willson, Ltd., London, purchased by Theodora Wilbour, 1938; Anonymous Gift in Memory of Charlotte Beebe Wilbour, September 8, 1938.

DESCRIPTION: The vase rests on a flat base with a simple molded foot. The body swells to a high shoulder and a narrow flaring neck. The vase is embossed with overlapping acanthus leaves around the foot and floral sprays above. A stepped molded section divides the body from the neck, which is embossed with leaves against a matted ground. The domed cover is embossed with acanthus leaves emanating from the central pomegranate finial.

CONSTRUCTION: The body of the vessel is formed of three pieces: a flat disk for the base, the raised, embossed, and chased section of the body, and the seamed and chased neck. Drawn, molded wire covers the joins. The domed embossed section of the cover is applied to the thick wire rim that forms the flange. The finial is composed of a cast and formed calyx enclosing a bud formed of two pieces. The gilding has been renewed.

The vase has been substantially reworked. The neck, which is out of proportion to the body and stiffly chased over false marks, appears to be a replacement. The embossed floral decoration on the body has also been retooled. The vase must have been one of a pair of smaller vases from a garniture of three or five pieces. Intended for a mantel, the garniture might have included long-necked jars[1] or tall beakers with flaring rims[2] in addition to high-shouldered vases like the present example. A pair of vases with high flaring necks and floral decoration in a style similar to the present vase sold recently in London.[3]

1. A garniture including a pair of jars by Thomas Jenkins was sold by Christie, Manson & Woods, London, November 26, 1980, lot 117.
2. A pair of vases from a similar garniture is in the Al-Tajir Collection, exhibited London, Christie's, 1990, cat. no. 33, p. 53.
3. Pair of vases, ca. 1680, maker's mark probably *NS* in script with mullets above and below, h. 25.4 cm, sold Christie's London, May 23, 1990, lot 228.

· 62 ·

COVERED VASE
London, marked 1667/8, with later alterations
Silver gilt
38.983

MARKS: inside rim of vase, *IG* a crescent below in a heart-shaped shield (Jackson, 1921, p. 129; rev. ed. 1989, p. 126); leopard's head

63

· 63 ·

QUAICH
William Law (apprenticed 1650, d. 1683)
Edinburgh, 1669–1675
Silver
62.168

MARKS: on rim, maker's mark *WL* a crown above a mullet below (Jackson, 1921, p. 499; rev. ed. 1989, p. 543); Edinburgh town mark; deacon's mark of Alexander Reid

ARMORIALS: engraved on handle, an unidentified coat of arms

INSCRIPTIONS: engraved in center of bowl, an unidentified cypher over a baron's coronet

H. 7.4 cm (2¹⁵⁄₁₆ in.); w. 27 cm (10⅝ in.); d. 18 cm (7¹⁄₁₆ in.)

WEIGHT: 442 gm (14 oz 4 dwt)

PROVENANCE: purchased from Firestone & Parson, Boston, February 14, 1962, Theodora Wilbour Fund in Memory of Charlotte Beebe Wilbour.

EXHIBITED: New York, Cooper-Hewitt Museum, 1985 (not in catalogue).

DESCRIPTION: The shallow rounded bowl rests on a straight foot with a flared rim. The two tapering handles are rectangular in section. The body of the bowl is engraved with square panels alternately plain or filled with a stylized flower. An engraved horizontal band divides the center of the bowl.

CONSTRUCTION: The body of the vessel is raised; the foot is seamed and formed. The handles are constructed of several joined pieces of sheet. The decoration is engraved.

This silver quaich's "lug" handles and engraved panels imitating staves echo its wood prototype. Quaiches were produced in silver in the later seventeenth and early eighteenth centuries in Glasgow, Aberdeen, and Edinburgh, in a range of sizes.[1] William Law served as deacon of the Edinburgh goldsmiths from 1675 to 1677. He made communion plate for at least thirteen parishes between 1665 and 1683, but he appears to have been most successful as a moneylender, and was able to purchase the castle and estate of Lauriston. At his death in 1683 he was worth £30,000 Scots.[2]

1. The term quaich is derived from the Gaelic word for cup, *cuach*. See Ian Finlay, *Scottish Gold and Silver Work* (London, 1956), pp. 112–115; Owen Evan-Thomas, *Domestic Utensils of Wood* (London, 1932), pp. 3–6.
2. See Edinburgh, Royal Museum of Scotland, *The Lovable Craft 1687–1987* (1987), catalogue by George Dalgleisch and Stuart Maxwell, p. 26.

TRAY

Jacob Bodendick (born Limburg, active in London after 1661, free by redemption 1673, not recorded after 1688)
London, 1669/70
Silver
1971.640

MARKS: on rim, maker's mark *IB* a pellet between a crescent and two pellets below in a plain shield (Jackson, 1921, p. 130; rev. ed. 1989, p. 128); leopard's head crowned; lion passant; date letter *M*

H. 8.1 cm (3³⁄₁₆ in.); w. 70.8 cm (27⅞ in.); d. 47.5 cm (18¹¹⁄₁₆ in.)

WEIGHT: 3,657 gm (117 oz 12 dwt)

PROVENANCE: Lord Heytesbury; sold anonymously at Christie, Manson & Woods, London, July 3, 1968, lot 89; purchased from Garrard & Co., London, December 8, 1971, Theodora Wilbour Fund in Memory of Charlotte Beebe Wilbour.

PUBLISHED: Christie, Manson & Woods, *Christie's Review of the Year 1967–1968*, p. 123; Moeller, 1974, pp. 4–23; Hawley, 1984, p. 339, fig. 9; Clayton, 1985a, p. 68, fig. 5.

DESCRIPTION: The tray is oval with a slight depression and rests on four flattened bun feet. At the center of the tray is an oval panel embossed with a scene of Hercules, wearing the skin of the Nemean lion, drawing his bow on the centaur Nessus, who carries away Deianira. The oval panel is enclosed by a band of laurel. The broad pierced border of the tray is embossed with naturalistically rendered flowers, including tulips, poppies, and lilies. The outer edge of the tray incorporates auricular motifs in low relief and flat-chased bubbles and waves. The two open handles are modeled with auricular and foliate motifs incorporating grotesque faces.

CONSTRUCTION: The body of the tray is formed from a single sheet, raised, embossed, chased, and pierced. The rim is strengthened by a thick round wire applied under the edge. The central relief panel is embossed and chased and secured on the back with four nuts. The front and back faces of the handles are cast separately and soldered together. The curved back of the tray is strengthened by two scrolled brackets under the handles. The mushroom-shaped feet are assembled from two formed pieces.

The design, function, and style of this tray have been discussed in an article by Robert Moeller published in 1974.[1] In summary, he records nine related trays or sideboard dishes, all oval in outline, with broad borders accommodating lush baroque foliage and enclosing a chased central panel. Some of the group have two handles like the present example, others have four; some have none. All incorporate auricular motifs in the design of the handles or around the borders. They range in date between 1668 and 1710; six of these were commissioned by the congregation of Sephardic Jews in London for presentation to the Lord Mayor.[2] The most closely related piece is a tray dated 1676/7 and marked by Bodendick; it has a central panel showing the same scene of abduction of Deianira by Nessus.[3] The floral border is composed of large, rather coarsely executed acanthus scrolls enclosing naturalistically rendered flowers. The design and execution of the later example are clumsy compared to that of the Boston tray, which has a dense but highly organized pattern in the floral border. In the chasing of the central panels the contrast is particularly evident; the turbulent surface of the water in the Boston tray is merely dimpled in the 1676 example. Moeller suggests that the later tray may be the work of an alien goldsmith submitted for assay under Bodendick's sponsorship. Moeller also discusses the relationship between this group of embossed plate to north German work, particularly that of Hamburg.[4]

To Moeller's list of related pieces three trays should be added: the first, dated 1669, with a central scene of Meleager and Atalanta and stylized acanthus borders[5]; the second, unmarked, with a central panel composed of a basket of flowers and naturalistic flowers in the borders arranged schematically like those on the Boston tray[6]; the third, at Knole, has in the center the Sackville arms and a border composed of birds against a pierced foliate ground.[7]

The composition of the scene on the central panel of the present tray is ultimately derived from an edition of Ovid's *Metamorphoses* with woodcut illustrations by Bernard Salomon, published in Lyon in 1557.[8] Salomon's depiction of the scene is the reverse of the composition on the tray: Hercules stands in the right foreground, drawing his bow against the centaur Nessus who has abducted his wife, carrying her across the river. Salomon's illustrations were the foundation for a number of later publications, including an edition illus-

64

trated by Virgil Solis in 1563, and another published in Leipzig in 1582. Bodendick may have known of a composition by Rubens executed for the Torre de la Parada, commissioned by Philip IV of Spain.[9] Two sketches attributed to Rubens are known; they represent only the figures of Nessus and Deianira. A related painting by a follower of Rubens shows the whole landscape, with Hercules represented in the left corner and cupid hovering above Nessus.[10] The subject was engraved by Willem Panneels (ca. 1600–after 1632), a student of Rubens and an engraver who often borrowed Rubens's compositions.[11]

It is likely that the handles and floral borders of the tray were based on a printed design, too. Crispin de Passe's pattern book, *Boutique Menuiserie,* published in Amsterdam in 1642, includes a sheet of auricular handle designs similar to those on the Boston tray.[12]

1. Moeller, 1974.
2. See Cecil Roth, "The Lord Mayor's Salvers," *Connoisseur* 95 (1935), pp. 296–299.
3. Sold Christie, Manson & Woods, March 31, 1971, lot 124.
4. Moeller, 1974, pp. 17–22.
5. Two-handled tray, 1669/70, maker's mark *AF* a mullet and two pellets below, w. 71 cm, sold by the Earl of Dudley at Christie, Manson & Woods, London, July 13, 1938, lot 137.
6. Four-handled tray, ca. 1670/1, unmarked, w. 67.3 cm, sold Sotheby Parke Bernet, New York, February 7, 1980, lot 767.
7. Four-handled tray, 1660/1, maker's mark illegible, ill. Penzer, 1961, p. 89.
8. Bernard Salomon, *La Metamorphose d'Ovid figurée* (Lyon, 1557).
9. Svetlana Alpers, *The Decoration of the Torre de la Parada,Corpus Rubenianum Ludwig Burchard, 9* (New York, 1971), pp. 80–100.
10. Hannover, Provinzialmuseum, *Katalog der Kunstsammlungen,* vol. 1 (Berlin, 1930), cat. no. 150, p. 95.
11. Recorded in Pierre François Basan, *Catalogue des Estampes gravées d'après P. P. Rubens* (1767), p. 90. I have not seen an image of this print.
12. Crispin de Passe, *Boutique Menuiserie* (Amsterdam, 1642), pl. 15.

147

· 65 ·

CIBORIUM
London, 1670/1
Silver gilt
60.944

MARKS: near rim of bowl, maker's mark *IS* crowned (Jackson, 1921, p. 136; rev. ed. 1989, p. 132); leopard's head crowned; lion passant (repeated on underside of foot); date letter *n*

H. 26 cm (10¼ in.); diam. 14.8 cm (5¹³⁄₁₆ in.)

WEIGHT: 890 gm (28 oz 12 dwt)

PROVENANCE: Sotheby & Co., London, November 17, 1955, lot 160 (unverified); purchased from John Hunt, Dublin, September 21, 1960, Theodora Wilbour Fund in Memory of Charlotte Beebe Wilbour.

PUBLISHED: Oman, 1957, p. 282, pl. 189.

DESCRIPTION: The standing cup rests on a stepped and domed foot that is decorated on the flat section of the top with cut-card work of foliate outline. The stem is in the form of a cylinder with bands of molding and twisted wire at the top, bottom, and mid-section. The vessel is hemispherical with cut-card work covering the lower third. Attached at regular intervals are small eyes from which bells dangle. The cover is stepped and domed with a flat central section that is decorated with cut-card foliage. At the center is a finial in the form of an orb and cross.

CONSTRUCTION: The foot of the cup is raised, with an applied wire rim and cut-card decoration. The detachable stem is screwed to the foot and bowl; it is formed of a single seamed sheet with applied moldings of profiled and twisted wire. The bowl is raised, with applied cut-card work. The bells are fabricated from two pieces. The cover is raised, with an interior wire bezel applied to the rim. The orb, fabricated from two pieces with applied beaded wire surmounted by a cast cross, is detachable.

Among the plate unique to the Catholic eucharist is the ciborium, used to contain the consecrated host. By tradition, the lining of the vessel is made of gold or silver, though few English examples in any medium have survived.

This ciborium is unusual for several reasons. Since recusant plate was not generally offered for public sale, it was rarely hallmarked, particularly during periods when the recusants were actively persecuted.[1] Though the bowl of this piece is fully marked and the foot bears the lion passant, none of the other parts is marked. The early use of cut-card decoration is also uncharacteristic of recusant silver, which tends to be conservative in design, though a parallel is found in the chalice and paten from St. Andrew Kingswood, marked by Jacob Bodendick in 1675/6.[2] This imposing piece has the familiar gothic foot and knop, with similar cut-card work at the base of the bowl and on the paten. The Museum's ciborium can be dismantled by unscrewing the foot, stem, and bowl, and has traditionally been thought to be designed for traveling like many of the recusant chalices.[3] This could also explain the austere design of the stem. The bells dangling from the bowl are also unusual and might possibly have served in place of an altar bell. They may be compared to the bells on the Royal Oak Cup in the Barber-Surgeons' Company, presented by Charles II.[4] When Pepys visited the Company in 1663, he drank from a standing cup of 1523 and wrote, "we drunk the King's health out of a gilt cup given by King Henry VIII to this Company, with bells hanging at it, which every man is to ring by shaking, after he hath drunk the whole cup."[5]

1. For a discussion of recusant plate, see Oman, 1957, pp. 257–261, 281–284.
2. St. Andrew, Kingswood, Surrey, Chalice and paten, 1675/6 maker's mark of Jacob Bodendick, h. 21.3 cm (chalice), ill. T. S. Cooper, *The Church Plate of Surrey* (London, 1902), p. 245.
3. See cat. no. 44.
4. Barber-Surgeons' Company, Cup, 1676, maker's mark *RM* in monogram, h. 41.9 cm, ill. Oman, 1970, pl. 4A.
5. Quoted in Judith Banister, "Pepys and the Goldsmiths," *Proceedings of the Society of Silver Collectors* 1, no. 10 (1968), pp. 10–11.

PAIR OF ANDIRONS
Jacob Bodendick (born Limburg, active in
London after 1661, free by redemption
1673, not recorded after 1688)
London, 1671/2
Silver with iron fittings
53.2000a,b

MARKS: at base of stem of each, date letter *O*;
lion passant; leopard's head crowned; maker's
mark *IB* a pellet between, a crescent and two
pellets below in a plain shield (Jackson, 1921,
p. 130; rev. ed. 1989, p. 128)

53.2000a: H. 49.2 cm (19⅜ in.); w. 26.4 cm
(10⅜ in.); d. (of silver) 14 cm (5½ in.).
53.2000b: H. 48.9 cm (19¼ in.); w. 26.4 cm
(10⅜ in.); d. (of silver) 12.7 cm (5 in.)

PROVENANCE: J. P. Morgan (1867–1943) (unverified); Gift of Mr. and Mrs. Winston F. C.
Guest, June 16, 1953.

DESCRIPTION: Each andiron rests on two
flattened bun-shaped feet. The base is in the
form of a scrolling volute and is chased with
acanthus leaves along the shoulders and clusters
of grapes on the apron at the front. In the center of the base is an oval cartouche surrounded
by a wreath of laurel leaves; there are traces of
obliterated engraving, probably a monogram or
armorials. The top of the base rises to a rectangular plinth with scrolling volutes. The baluster
shaft of the andiron is composed of three bun-
shaped sections chased with acanthus leaves,
separated by molded spool-shaped dividers. The
whole is surmounted by a finial in the form of a
flame.

CONSTRUCTION: All silver parts of the andirons are raised or fabricated and embossed. The
silver base is formed around a wrought iron
frame to which it is secured at each foot. There
are six silver pieces that form the upright, each
composed of two formed sections, joined in the
middle with a molded wire. They are secured
by an iron shaft that is attached to the flame
finial at the top. The base of the shaft is bolted
through the silver, the iron frame, and the iron
billet bar. Both andirons have been repaired extensively in the area around the feet. The iron
billets are modern. Two small holes on either
side of the apron that extends between the feet
might possibly have been used to affix an addi-
tional pendant piece, now missing.

Though a relatively large number of English baroque silver andirons have survived,[1] this is the only pair marked by
Bodendick.[2] It is also among the earliest
pairs known. The set of silver hearth fur-

niture from Ham House, which included
bellows, a shovel, a brush, and tongs,
suggests the appearance of the complete set
to which these andirons would have belonged.[3] The shaped base incorporating architectural and figural motifs was well
established on the Continent by the middle
of the century; a drawing of about 1640 by
Jean Cotelle shows the scrolling supports
for the feet and a pedestal supporting an
urn with a flame finial, all standard features
of English silver andiron designs from the
1670s to about 1700.[4] The design of the
present pair, with its overall acanthus embossing and graduated baluster uprights,
appears to be a unique survival; most of
the other andirons of the following decade
show the influence of the Huguenot style
in the use of gadrooning and other geometric embellishments.[5] The most closely
related examples are an unmarked pair, also
of about 1670, chased with acanthus leaves
incorporating putti and lions' masks,[6] a
similar pair in the collection of the Duke of
Buccleuch,[7] and a pair from Mentmore.[8]
These three sets have been associated on
stylistic grounds; the present pair of andirons is less boldly chased and the embossed
acanthus decoration is less integral to the
design.

1. For example: Knole, Pair of andirons, ca.
1670, h. 63.5 cm, ill. Penzer, 1961a, p. 180, fig.
11; Knole, Pair of andirons, ca. 1680, exhibited
Washington, National Gallery of Art, 1985, cat.
no. 136, pp. 211–212; Her Majesty the Queen,
Pair of andirons, ca. 1660–1685, unmarked, h.
83.8 cm, ill. N. M. Penzer, "The Royal Fire
Dogs," *Connoisseur* 133 (1954), p. 11; Her Majesty the Queen, Pair of andirons, 1696/7, h. 43
cm, ill. ibid. p. 10; Gilbert Collection, Pair of
andirons, ca. 1670, maker's mark *CG* in cipher,
h. 46.5 cm, ill. Schroder, 1988, cat. no. 24,
pp. 107–111.
2. For other work by Bodendick, see cat. nos.
56, 59, 64, 75, 82.
3. Exhibited Washington, National Gallery of
Art, 1985, cat. no. 135, pp. 210–211. For further information about the components of the
chimney piece, see Christopher Gilbert and Anthony Wells-Cole, *The Fashionable Fire Place
1660–1840* (Leeds, 1985).
4. See Peter Thornton, *Seventeenth Century Interior Decoration in England, France, and Holland*
(New Haven, 1978), p. 262, fig. 247. English
silver examples that incorporate these elements
include the pair of about 1680 at Knole, illustrated in Jackson, 1911, vol. 1, p. 249.

66 (Color Plate XIV)

5. See, for example, the pair of 1697 by Benjamin Pyne in the Metropolitan Museum of Art, Untermyer Collection, published in Hackenbrock, 1963, no. 153, p. 73, pl. 161.

6. Pair of andirons, ca. 1670, unmarked, h. 48.3 cm, sold Sotheby & Co., London, June 17, 1971, lot 165.

7. Collection of the Duke of Buccleuch, Pair of andirons, ca. 1670, unmarked, ill. Oman, 1970, pl. 83B.

8. Pair of andirons, ca. 1685, maker's mark GC duplicated in reverse, h. 51 cm, sold Sotheby Parke Bernet, at Mentmore, May 23, 1977, lot 1718.

67

· 67 ·

STANDING CUP
London, 1672/3
Silver
35.1566

MARKS: on rim, leopard's head crowned, maker's mark *RS* between mullets (Jackson, 1921, p. 132; rev. ed. 1989, p. 128); lion passant; date letter *P*

INSCRIPTIONS: pounced on side of cup, *E*P*

H. 10.5 cm (4⅛ in.); diam. of rim 7 cm (2¾ in.)

WEIGHT: 89.4 gm (2 oz 17 dwt)

PROVENANCE: Walter H. Willson, Ltd., London, purchased by Frank Brewer Bemis, 1929, Bequest of Frank Brewer Bemis, November 7, 1935.

DESCRIPTION: The cup rests on a trumpet-shaped stem that is divided into six lobes with vertically chased lines. The body of the cup has flaring sides and is hexafoil in section.

CONSTRUCTION: The trumpet-shaped stem is raised and chased. It is soldered at the top to an inverted spreading cone. The body of the vessel is raised and chased, with a let-in flat base that is soldered to the top of the inverted cone. This join has been repaired with soft solder.

A relatively small number of modest domestic wine cups such as this have survived from the seventeenth century. They are of light gauge and simple construction, and must have been made in quantity, though there is nothing to suggest that they were made in sets. The earliest examples are from the period of the Commonwealth; they have a spreading trumpet-shaped foot and are chased and matted with simple symmetrical ornament.[1] A cup in the Untermyer Collection at the Metropolitan Museum of Art has a fluted body with chased and matted panels.[2]

Even closer in design to the present cup is a cup sold in New York in 1979; it bears only a maker's mark and was catalogued tentatively as Dutch, mid-seventeenth century.[3] The upper section of the cup has ribbed vertical fluting and a flat base; the stem is taller and has a knop resting on a lobed foot. A similar cup in the Metropolitan Museum bears London marks for 1664/5 and the maker's mark *HM*.[4]

The fluted form of these silver cups may have been based on glass designs. Venetian and Netherlandish glasses were available in England in the mid-seventeenth century, and the flaring sides, flat bottom, and ribbing appear on mold-blown examples of the 1670s–1680s.[5]

1. For example, see Wine cup, 1654, maker's mark *GS* with a shepherd's crook, h. 7.9 cm; Wine cup, York, 1655, maker Robert Williamson, h. 11 cm, ill. Clayton, 1985a, p. 52, figs. 5–6.
2. Wine cup, silver gilt, 1653, maker's mark *ET* with a crescent below, h. 8.5 cm, ill. Hackenbroch, 1969, p. 23, pl. 40.
3. Standing cup, mid-seventeenth century, maker's mark *HM* conjoined in a circle, h. 9.4 cm, sold Sotheby Parke Bernet, New York, April 25, 1979, lot 117.
4. Untermyer Collection, acc. no. 1970.131.9, Standing cup, 1664/5, maker's mark *HM*.
5. See R. J. Charleston, *English Glass* (London, 1984), pls. 21a, 26b.

68

· 68 ·

TWO-HANDLED COVERED BOWL
Thomas Jenkins (active by 1668, d. 1706)
London, 1672/3
Silver
35.1565

MARKS: on rim of cover and rim of bowl, maker's mark *TI* between scallops in a shaped shield (Jackson, 1921, p. 130; rev. ed. 1989, p. 128); leopard's head crowned; lion passant; date letter *P*

ARMORIALS: engraved on rim of cover and rim of bowl, the crests of Charlton and Lechmere for the Lechmere-Charlton family

H. 14.6 cm (5¾ in.); w. 27 cm (10⅝ in.); diam. of rim 20.6 cm (8⅛ in.)

WEIGHT: 686 gm (22 oz 1 dwt)

PROVENANCE: C. Coltman Rogers, Esq., Stanage Park, Shropshire (unverified); Walter H. Willson, Ltd., London, purchased by Frank Brewer Bemis, 1930, Bequest of Frank Brewer Bemis, November 7, 1935.

PUBLISHED: Buhler, 1936, p. 80; Buhler, 1952, p. 229, no. 8; Grimwade and Banister, 1982, p. 188.

EXHIBITED: Austin, University of Texas at Austin Art Museum, 1969, cat. no. 14.

DESCRIPTION: The low rounded bowl rests on three claw-and-ball feet. The underside of the bowl is undecorated; the sides are embossed and chased with twelve teardrop-shaped lobes interspersed with acanthus leaves. The C-shaped handles are modeled with the bust of a woman and scrolls. The removable cover is slightly domed and is embossed around the rim with teardrop-shaped lobes similar to those on the body of the bowl. The center of the cover is filled with a naturalistically modeled, chased, and embossed flower.

CONSTRUCTION: The body and cover of the bowl are raised, embossed, and chased. The handles and feet are cast. The feet and handles have been reattached to the body. At the center of the cover a large patch of solder is visible on the inside, where a finial must have been attached. The surface has been mechanically buffed and may originally have been gilt.

Shallow covered bowls of this type are extremely rare. The earliest related example is a lobed basin of 1640 in the collections of King's College, Cambridge, that is described as having an internal spice strainer to be used for mulled wine.[1] The only example that is related in style is a covered bowl of 1677 made for the parish of Withycombe Raleigh, formerly in the Hearst collection.[2] It has a cover with three scroll feet that may be inverted for use as a stand. It is interesting that the cast and scrolled handles on the Hearst bowl are identical in design to those on a larger lobed bowl sometimes described as an artichoke dish.[3] Jackson, discussing a third related example of 1668, suggests that such covered bowls were probably used as serving dishes for both savory and sweet foods.[4] Like the Hearst bowl, the 1668 bowl has three feet on the cover. The embossed decoration on the body and cover are in the auricular style, but as on the Boston bowl, the decoration is divided into twelve lobed panels on the cover, and the cover fits over the rim of the body. Judith Banister suggested that the Boston bowl may have been part of a toilet service,[5] though in scale it is considerably larger than the ecuelles usually included. With so few surviving examples it is difficult to propose either the function of the bowl or the design of the missing finial.

Jenkins's activity and the range of his style have been discussed at some length.[6] Though incomplete, this is a representative example of his bold chasing.

1. Three-footed lobed basin with cover, 1640/41, maker's mark *RL* with a pellet between and a trefoil below in a plain shield, diam. 30.5 cm. Exhibited Cambridge, Fitzwilliam Museum, 1975, cat. no. BO1, p. 47.
2. Covered bowl, 1679/80, maker's mark *AR* mullet and two pellets below, w. 30.5 cm, sold Sotheby & Co., London, November 17, 1937, lot 78.
3. Bowl, 1675, maker's mark *AH,* diam. 28 cm. See also Clayton, rev. ed., 1985, fig. 42, p. 42, where a second artichoke dish is illustrated, and its function discussed. A finial in the shape of an artichoke on a dish of 1680 (maker's mark *JS,* w. 23.5 cm), suggests the function of the bowl. For a discussion see Oman, 1970, p. 51, pl. 58A.
4. Covered dish, 1668, maker's mark *WW* over a fleur-de-lys and two pellets in a shaped shield, diam. 26 cm. See Jackson, 1911, vol. 2, p. 810.
5. Grimwade and Banister, 1982, p. 190.
6. Grimwade and Banister, 1977 and Grimwade and Banister, 1982, pp. 185–193.

PEG TANKARD

John Thompson (free 1633, d. 1692)
York, 1673/4
Silver
33.71

MARKS: on cover and on underside of base, maker's mark *IT* in a shaped shield (Jackson, 1921, p. 289; rev. ed. 1989, p. 462); York town mark; date letter *R*

H. 20.6 cm (8⅛ in.); w. 20.9 cm (8¼ in.); diam. of base 13.9 cm (5½ in.)

WEIGHT: 995.1 gm (32 oz)

PROVENANCE: Anonymous Gift in Memory of Charlotte Beebe Wilbour (1833–1914), March 2, 1933.

EXHIBITED: Boston, Museum of Fine Arts, 1933 (no catalogue).

PUBLISHED: Hipkiss, 1933, p. 28; Oman, 1962, pl. 23, fig. 79.

DESCRIPTION: The tankard rests on three ball feet modeled as pomegranates with leaves extending above to the smooth side of the tankard. The vessel has a flat base, straight sides, and a slightly domed cover that is attached to the handle with a large knuckle hinge and a thumbpiece composed of two intertwined pomegranates. On the interior of the tankard is a vertical line of six cylindrical pegs. The handle is ear shaped, with a reverse curve near the shield-shaped terminus; it is D-shaped in section.

CONSTRUCTION: The body of the tankard and the cover are raised. The feet and thumbpiece are cast in two pieces and applied. The handle is fabricated. The surface of the tankard has been restored to remove engraving or chasing. The handle and the thumbpiece have been reattached.

The design of the large cylindrical tankard standing on three feet, usually in the form of pomegranates or lions, is Scandinavian in origin.[1] The pegs on the interior of the tankard mark each drinker's portion. The form became a speciality of the York goldsmiths, particularly the prolific John Plummer, who often covered the plain surface with finely engraved botanical subjects.[2] The worn surface of this tankard raises the possibility that it might once have been similarly decorated.

1. See Hernmark, 1977, vol. 1, pp. 124–125. See also the numerous examples of this form illustrated in Lightbown, 1975.
2. See Oman, 1978, pp. 66–69.

69

OSTRICH EGG EWER
London, ca. 1675
Ostrich egg with silver gilt mounts
63.1257

Unmarked
INSCRIPTIONS: engraved on base, *IX* in a circle

H. 27.5 cm (10¹³⁄₁₆ in.); w. 22.2 cm (8¾ in.);
d. 13 cm (5⅛ in.)

PROVENANCE: the Earl of Yarborough by 1911; purchased from S. J. Phillips, Ltd., London, September 18, 1963, Theodora Wilbour Fund in Memory of Charlotte Beebe Wilbour.

PUBLISHED: Jackson, 1911, vol. 1, p. 235, fig. 245 (property of the Earl of Yarborough); Smith, 1968, p. 229; Clayton, rev. ed. 1985, p. 254 (mentioned).

DESCRIPTION: The ewer is composed of an ostrich egg set vertically on a stepped spreading foot that is embossed with acanthus leaves against a matted ground. Four flat vertical straps with a foliate outline support the egg and are attached at the top to a spool-shaped neck that is embossed with bands of acanthus foliage. The spout is in the form of an ostrich's neck and head. The S-shaped handle is modeled with acanthus foliage and abstract auricular motifs surrounding a claw. The domed cover is embossed with acanthus foliage; it has a finial in the form of a berry and a thumbpiece in the form of bud.

CONSTRUCTION: The foot is raised, embossed, and chased and has an applied base wire. It is soldered to a raised cup-shaped disk with a pierced and engraved border that supports the base of the egg. The four straps are formed of flat sheet with pierced and engraved borders; they are hinged at the base to the disk and at the top to the shoulder of the ewer. The shoulder and neck are formed of three raised pieces, embossed and chased. The handle is cast in two pieces; it is pinned to a cast cluster of acanthus leaves soldered onto one of the straps.

The top of the handle is pierced to receive a leaf-shaped pin that is soldered onto the shoulder of the ewer. The spout is cast in two pieces. The cover is raised, embossed, and chased; the finial and thumbpiece are cast. The ends of the straps have been extended, probably to accommodate replacement of the egg. The heavy gilding, which covers the interior sections of the silver, appears to have been renewed; it is flaking in some places.

The enthusiasm for exotic materials such as porcelain, rock crystal, coconut, and mother-of-pearl mounted in silver had reached a peak by the last quarter of the sixteenth century.[1] Primarily a Mannerist invention, nautilus shells and ostrich eggs with baroque mounts are rare.[2]

Though unmarked, this mounted ostrich egg may be considered to be English because of the organized arrangement of the tightly scrolled acanthus leaves and the bold matting of the background. The style may be compared to the work of Thomas Jenkins, which features similar bands of finely chased acanthus leaves and cast leaves like those at the base of the handle.[3] The handle, with its cartilaginous terminus and protruding claw, is based on a German design that was widely used and adapted in England.[4] For example, Thomas Jenkins used the model on a pair of tankards at Dunham Massey.[5]

1. See the entries of the 1574 inventory of Queen Elizabeth's holdings in Collins, 1955, pp. 317–355.
2. A pair of ostrich eggs mounted as jugs and apparantly dating from the third quarter of the seventeenth century are illustrated in Oliver Impey, *Chinoiserie* (London, 1977), p. 55.
3. Grimwade and Banister, 1982, pp. 185–193.
4. See Jacob Bodendick's use of this design, cat. nos. 56, 59.
5. Pair of tankards, Thomas Jenkins, 1671, h. 25 cm, ill. Glanville, 1987, p. 63, fig. 24.

WAX JACK
London, ca. 1675–1685
Silver
61.185

MARKS: on top of taper holder, maker's mark *PR* in monogram a pellet below in a shaped shield (Jackson, 1921, p. 140; rev. ed. 1989, p. 139) (repeated on underside of each horizontal frame support); leopard's head crowned; lion passant; indecipherable date letter

H. 22.9 cm (9 in.); w. 22.6 cm (8⅞ in.); d. 16.5 cm (6½ in.)

WEIGHT: 1,221.9 gm (39 oz 6 dwt)

PROVENANCE: according to tradition, presented by Charles II to Benjamin Fellows, London, by descent, to Colonel C. T. Fellows, sold Sotheby & Co., London, December 18, 1930; William Randolph Hearst, sold Sotheby & Co., London, November 17, 1937, lot 31; Mrs. R. Makower, sold Sotheby & Co., London, March 16, 1961, lot 140 [Thomas Lumley, Ltd., London], purchased April 12, 1961, Theodora Wilbour Fund in Memory of Charlotte Beebe Wilbour.

EXHIBITED: London, South Kensington Museum, 1862, p. 489, cat. 5,866.

PUBLISHED: *Antiques* 19, no. 5 (1931), p. 400; G. Bernard Hughes, "Wax Taper Winders and Holders," *Country Life* 120 (1956), p. 1184, fig. 1; Gruber, 1982, p. 251, fig. 368; Brett, 1986, p. 134, fig. 467; Finlay, 1990, p. 187, fig. 337.

DESCRIPTION: The wax jack consists of a spool in a frame that rests on four feet. The ends of the spool are circular disks of silver, pierced and embossed with naturalistic foliage. The rectangular frame enclosing the spool is formed of flat strips that are pierced with a heart-shaped pattern. The legs are composed of two elongated C-shaped pieces; each foot is in the form of a lion's paw with a beaded appliqué. At the juncture of the legs with the frame, there is a cast ornament in the form of a putto's head. Each end of the frame is surmounted by a finial in the form of a flame. The end of the wax is held in a disk-shaped clamp with a handle in the form of two embossed birds. At the center is a finial in the shape of a putto's head.

CONSTRUCTION: The central spool has a solid wood core, with silver disks at either end that are formed, embossed, chased, and pierced. They are threaded though the center of the core with a seamed hollow silver rod. The spool is attached to the frame with a second silver rod that runs through the center of the first. The base of the frame is formed of three pieces: the two legs, formed and pierced, with an applied wire and cast feet, and the pierced cross bar,

which is soldered to the underside of the legs. The rectangular section of the upper frame is formed of a single piece and pierced; the cast flame finials and putti's heads are applied. The frame is attached to the base with posts threaded through a steel bar that runs underneath the cross bar. A twisted wire is applied to the rim of the clamp; the handles are embossed, chased, and pierced. A steel spring with a decorative outline is riveted to the inside of the handle. The clamp is secured to the frame with a threaded post and a nut in the form of a cast putto's head. The underside of one leg has been patched.

Though the date letter is indistinct,[1] this wax jack may be dated about 1675–1685. Several stylistic features show a strong Dutch influence, most notably the embossed ends of the spools, with naturalistic flowers filling each pierced lobe. This convention is related to the treatment of a group of Dutch dishes and it also appears on a series of English dishes of the early 1670s.[2] The symmetrically arranged pierced hearts on the bracket and legs of the wax jack and the cast putti's heads (possibly from a thumbpiece model) are familiar English motifs.[3]

It is unclear precisely how this wax jack would have been used. The present mounting with a spool of sealing wax is most likely incorrect. Later examples, usually with a vertical spool of wax, were often equipped with snuffers and were probably used for burning a coiled taper as a source of light.[4]

The present example and a brass wax jack in the Victoria and Albert Museum[5] are among the only such pieces to have survived from the late seventeenth century. Their imposing size and extensive decoration suggest that they may have been reserved for ceremonial occasions. They were most likely lighted only briefly to melt sealing wax before it was applied to a letter or a document. The importance of the plate that furnished the writing table in a state office is documented by the order placed in 1686 for silver for the Privy Council: each member was to have his own snuffer and tray and inkstand.[6] A snuffer and tray belonging to the Privy Council and dated 1685 has pierced work and applied beading that relate to the present example.[7] The innovative design and meticulous craftsmanship of this wax jack suggest that it was used for official business by a person of high rank.

71 (Color Plate xv)

1. It might possibly be a Q for 1673/4.
2. See the dish in the Cleveland Museum of Art by the maker *WW* above a fleur-de-lys, 1673/4, diam. 36.7 cm, discussed in Hawley, 1984, pp. 334–340.
3. The geometric piercing is found on casters of the 1680s; see, for example, Oman, 1970, pl. 53B.
4. See G. Bernard Hughes, "Wax Taper Winders and Holders," *Country Life* 120 (1956), p. 1,184, fig. 1.
5. Acc. no. 853–1897, Wax jack, brass, ca. 1675–1700, ill. Rupert Gentle, *English Domestic Brass* (New York, 1975), p. 130, fig. 72.
6. Oman, 1970, pp. 56–57.
7. H. M. Privy Council, Snuffers and tray, 1685, w. 21.5 cm, ill. Oman, 1970, fig. 67B.

72

• 72 •

PORRINGER
London, ca. 1675
Silver
33.69

MARKS: on rim near handle, maker's mark *WS* a mullet and two pellets above and below in a circle (Jackson, 1921, p. 136); maker's mark *RN* or *RM* a mullet below (possibly Jackson, 1921, p. 132; rev. ed. 1989, p. 134); leopard's head crowned; lion passant; indecipherable date letter

ARMORIALS: engraved on handle, an unidentified coat of arms (a stag statant, differenced with a crescent for second son)

INSCRIPTIONS: engraved on underside of base, *H*L*

H. 4.3 cm (1¹¹⁄₁₆ in.); w. 19.6 cm (7¾ in.); diam. of rim 13 cm (5⅛ in.)

WEIGHT: 221.1 gm (7 oz 2 dwt)

PROVENANCE: Lord Ashbrook, American Art Galleries, New York, March, 1922, lot 524; Anonymous Gift in Memory of Charlotte Beebe Wilbour (1833–1914), March 2, 1933.

EXHIBITED: Boston, Museum of Fine Arts, 1933 (no catalogue).

DESCRIPTION: The round bowl has a flat base, with curved sides rising to a straight rim.

The cartouche-shaped handle is pierced with shields and hearts in a symmetrical pattern.

CONSTRUCTION: The bowl is raised. The cast handle is soldered to the rim.

The precise name for one-handled bowls such as this is not certain. As Philippa Glanville has pointed out, there is considerable variation in contemporary terminology, ranging from "saucers with one ear" to "bleeding" or "cupping" bowls. American examples of the form are invariably called porringers; Samuel Pepys made a christening gift of a porringer and spoons, though it is not clear if he was referring to a bowl with a single handle or a two-handled cup.[1] Miss Wilbour believed this bowl to be a forgery; in her correspondence with the curator, Edwin Hipkiss, she stated "The rim only is genuine, made from a spoon. I send it as a lesson to beginners. It was one to me." While there has been some reworking and the marks are problematic, the bowl is not assembled from a spoon. The second maker's mark may represent a repairer.

1. Glanville, 1990, p. 439.

73

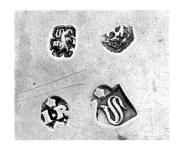

· 73 ·

MUG
London, 1675/6
Silver
40.617

MARKS: on underside of base, maker's mark *IR* between rosettes a pellet between, rosettes above and below in an oval (Jackson, 1921, p. 132; rev. ed. 1989, p. 130) (struck twice); lion passant; leopard's head crowned; date letter *S*

INSCRIPTIONS: pricked on top of handle, *W.G**

H. 6 cm (2⅜ in.); diam. of rim 7 cm (2¾ in.)

WEIGHT: 102.1 gm (3 oz 6 dwt)

PROVENANCE: Anonymous Gift in Memory of Charlotte Beebe Wilbour (1833–1914), October 10, 1940.

DESCRIPTION: The cup has a flat base, straight sides, and a slightly flared rim. The strap handle is ear shaped, with a tapered end and a rounded, curved tailpiece.

CONSTRUCTION: The cup was raised from a single sheet. The handle is formed. Below the pricked initials on the handle, traces of a former inscription are visible.

Mugs of this form have not survived in quantity,[1] but they belong to a larger category of modest domestic drinking vessels that includes simply formed tumbler cups, beakers, and thistle-shaped cups.[2] These forms, particularly suited to metalwork, do not seem to have counterparts in ceramics.

1. A similar cup of 1655, with the maker's mark *HN* a bird between, has been variously described as a christening mug and a tot cup. See Sotheby Parke Bernet, London, November 27, 1975, lot 129, and Christie, Manson & Woods, New York, June 14, 1982, lot 124. A Norwich example of 1688 was sold by Christie, Manson & Woods, London, April 27, 1983, lot 191.
2. See, for example, the cups in the Metropolitan Museum of Art, Untermyer Collection: a thistle-shaped cup of 1684, maker's mark *IS* a pillar between, h. 10.1 cm, ill. Hackenbroch, rev. ed. 1969, no. 64; a double cup with matted ground of 1685, maker's mark *TC* in monogram, ill. Hackenbroch, rev. ed. 1969, no. 72; and a nest of silver-gilt beakers, 1688, maker's mark *PH* in a dentated reserve, ill. Hackenbroch, rev. ed. 1969, no. 74.

74

· 74 ·

TWO-HANDLED CUP
London, 1676/7
Silver
57.58

MARKS: on rim, maker's mark *EI* a pellet below in a heart-shaped shield (unrecorded); leopard's head crowned; lion passant; date letter *T*

ARMORIALS: engraved on the side of the cup, the arms of Wethered or Wetherid impaling Daderon, Levinge, or Levins, probably added in the early 18th century

H. 7 cm (2¾ in.); w. 15.6 cm (6⅛ in.); d. 11.9 cm (4¹¹⁄₁₆ in.)

WEIGHT: 138 gm (4 oz 9 dwt)

PROVENANCE: Gift in Memory of Dr. George Clymer, January 10, 1957.

DESCRIPTION: The cup rests on a flat base. The body has slightly flaring sides and is decorated on the lower third with a chased and embossed band of stylized acanthus leaves and flower buds. The engraved coat of arms on the front is surrounded by foliage. The ear-shaped handles terminate in a reverse curve and have beaded decoration on the upper section.

CONSTRUCTION: The cup is raised from a single sheet, and embossed and chased. The cast handles have been reattached. Four patched repairs are visible on the interior: two on the decorated band, one on the right handle, and one on the back rim.

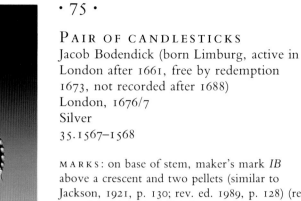

PAIR OF CANDLESTICKS
Jacob Bodendick (born Limburg, active in London after 1661, free by redemption 1673, not recorded after 1688)
London, 1676/7
Silver
35.1567–1568

MARKS: on base of stem, maker's mark *IB* above a crescent and two pellets (similar to Jackson, 1921, p. 130; rev. ed. 1989, p. 128) (repeated on rim of nozzle); lion passant (repeated on rim of nozzle); date letter *J* (indecipherable on 35.1567); leopard's head crowned (indecipherable on 35.1567)

ARMORIALS: engraved on embossed shield on base, the crest of Gunning, Somerset

35.1567: H. 17.2 cm (6¾ in.); w. 17.2 cm (6¾ in.). 35.1568: H. 17.5 cm (6⅞ in.); w. 17.2 cm (6¾ in.)

WEIGHT: 35.1567: 413.9 gm (13 oz 6 dwt). 35.1568: 433.8 gm (13 oz 9 dwt.)

PROVENANCE: according to tradition, descended from Peter Gunning, Bishop of Ely (1614–1684), sold Sotheby & Co., London, July 27, 1922, lot 65; Walter H. Willson, Ltd., London, purchased by Frank Brewer Bemis 1924, Bequest of Frank Brewer Bemis, November 7, 1935.

EXHIBITED: Hartford, Wadsworth Atheneum, *Let There Be Light* (1964), cat. no. 45; University Park, Pennsylvania, Pennsylvania State University Museum of Art, 1982, cat. no. 92.

PUBLISHED: Hipkiss, 1929, p. 37; Buhler, 1952, p. 229, no. 9; Buhler, 1970, p. 73, fig. 10; Moeller, 1974, pp. 13–14, fig. 10.

DESCRIPTION: The candlesticks rest on a flat base of shaped outline that is embossed with overlapping acanthus foliage. The stem is formed of three sections: the lower third consists of a cast disk of acanthus leaves above which rests an open calyx of four acanthus leaves; the middle section is formed by an inverted pear-shaped baluster knop that is chased with acanthus leaves; the nozzle is of a cluster-column design with small moldings at the upper and lower edges.

CONSTRUCTION: The base of the candlestick is formed from a sheet, embossed and raised at the base of the stem. On both candlesticks there have been extensive repairs at the juncture of the base and the stem. The underside of the rim is strengthened by an applied wire. The acanthus-decorated disk is cast. The stem of the candlestick screws into the pierced disk. The open calyx is cast, the baluster knop is raised and chased, and the nozzle is formed from a seamed sheet, with wire moldings applied at the top and bottom.

75

Bodendick's German training is evident in the baroque form of this candlestick, which he made with numerous variations. The design is identical to that of a gilt pair marked by Bodendick that were purchased recently by the Victoria and Albert Museum.[1] These are larger in scale, heavier in gauge, and more finely chased than the present example. In addition, they have retained their wax pans, which echo the outline of the base. An alternative design for a wax pan, with a foliate outline, appears on another pair which are more similar in scale and quality to the present pair.[2] While many of Bodendick's pieces are very precisely chased and monumental in scale, there is also a body of more modest domestic work, to which these candlesticks belong. It is possible that they were made for a toilet service, though there are no surviving services that include a pair of candlesticks with the spreading acanthus-decorated base. A related design was used on a pair of candlesticks from a toilet service marked in part by Bodendick; these have heavily cast bases with a similar acanthus pattern and a short nozzle in a boldly modeled calyx.[3]

By the mid-seventeenth century the columnar candlestick was being produced in France, the Netherlands, Germany, and England. The earliest models have square bases with a vertically reeded stem; later variations include domed, lobed, or pierced bases.[4] Other related candlestick designs by Bodendick include an octagonal base with acanthus leaves chased around the stem[5] and a base composed of four shell-like lobes.[6]

1. Victoria and Albert Museum, acc. no. M261a-c-1984, Pair of candlesticks, silver gilt, ca. 1665, maker's mark only, h. 24.5 cm. Exhibited London, British Museum, *Treasures for the Nation*, 1988, cat. no. 53, p. 78.
2. Pair of candlesticks, ca. 1675, h. 20.3 cm, sold Christie, Manson & Woods, London, on July 22, 1936, lot 136 and again on November 6, 1980, lot 270. The authenticity of these candlesticks has apparantly been questioned. When they were sold again on July 11, 1984, lot 403, the marks had been removed. In view of the other candlesticks by Bodendick of similar design, and in view of the fact that the identity of

the silversmith was not established until 1970, it seems unlikely that they could be forgeries.
3. Private collection. See exh. cat., Ormeley Lodge, Surrey, *Masterpieces of British Art and Craftsmanship*, 1954, cat. no. 45.
4. For a discussion of the general development of the form in base metal, see Ronald F. Michaelis, *Old Domestic Base-Metal Candlesticks from the 13th to the 19th Century* (Woodbridge, 1978), pp. 86–95. See also Clayton, rev. ed., 1985, pp. 54–55.
5. Harthill, Yorks, Candlestick, silver-gilt, 1675, h. 35.25 cm; see Oman, 1957, pl. 142.
6. Ashmolean Museum, Oxford, Candlestick, 1673, h. 29.8 cm. See Oman, 1970, pl. 61A.

· 76 ·

SUGAR BOX AND COVER
London, 1676/7
Silver gilt
55.930

MARKS: on underside of base and on dome of cover, maker's mark *WW* above a fleur-de-lys between two pellets in a shaped shield (Jackson, 1921, p. 131; rev. ed. 1989, p. 128); leopard's head crowned; lion passant; date letter *T*

ARMORIALS: engraved on each side of rim of box, the crest of Child, for Sir Richard Child of Wanstead, Essex (1679–1749), as Viscount Castlemaine of co. Kerry

H. 13.9 cm (5½ in.); w. 19.5 cm (7¹¹/₁₆ in.); d. 16.9 cm (6¹¹/₁₆ in.)

WEIGHT: 765.5 gm (24 oz 12 dwt)

PROVENANCE: purchased from Spink & Son, London, November 10, 1955, Theodora Wilbour Fund in Memory of Charlotte Beebe Wilbour.

DESCRIPTION: The base of the box is oval in section with bombé sides; the removable cover is domed, with a crimped rim and an interior bezel. The box rests on four scroll feet and is embossed and chased with shells and acanthus leaves against a matted ground. The cover is similarly decorated, with a handle formed of coiling tendrils enclosing a salamander.

CONSTRUCTION: The body and the cover are each raised, embossed, and chased. The feet are cast; two have been repaired. The handle is composed of a coiled wire; the salamander in the center is cast. The gilding has been renewed.

76

The viscount's coronet over the crest indicates that the engraving must have been added between 1718, the year of the creation of the peerage, and 1731, when Lord Castelmaine was elevated to the Earldom of Tylney. Sir Richard Child succeeded his brother and inherited the family estates January 10, 1703/4; he was created Baron Newtown, of co. Donegal, Viscount Castelmaine of co. Kerry April 24, 1718, and Earl Tylney of Castelmaine January 11, 1731.

Sugar boxes of this design are generally fitted with a hinge and clasp, although it is not clear that this box has been altered by the removal of these fittings. Such an alteration would have occurred before the engraving of the crest, which predates 1732.

While the twisted wire and salamander handle and scroll feet on this box are typical features of such boxes, the overall acanthus decoration is unusual. More commonly, the base is lobed and occasionally embellished with acanthus leaves between.[1] The style of the chasing is consistent with other work bearing the mark *WW* above a fleur-de-lys between two pellets, which is characterized by richly chased baroque motifs against a matted ground. For a further discussion of this maker's work, see cat. no. 61.

1. See for example the box by Thomas Jenkins of 1677, sold at Christie, Manson & Woods, June 25, 1980, lot 94.

77

· 77 ·

BEAKER
London, 1679/80
Silver
35.1569

MARKS: on underside of base, indistinct maker's mark, probably *TE* in monogram, a coronet above in a shaped shield (Jackson, 1921, p. 137; rev. ed. 1989, p. 135); leopard's head crowned; lion passant; date letter *b*

INSCRIPTIONS: pricked on side of beaker, indecipherable initials, *1680*

H. 10.2 cm (4 in.); diam. of rim 9.4 cm (3¹¹⁄₁₆ in.)

WEIGHT: 161.6 gm (5 oz 4 dwt)

PROVENANCE: Lieutenant General Sir Charles Craufurd Fraser, sold Christie, Manson & Woods, London, April 21, 1869, lot 145, purchased by Spink & Son, London; Arthur Bateman, sold Christie, Manson & Woods, London, April 3, 1903, lot 51, purchased by Welby; Christie, Manson & Woods, London, June 28, 1907, lot 78; William E. Godfrey, New York, purchased by Frank Brewer Bemis, 1924, Bequest of Frank Brewer Bemis, November 7, 1935

PUBLISHED: Buhler, 1936, p. 80, fig. 5.

DESCRIPTION: The beaker has a flat base with a molded foot and slightly flaring sides with an everted rim. It is embossed with acanthus leaves along the base and inverted tulips dangling from a horizontal band of foliage below the rim.

CONSTRUCTION: The beaker is raised and chased. The drawn wire molding is applied to the base.

· 78 ·

COMB CASE
Possibly mounted in London, ca. 1680
Tortoiseshell (Jamaica) with silver mounts
60.1173a,b

Unmarked
H. 18.4 cm (7¼ in.); w. 11.8 cm (4⅝ in.);
d. 1.1 cm (⁷⁄₁₆ in.)

PROVENANCE: Percival D. Griffiths; How (of Edinburgh), London; Gift of Mrs. Samuel Cabot, October 13, 1960.

PUBLISHED: Frank Cundall, "Tortoiseshell Carving in Jamaica," *Connoisseur* 72 (1925), p. 157, no. 5.

DESCRIPTION: The rectangular box is open on one side. On each face, the four corners are fitted with silver mounts that are engraved with stylized flowers. The borders of the tortoiseshell are engraved with an egg-and-dart pattern. One face is engraved with a nut-bearing tree and two pineapples (?) and is inscribed, *A CASHV TREE*. The reverse is engraved with the arms of Jamaica supported by standing men wearing loincloths, one bearing a bow and arrow and the other a spear. Below is the engraved motto, *INDVS VUERQUE SERVIET VNI*. The interior of the box is lined with silk. The flat comb has rounded corners, long, widely spaced teeth and is engraved on the handle with stylized foliage.

CONSTRUCTION: The flat faces of the box are composed of single sheets of tortoiseshell. The silver corner mounts are cut from sheet and engraved. The box is assembled with rivets through the narrow sides. The comb is carved from a single sheet of tortoiseshell.

A letter written by Sir Thomas Lynch, Governor of Jamaica, on March 2, 1671/2 refers to gifts sent by his wife to Lady Herbert, including "400 pounds of the best white sugar from Barbados, and a tortoiseshell box from here with combs."[1] Many of the numerous examples of these combs[2] are inscribed with a date; none, however, predates this letter. The exotic subjects of the engravings—including na-

78

tive produce such as cashews, pineapples, coconut palms, and sugar canes—indicate that they were made as souvenirs to represent the bounty of Jamaica to Londoners. Cundall suggests that Lady Lynch had commissioned them all as gifts to be sent to her English friends, though the latest dated comb is inscribed 1692,[3] and Lady Lynch died in 1682. In view of the size of these combs, it is unlikely that they were intended to be portable as has been proposed. Several of the cases are inscribed with the name of the city of manufacture, Port Royal. Only one other case besides the present example bears silver mounts.[4] Though the mounts are unmarked, the fact that the engraving of the tortoiseshell is completed beneath the mounts suggests that the silver may have been applied in England. It is also possible, however, that the mounts were fashioned in Jamaica; by 1681 there were at least five goldsmiths active in Port Royal.[5]

1. Quoted in Frank Cundall, "Tortoiseshell Carving in Jamaica," *Connoisseur* 72 (1925), p. 159.
2. In addition to the eight combs listed by Cundall (op. cit.), Geoffrey Wills records eight more; see Geoffrey Wills, "Jamaican Engraved Tortoiseshell Wig-combs," *Connoisseur Year Book, 1957* (London, 1957), pp. 76–77.
3. Wills, op. cit., p. 77.
4. Cundall, op. cit., p. 157, no. 6.
5. Robert Barker, "Jamaican Goldsmiths, Assayers and Their Marks from 1665 to 1765," *Proceedings of the Silver Society* 3, no. 5 (1986), p. 133.

PAIR OF TWO-HANDLED CUPS AND COVERS

London, ca. 1680
Silver and silver gilt
66.284a,b

MARKS: on plate on underside of base of each, maker's mark *RC* three pellets above and below in a dotted circle (Jackson, 1921, p. 139; rev. ed. 1989, p. 137) struck twice

66.284a: H. 18.5 cm (7¼ in.); W. 22.1 cm (8¹¹⁄₁₆ in.); D. 14.8 cm (5¹³⁄₁₆ in.). 66.284b: H. 19.4 cm (7⅝ in.); W. 21.6 cm (8½ in.); D. 13.7 cm (5⅜ in.)

WEIGHT: 66.284a: 1,241.7 gm (39 oz 18 dwt). 66.284b: 1,291.6 g (41 oz 11 dwt)

PROVENANCE: Spink & Son, Ltd., London by 1928; purchased from Michael Clayton, London, May 11, 1966, Theodora Wilbour Fund in Memory of Charlotte Beebe Wilbour.

EXHIBITED: London, British Antique Dealer's Association, 1928, p. 111, cat. no. 934 (lent by Spink & Son, Ltd., London).

PUBLISHED: Gruber, 1982, p. 154, fig. 204.

DESCRIPTION: The cups rest on three ball feet. They are straight-sided with simple moldings at the rim and the base and two S-shaped handles incorporating foliage and female heads. The body consists of a plain gilt inner lining with a pierced outer sleeve in the form of an open-ended cylinder. The sleeve is white, and is embossed and pierced with figures of putti and lions against a ground of acanthus foliage. The flat covers are stepped, with twisted wire applied around the rim. Like the body, the cover consists of a plain gilt substructure with an openwork white sleeve that is embossed and pierced with figures and foliage. At the center is a finial in the form of a bud enclosed in a calyx of acanthus leaves.

CONSTRUCTION: The ball feet are formed in two pieces and seamed. They are soldered to a disk with an applied wire rim. The inner body of the vessel is raised, and has an applied wire rim. It is fitted in the center of the base with a threaded post. The white sleeve is formed from two rectangular pieces, seamed, embossed, pierced, and chased. The sleeve fits over the vessel and is secured by the base, which is pierced to accommodate the threaded post. A circular plate with a shaped outline fits between the nut and the base. The raised cover has an applied inner bezel and a rim decorated with twisted wire. The white sleeve, which is raised, embossed, pierced, and chased, fits over a threaded post at the center of the cover. The finial, which is fabricated and cast, secures the sleeve.

More than twenty sleeve cups have survived, though this set and another made in Ireland are the only pairs known.[1] With the exception of the Irish examples, which are dated 1696–1699, the surviving sleeve cups probably range in date between 1668 and 1685; the majority are not hallmarked. They share a limited decorative vocabulary. The feet are most often in the form of balls, but shells, birds, or claw-and-ball feet also appear. The handles are invariably ear shaped, incorporating female heads, acanthus leaves, or auricular scrolls. The finials are composed of either buds, acanthus leaves, rosettes, or birds.[2]

With only a few exceptions, the pierced sleeves of this large group seem to be based on a single series of designs. The field of these cups is filled with naturalistically rendered flowers and foliage; at the center of each side is usually a bird. These are similar in spirit to the engraved designs of Dietrich Meyer (1572–1658), though the backgrounds of Meyer's designs are composed of scrolling acanthus foliage.[3]

It has been suggested that the pierced sleeves may be either the work of a German-trained maker who provided them to the English trade,[4] or imported from the Continent and fitted with English-made cups.[5] Sleeve cups by the maker *RC* a pellet above and below in a dotted circle, however, differ from most sleeve cups in several respects.[6] The design of the inhabited foliate ground and the style of the awkwardly rendered putti with lions emerging from acanthus foliage are unique to this maker. The stiff figures and foliage of this pair of cups are purely English in character.

1. For the Irish examples, see Clayton, rev. ed. 1985, p. 220, pl. 43. They bear Dublin marks for 1696/99.
2. Representative examples are in the Untermyer Collection at the Metropolitan Museum of Art (Two-handled cup and cover, ca. 1680, unmarked, h. 19 cm, ill. Hackenbroch, rev. ed. 1969, cat. no. 61); in the Victoria and Albert Museum (acc. no. 290-1854, Two-handled cup and cover, 1669/70, maker's mark *CG* in monogram with a sun, h. 17.8 cm, ill. Oman, 1965, pl. 65); in the Cleveland Museum of Art (acc.

79

no. 58.422, Two-handled cup and cover, 1677/
8, maker's mark *IA* in a dotted circle, h. 17.9
cm, ill. Miles, 1976, p. 32, no. 29); and the
British Museum (Two-handled cup and cover,
1685, maker's mark of Thomas Jenkins, h. 17.8
cm, ill. Read, 1928, cat. no. 93, p. 35).
3. See Berliner, 1925, vol. 2, pl. 315, no. 2.
4. Oman, 1970, p. 18.
5. C. J. Shrubsole, "Silver Gilt Sleeve Cups,"
The Antique Dealer and Collectors Guide (1978),
p. 75.

6. Examples marked by the maker *RC* three
pellets above in a dotted circle include: Two-
handled cup and cover, ca. 1680, maker's mark
only, h. 19.7 cm, sold Sotheby & Co., London,
January 24, 1957, lot 133; Two-handled cup and
cover, ca. 1680, maker's mark only, sold Christie, Manson & Woods, January 31, 1945, lot 99;
Two-handled cup and cover, 1680, collection of
the Earl of Carysfort, exhibited London, Burlington Fine Arts Club, 1901, p. 71, no. 8, pl.
111, fig. 3.

80

81

DECORATIVE HOOK, POSSIBLY FROM A SWORD BELT
English, ca. 1660–1680
Silver
1972.977

MARKS: on reverse (struck twice) maker's mark *IS* a pellet between and a pellet below, a crown above in a shaped shield (unrecorded)

H. 5.6 cm (2³⁄₁₆ in.); w. 3.5 cm (1³⁄₈ in.)

WEIGHT: 8.5 gm (5 oz)

PROVENANCE: Gift of Malcolm Stearns, Jr., in Acknowledgment of Kathryn C. Buhler's Scholarship and Her Recent Catalogue, November 8, 1972.

DESCRIPTION: The flat hook is trefoil shaped and is engraved on the front with a tulip. Two hooks are applied to the back: the upper, perpendicular, and the lower, flush.

CONSTRUCTION: The hook is formed from a cut and engraved sheet with applied round wires.

· 81 ·

MUG
Possibly England, ca. 1680
Hard-paste porcelain (China, Dehua, Fukien Province, for export) with silver mount
63.487

MARKS: on rim, maker's mark *IW* a pellet below in a shaped shield (unrecorded)

H. 9.2 cm (3⅝ in.); w. 11.1 cm (4⅜ in.); diam. of rim 6.7 cm (2⅝ in.)

PROVENANCE: Christie, Manson & Woods, London, March 20, 1963, lot 29 [Garrard & Co., London], purchased May 8, 1963, Theodora Wilbour Fund in Memory of Charlotte Beebe Wilbour.

EXHIBITED: New York, China House Gallery, 1980, cat. no. 2, p. 26.

PUBLISHED: Fontein, 1982, no. 277.

DESCRIPTION: The body of the mug is made of hard-paste porcelain. It is bulbous, with a straight neck with horizontal ribbing. Around the plain foot and below the neck is an incised chevron pattern. The handle is ear shaped. The plain silver rim has a foliate border.

CONSTRUCTION: The mug is wheel thrown from a fine, translucent white porcelain. The ribbed section of the neck is incised, and the chevron borders are applied with slip. The silver collar is constructed of two seamed pieces of sheet, joined along the rim with a small wire applied to the lower edge. The border is cut, pierced, and engraved.

By the mid-seventeenth century, porcelain wares from the kilns at Dehua (Fukien Province) were available in Europe in considerable quantity.[1] The form of this mug is related to the stoneware models produced at Fulham by John Dwight after 1673, which was, in turn, influenced by German salt-glazed prototypes. The form was also produced in silver and glass.[2] The lustrous porcelain body was embellished in several ways—with polychrome enamels in Holland, with raised gilding in Saxony,[3] and with silver mounts. The mark on the present mug, unrecorded in England, could also be that of a Continental maker.

1. See Le Corbellier, 1974, p. 22.
2. For an example in silver see cat. no. 88; for an example in glass see Robert J. Charleston, *English Glass and the Glass Used in England* (London, 1984), pl. 25.
3. See Elinor Gordon, ed., *Chinese Export Porcelain, an Historical Survey* (New York, 1977), pp. 103, 108.

82

PAIR OF CANDLESTICKS

Jacob Bodendick (born Limburg, active in London after 1661, free by redemption, 1673, not recorded after 1688)
London, ca. 1680
Silver
60.947a,b

MARKS: on base of stem of each, maker's mark *IB* a pellet between, a crescent and two pellets below, three pellets above (similar to Jackson, 1921, p. 130; rev. ed. 1989, p. 128)

H. (of each) 14.8 cm (5¹³⁄₁₆ in.); w. of base 11 cm (4⁵⁄₁₆ in.)

WEIGHT: 60.947a: 340.2 gm (10 oz 18 dwt). 60.947b: 357.2 gm (11 oz 10 dwt)

PROVENANCE: purchased from Thomas Lumley, Ltd., London, September 21, 1960, Theodora Wilbour Fund in Memory of Charlotte Beebe Wilbour.

DESCRIPTION: The candlesticks rest on stepped bases of square outline with cropped corners. The base rises to a baluster stem, with a large central knop of inverted pear shape. The nozzle is in the form of a cylinder. The surface is decorated on the base, central knop, and nozzle with flat-chased chinoiserie birds and foliage.

CONSTRUCTION: The base of each candlestick is raised, with the rim strengthened by an applied wire. The stem is cast in several pieces; the nozzle is seamed, with wires applied to each rim. The flat-chased decoration and the marks are worn.

Jacob Bodendick[1] is best known for his chased and embossed wares that reflect his Continental training and the taste of his English patrons for the floral baroque. His mark also appears, however, on objects that are strictly English in style. These candlesticks are of a scale that was often included in a toilet service. They may have once belonged to a service partially marked by Bodendick consisting of a mirror, five boxes of varying sizes, a brush, a pincushion, and a pair of small covered jars.[2] The boxes are fully marked for 1680/1, the pincushion bears only Bodendick's mark, and the mirror is unmarked. The cropped corners and moldings of the boxes and pincushion and the details of the flat-chased chinoiserie decoration are identical to those on the candlesticks.[3]

1. For a brief biography of Bodendick, see cat. no. 59. See also cat. nos. 56, 64, 66, 75.

2. Sold Christie, Manson & Woods, London, November 21, 1973, lot 127.

3. It is generally assumed that the flat-chased chinoiserie schemes were the work of a single specialized workshop (see Dauterman, 1964). The similarities between the candlesticks and the boxes are so close that they must have been decorated simultaneously. The outer border of the large casket in the toilet service, for example, is empty save for curling leaves reaching down from the matted border; the same treatment appears on the candlesticks. For further discussion of chinoiserie decoration see cat. nos. 85 and 91.

83

· 83 ·

PORRINGER
London, 1681/2
Silver
33.72

MARKS: on rim near handle, leopard's head crowned; maker's mark *EG* in a rectangle (Jackson, 1921, p. 131; rev. ed. 1989, p. 129); lion passant (repeated on underside of handle); date letter *d*

INSCRIPTIONS: pricked on handle, *HS/CH/1684*

H. 4.5 cm (1¾ in.); w. 20.6 cm (8⅛ in.); diam. of rim 13.2 cm (5³⁄₁₆ in.)

WEIGHT: 207 gm (6 oz 13 dwt)

PROVENANCE: Christie, Manson & Woods, London, December 6, 1899, lot 138; Anonymous Gift in Memory of Charlotte Beebe Wilbour (1833–1914), March 2, 1933.

EXHIBITED: Boston, Museum of Fine Arts, 1933 (no catalogue).

DESCRIPTION: The round bowl has a slightly domed base, with curved sides rising to a straight rim. The handle is pierced with shields and quatrefoils in a symmetrical pattern.

CONSTRUCTION: The bowl is raised. The cast handle is soldered to the rim.

· 84 ·

MONTEITH
Probably George Garthorne (apprenticed 1669, d. 1730)
London, 1685/6
Silver
1975.711

MARKS: on underside of base, maker's mark *GG* a pellet below (Jackson, 1921, p. 142; rev. ed. 1989, p. 139); leopard's head crowned; date letter *h*; lion passant

ARMORIALS: engraved on side panel, the crest of Cayley

INSCRIPTIONS: engraved on base, *27–3–0*

H. 12.4 cm (4⅞ in.); diam. of rim 26.3 cm (10⅜ in.)

WEIGHT: 782.5 gm (25 oz 3 dwt)

PROVENANCE: purchased by Mrs. Andrew B. McClary from Louis Wine, Ltd., Dublin, Gift of Mrs. Andrew B. McClary, December 10, 1975.

PUBLISHED: Lee, 1978, p. 63.

84

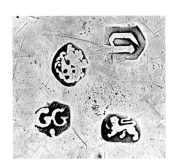

DESCRIPTION: The monteith rests on a low molded foot. The gently sloping sides are divided into six lobes separated by panels of matting. The lobes are decorated with flat-chased chinoiserie figures, foliage, and architectural ruins. The rim of the bowl is scalloped and reinforced on the outside with a border of applied foliage.

CONSTRUCTION: The bowl is raised from a single sheet with chased ribs dividing the panels. The foot is formed of two seamed pieces. The rim is reinforced with an applied wire and a cast floral border. The bowl is decorated with flat-chased and matted panels. The underside of the bowl is extensively pitted and the foot has been reattached.

Chinoiserie decoration was favored for monteith bowls, and examples of essentially the same design as the present example were marked by several makers.[1] Garthorne's own variations on this design included a removable rim, which allowed the monteith to be used as a punchbowl,

and the addition of lion's mask handles.[2] This bowl has suffered considerable damage, and the difference between the scratch weight and the present weight suggests the possibility that the foot was replaced in the course of the repairs.

1. See the following examples: Monteith, 1685/6, maker's mark *DB,* diam. 28.6 cm, Art Institute of Chicago, acc. no. 47.483, exhibited San Francisco, Fine Arts Museums of San Francisco, 1966, cat. no. 104; Monteith, 1688/9, maker's mark *IA* in monogram, h. 14.6 cm, Colonial Williamsburg Foundation, ill. Davis, 1976, cat. no. 32, pp. 42–43; Monteith, 1689, maker's mark *TD,* diam. 31.8 cm, ill. Spink & Son, London, *An Exhibition of Early English Silver* (London, 1975), cat. no. 20.
2. For example, see Monteith, George Garthorne, 1687, diam. 27 cm, sold Christie, Manson & Woods, Geneva, November 20, 1979, lot 45; Monteith, George Garthorne, 1685, diam. 28.2 cm, sold Sotheby's, London, June 19, 1986, lot 94.

85

TANKARD AND SALVER
London, 1685/6
Silver
50.2724–2725

MARKS: on cover of tankard, on body of tankard near handle, and on rim of salver, maker's mark *SH* conjoined in a circle (Jackson, 1921, p. 139; rev. ed. 1989, p. 137) (repeated on handle of tankard and on rim of salver); leopard's head crowned; lion passant; date letter *h*

ARMORIALS: engraved on the tankard and salver, the arms and crest of Hoo, Staffordshire

INSCRIPTIONS: engraved on base of tankard and salver, *My Mothers Gift to me Margaret Hoo*

50.2724 (tankard): H. 19.1 cm (7½ in.); w. 23 cm (9¹⁄₁₆ in.); d. 15.5 cm (6⅛ in.). 50.2725 (salver): H. 9.7 cm (3³⁄₁₆ in.); diam. 34.3 cm (13½ in.)

WEIGHT: 50.2724 (tankard): 1,040.4 gm (33 oz 9 dwt). 50.2725 (salver): 969.6 gm (31 oz 3 dwt.)

PROVENANCE: Mrs. N. d'Arcy, sold Christie, Manson & Woods, London, July 26, 1950, lot 21 [Goldsmiths' and Silversmiths' Co., London], purchased September 18, 1950, Theodora Wilbour Fund in Memory of Charlotte Beebe Wilbour.

PUBLISHED: Hipkiss, 1951, p. 15; Frank Davis, "English Tankards and Casters," *The Illustrated London News,* August 26, 1950, p. 336; Owsley, 1966, pp. 34–35; Gruber, 1982, pls. 75, 178.

DESCRIPTION: The circular salver rests on a low trumpet-shaped foot. It has a chased molded rim, and the plain surface is decorated overall with flat-chased chinoiserie figures including men and women in exotic dress, foliage, and birds. Around the outer border are small clouds, behind one of which the sun is visible. In a circle reserved at the center are engraved a coat of arms and crest within mantling. The tankard has a flat base with a simple molded rim, tapering sides, and a flat stepped cover with a broad rim that is shaped on the front edge. The handle is S-shaped and is D-shaped in section. The thumbpiece represents intertwined dolphins. The surface of the tankard is decorated overall with flat-chased chinoiserie figures, exotic birds, and foliage.

CONSTRUCTION: The salver is formed of a single sheet, with a chased molded border and flat-chased decoration. The raised foot is applied. The body of the tankard is raised from a single sheet, with a thickened and incised rim, and an applied wire molding at the foot. The cover is raised and flat-chased; the hinge and thumbpiece are cast. The handle is formed of two pieces, with an applied shaped terminus.

The large group of objects embellished with flat-chased chinoiserie decoration suggests the popularity of this exotic taste. The chasing on the present tankard and salver is among the most ambitious and confidently executed in this group. Often applied to otherwise plain domestic forms, such as monteiths,[1] tankards,[2] or mugs,[3] flat-chased chinoiserie appears on objects marked by a large number of makers between about 1680 and 1690. Characteristic features are the highly stylized figures, usually shown in profile and gesturing dramatically, wearing richly patterned fanciful costumes with elaborate plumed hats, drapery, or parasols. Birds, dragons, and oversized tropical foliage are depicted against rocky landscapes or architectural ruins. A single graphic source for these designs has not yet been identified; they share characteristics with contemporary Indian textiles and European travel books. In discussing a toilet service in the Metropolitan Museum of Art, Carl Dauterman proposed that a single designer may have supplied paper patterns to goldsmiths who executed the flat-chased designs.[4] Charles Oman made the more plausible suggestion that a single shop specializing in flat-chasing received the finished wares from various goldsmiths for decoration.[5] While there is remarkable homogeneity in motifs, there does seem to be a range of quality, suggesting that several hands or workshops may have been involved.

The arms have been incorrectly engraved. The 1663 Visitation of Staffordshire records them as quarterly sable and argent within a bordure erminois; the bordure has been omitted on the salver. It is impossible to date the inscription precisely; it may have been added to a piece inherited by a Margaret Hoo in the early eighteenth century, or the set may have been purchased with a sum of money given or bequeathed to a Margaret Hoo by her mother around 1685. Three Margaret Hoos are recorded in the 1663 Visitation of Staffordshire: Margaret, daughter and coheir to Richard Wilks of Bilston, Staffordshire, and wife of Anthony Hoo of Bradley (d. 1614); their daughter, Margaret, who married John Bisby of Whixhall, Shropshire; and Margaret, sister of John Hoo (d. 1719/20) and wife of William Bendy of Shuttend.[6]

1. See cat. no. 84.
2. For example, see at the Victoria and Albert Museum, acc. no. M31–1948, Tankard, 1684/5, maker's mark *IS* above a cinquefoil, h. 21.6 cm, ill. Oman, 1965, pl. 87.
3. For example, see in the Huntington Collection, acc. no. 59.35, Mug, 1684/5, maker's mark *IG* a pellet below, h. 7.6 cm, ill. Wark, 1978, cat. no. 50, p. 23.
4. Dauterman, 1964, p. 21. For further examples of chinoiserie-decorated silver in the Museum of Fine Arts, see cat. nos. 84, 90, 91. For a more general discussion of chinoiserie themes see Hugh Honor, *Chinoiserie, The Vision of Cathay* (New York, 1961).
5. Oman, 1970, p. 16
6. H. Sydney Grazebrook, ed., *The Heraldic Visitations of Staffordshire* (London, 1885), pp. 178–180.

86

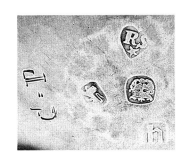

· 86 ·

TUMBLER
London, 1685/6
Silver
42.6

MARKS: on base, maker's mark *RS* a mullet below in a heart-shaped shield (Jackson, 1921, p. 143; rev. ed. 1989, p. 140); leopard's head crowned; lion passant; date letter *h*

INSCRIPTIONS: engraved on base, *C-P*

H. 5.7 cm (2¼ in.); diam. 7.6 cm (3 in.)

WEIGHT: 85 gm (2 oz 14 dwt)

PROVENANCE: Anonymous Gift in Memory of Charlotte Beebe Wilbour (1833–1914), January 8, 1942.

DESCRIPTION: The round cup rises from a curved base to a straight rim.

CONSTRUCTION: The tumbler is raised. The planishing marks are plainly visible.

87

· 87 ·

SALVER
London, 1686/7
Silver
37.567

MARKS: on rim, maker's mark *RC* three pellets above and below in a dotted circle (similar to Jackson, 1921, p. 139; rev. ed. 1989, p. 137); leopard's head crowned; lion passant (repeated on underside of foot); date letter *i*

ARMORIALS: engraved on center of salver, the arms of Dodsworth differenced with a crescent for the second son

INSCRIPTIONS: scratched on rim of base, *30=18=0;* scratched on underside of salver, *E*D 30=11*

H. 8.6 cm (3⅜ in.); diam. of rim 31.8 cm (12½ in.)

WEIGHT: 935.6 gm (30 oz 2 dwt)

PROVENANCE: Sotheby & Co., London, April 8, 1937, lot 207; Walter H. Willson, Ltd., London, purchased by Theodora Wilbour, 1937, Anonymous Gift in Memory of Charlotte Beebe Wilbour (1833–1914), August 12, 1937.

DESCRIPTION: The circular salver has a molded rim and a trumpet-shaped foot.

CONSTRUCTION: The salver is formed from a piece of sheet, with an applied raised foot.

· 88 ·

MUG
London, 1688/9
Silver
62.509

MARKS: on underside of base, maker's mark *ID* three pellets above and a gerbe between pellets below (Jackson, 1921, p. 132; rev. ed. 1989, p. 130); leopard's head crowned; date letter *l;* lion passant

INSCRIPTIONS: engraved on center of body, *ATH* in monogram, engraved on base, *L* over *C*S*

H. 9.9 cm (3⅞ in.); w. 13 cm (5⅛ in.); diam. of rim 7.6 cm (3 in.)

WEIGHT: 224.3 gm (7 oz 3 dwt)

PROVENANCE: Sir Andrew Noble, John Noble, and Michael Noble, sold Christie, Manson & Woods, London, March 28, 1962, lot 116 [Garrard & Co., London], purchased June 6, 1962, Theodora Wilbour Fund in Memory of Charlotte Beebe Wilbour.

DESCRIPTION: The mug has a bulbous body, a straight ribbed neck, and an ear-shaped handle. It rests on a plain low foot.

CONSTRUCTION: The body of the mug is raised; the ridges around the neck are incised. The foot ring, formed of a heavy piece of half-round wire, is applied. The handle is formed.

The form of this mug is copied after stoneware vessels first produced in Fulham in the mid-1670s by John Dwight and later by the Nottingham potters.[1] It was also manufactured in the translucent porcelain body known as blanc-de-Chine, made at Dehua (Fukien Province) for the English and the Continental markets.[2] Tiny pits and scratches on the surface of the body and the even and coarse hammer marks that are clearly visible suggest that decoration has been removed from the lower part of this mug. It is likely to have been flat-chased chinoiserie decoration, a popular treatment of mugs of this form.[3] It may have been done at the time the engraved monogram was added, possibly in the nineteenth century. The date of 1688 coincides with the period of greatest activity of the London-based workshop or shops that specialized in decoration of this style.[4]

1. Adrian Oswald, *English Brown Stoneware, 1670–1900* (London, 1982), pp. 27, 110. German salt-glazed stoneware vessels provided the model for a bulbous jug with a straight neck, but the short form with a wide, ribbed neck was an English innovation.
2. See cat. no. 81. Clare Le Corbellier (1974, pp. 22–23) addresses the question of the interest in European pottery in the Far East and the possibility of the German vessels having determined the shape of these Dehua mugs.
3. See, for example, in the Huntington Collection, acc. no. 59.35, Mug, 1684, maker's mark *IG* a pellet below, h. 7.6 cm, ill. Wark, 1978, cat. no. 50, p. 23. Another example of 1693/4 in the Miles Collection at the Wadsworth Atheneum, Hartford, bears the maker's mark *IR*. See Miles, 1976, cat. no. 40, p. 44.
4. See Dauterman, 1964, pp. 11–25. See also cat. nos. 85 and 91.

88

89 (Color Plate XVI)

TEAPOT (?)

London, ca. 1690
Silver gilt
55.193

MARKS: on underside of base, maker's mark *FS* over *s* a crown above in a shaped shield (unrecorded)

H. 11.8 cm (4⅝ in.); w. 15.1 cm (5¹⁵⁄₁₆ in.); d. 8.3 cm (3¼ in.)

WEIGHT: 311.8 gm (10 oz)

PROVENANCE: Miss P. E. Lewis, sold Christie, Manson & Woods, London, December 8, 1954, lot 78 [Garrard & Co., London], purchased April 14, 1955, Theodora Wilbour Fund in Memory of Charlotte Beebe Wilbour.

EXHIBITED: Austin, University of Texas at Austin Art Museum, 1969, cat. no. 25.

PUBLISHED: Yvonne Hackenbroch, "Gribelin's Designs Engraved on English Silver," *Connoisseur* 168, no. 676 (1968), p. 138, fig. 6; Gruber, 1982, p. 92, fig. 94; Clayton, 1985a, p. 84, fig. 2.

DESCRIPTION: The pear-shaped pot rests on three feet in the form of dolphins' heads. A cut-card leaf is applied to the body at the juncture of each foot. The curved spout tapers to a dolphin's head at the opening; a line of oval beads is applied to the outside. The handle is S-shaped and modeled with auricular decoration, terminating in the head of a dolphin. There is a small wire eye on the front of the rim opposite the spout. The cover is stepped and slightly domed and the rim is decorated with an applied crimped wire. The finial is in the form of a bud, and a band of foliage is engraved on the cover around the finial. The body of the pot is engraved with a scene of a mounted hunter spearing an attacking lion, and on the other side with a hunter and a boar. The background is engraved with scrolling foliage.

CONSTRUCTION: The body of the pot is raised. The handle and spout are cast in two sections and chased; the fabricated beaded decoration is applied separately. The cover is raised with an applied crimped wire around the rim and an applied wire bezel; the cast feet, thumbpiece, and finial are chased and applied.

The *FS* over *s* maker, as yet unidentified, is associated with exceptionally fine engraved ornament including scrolling foliage inhabited by figures or animals. Other examples of his work include a covered cup

and stand in the Metropolitan Museum of Art and a pair of two-handled cups and covers at Temple Newsam House, Leeds.[1] His mark invariably appears on small objects of Continental form, including beakers, double spice boxes, or small pots similar to the present example. A few pieces bearing his mark are not engraved, such as a pot in the Metropolitan Museum.[2] Fully marked examples of his work are extremely rare.[3] The precisely worked cut-card and beaded applications to this pot are not English in style, nor does the form have an English prototype. The very distinctive forms and ornament on this group of objects suggest that *FS* over *s* was a Continental maker active in London around 1690. The style of the mark itself is similar to French makers' marks.[4]

The sources for the engraved decoration on these pieces are varied. Yvonne Hackenbroch suggested that the engraving on this pot and on a large group of related objects by other makers was influenced by Simon Gribelin (1661–1731), whose ornament designs first appeared in London in 1682.[5] The figures on this pot of a mounted hunter defending himself from an attacking lion are taken from a composition engraved by Antonio Tempesta (1555–1630).[6] The scene on the opposite side showing a boar hunt is less closely dependent on Tempesta, but seems to be taken from another of his hunting scenes.[7] Tempesta did engrave grotesque ornament panels that might have served as models for some of the other *FS* over *s* pieces, but they are more strictly antique, and do not show the fanciful scrolling foliage inhabited by birds and insects that are so characteristic of these objects. Closer comparisons can be found in the ornament sheets of Theodor Bang (active after 1606) and Henri Le Roy (1579–1631). Designs by Le Roy incorporate naturalistic birds and animals in scrolling foliage, while those by Bang include hunt scenes similar in character to those on this pot.[8]

Recent efforts to identify the engraver of this group of objects have focused on a set of six covered cups and stands sold in London in 1989. The engraver has been associated with the unidentified master H. R. who was responsible for the richly decorated table top in the Queen's collection.[9]

The characteristic motif is thought to be the tightly composed acanthus leaves with pinecones surrounding the borders of the table and the cups. It is also suggested that Blaise Gentot, recently identified by Arthur Grimwade as the "Master of George Vertue,"[10] may have engraved some of the cups in the set. The distinctive acanthus and pinecone borders appear on only a small subset of objects decorated in this style, and may characterize the work of a single engraver. It appears that there may have been several workshops in London specializing in this engraved ornament.

It is unclear how this pot was meant to be used. In the 1690s teapots in silver were a novelty.[11] The bulbous shape of this pot must have been inspired by Chinese pear-shaped wine or sauce ewers.[12] The uninsulated handle of this pot would have been inappropriate for serving hot tea, though it should be noted that the small *FS* over *s* pot in the Untermyer collection at the Metropolitan Museum of Art has a wood handle and no spout. The small eye on the Museum's pot must have held a chain attached to a stopper for the spout, similar to somewhat later French and German examples. It may have been intended to hold warm brandy, cordial, or saffron tea.

1. Covered bowl on stand, maker's mark only, *FS* over *s,* ca. 1680, h. 8.9 cm, ill. Hackenbroch, rev. ed. 1969, cat. no. 82, p. 44; Temple Newsam House, Leeds, Pair of two-handled cups and covers, acc. no. 21/76, maker's mark only, *FS* over *s,* ill. Yvonne Hackenbroch, "Gribelin's Designs Engraved on English Silver," *Connoisseur* 168, no. 676 (1968), p. 139 fig. 9.
2. Pot, maker's mark only, *FS* over *s,* h. 11.4 cm, ill. Hackenbroch, rev. ed. 1969, cat. no. 81, p. 44.
3. A pair of covered bowls by *FS* over *s* with London marks for 1688 is in a private collection in Toronto. A pair of candlesticks with marks for London, 1690, seems to have had the *FS* over *s* mark overstriking another. See Christie's, New York, April 18, 1991, lot 334.
4. The fact that Jackson did not record the mark suggests that he may have thought it was a Continental maker's mark.
5. Yvonne Hackenbroch, "Gribelin's Designs Engraved on English Silver," *Connoisseur* 168, no. 676 (1986), pp. 136–144.
6. See Sebastian Buffa, ed., *The Illustrated Bartsch,* vol. 36 (New York, 1983), no. 1026. I am grateful to Liana Paredes-Arend for her assistance.
7. Ibid, vol. 37 (1984), no. 1125. See also no. 1145, a similar scene from which the figure of the boar and the costume of the hunter seem to be taken.
8. I am grateful to Edith I. Welch for these comparisons. For Bang, see Berliner, 1925, vol. 2, pp. 63–64, pls. 228–229. For Le Roy, see examples in the British Museum Print Room.
9. See the set of six covered cups and stands sold by Sotheby's, London, October 19, 1989, lot 521. The cups are marked by three different makers, David Willaume, *IC* below a crown between two mullets, and *FS* over *s.* For the table, see Oman, 1978, p. 64.
10. Arthur Grimwade, "The Master of George Vertue," *Apollo* 127, no. 312 (1988), pp. 83–89.
11. The earliest known silver English teapot, a large tapering vessel with a short spout, is dated 1670. Victoria and Albert Museum, acc. no. 02641, Teapot, 1670/1, maker's mark *TL,* h. 34.3 cm, ill. Oman, 1965, pl. 66.
12. For example, see a porcelain ewer with underglaze blue decoration from Jingdezhen, exhibited National Gallery of Victoria, Melbourne, *Oriental Trade Ceramics in Southeast Asia,* 1980, cat. no. 52, p. 46.

90

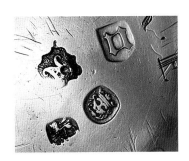

• 90 •

COVERED BOWL, PROBABLY FROM A TOILET SERVICE

Anthony Nelme (free 1679, d. 1723)
London, 1690/1
Silver
62.979

MARKS: on underside of base of bowl, maker's mark *AN* in monogram in a shaped shield (Jackson, 1921, p. 146; rev. ed. 1989, p. 144) (repeated on inside of cover); lion passant; leopard's head crowned; date letter *n*

ARMORIALS: engraved on the bowl the arms and on the cover, the crest of Jolley or Jolly of Hatton Garden, London, granted 1692

INSCRIPTIONS: engraved on underside of base, *R*E*I; 14/7*

H. 8.9 cm (3½ in.); w. 17.9 cm (7⅛ in.); d. 13.7 cm (5⅜ in.)

WEIGHT: 439.4 gm (14 oz 2 dwt)

PROVENANCE: purchased from Firestone & Parson, Boston, November 14, 1962, Theodora Wilbour Fund in Memory of Charlotte Beebe Wilbour.

EXHIBITED: San Francisco, Fine Arts Museums of San Francisco, 1966, no. 106.

PUBLISHED: Owsley, 1966, p. 38.

DESCRIPTION: The low round bowl rests on a plain foot rim. It has gently sloping sides and two S-shaped handles in the form of grotesque animals. The removable cover is flat, with a plain broad rim, and a C-shaped handle in the center. The surface of the bowl and the cover is flat-chased with chinoiserie figures in exotic dress, birds, and foliage.[1]

CONSTRUCTION: The bowl is raised. The applied foot is constructed of two wires. The raised cover has an applied interior flange fitting. The handles and finial are cast. The decoration is chased and matted.

1. For chinoiserie decoration see cat. no. 85.

TWO-HANDLED CUP AND COVER AND SALVER

London, cup marked 1677/8; salver marked
1691/2; both with later alterations
Silver gilt
64.518a,b–519

MARKS: 64.518a,b (cup): on rim, maker's mark
TM in monogram (Jackson, 1921, p. 138; rev.
ed. 1989, p. 127); leopard's head crowned; lion
passant; date letter *v* (repeated on cover). 64.519
(salver): on rim, *RL* a fleur-de-lys below in a
shaped shield (Jackson, 1921, p. 144; rev. ed.
1989, p. 137); leopard's head crowned; lion passant (repeated on foot); date letter *o*

ARMORIALS: engraved on the cup and the salver, the arms of the Commonwealth under the
Protector, Oliver Cromwell

INSCRIPTIONS: engraved on the foot of the
salver and the cup, *EC*

64.518: H. 17.6 cm (6^{15}/16 in.); W. 23 cm (9^{1}/16
in.); D. 16 cm (6^{5}/16 in.). 64.519: H. 9.6 cm (3¾
in.) diam. 34.6 cm (13⅝ in.)

WEIGHT: 64.518: 995 gm (32 oz). 64.519:
1,330 gm (42 oz 15 dwt)

PROVENANCE: Lord Brownlow, Belton
House, Lincolnshire, sold Christie, Manson &
Woods, London, May 29, 1963, lot 22; pur-
chased from Garrard & Co., London, April 8,
1964, Theodora Wilbour Fund in Memory of
Charlotte Beebe Wilbour.

EXHIBITED: London, Burlington Fine Arts
Club, 1901, cat. no. 31, case I, p. 82, pl. 105,
fig. 1 (salver only); London, St. James's Court,
1903, cat. case D, no. 2, pl. 72, fig. 1 (cup
only); London, Park Lane, 1929, cat. nos. 771–
772, pl. 15.

PUBLISHED: Christie, Manson & Woods,
*Christie's Review of the Year, October, 1962–Au-
gust, 1963* (London, 1963), p. 45; Oman, 1970,
fig. 15B[1]; Owsley, 1966, p. 38.

DESCRIPTION: The circular salver rests on a
low trumpet-shaped foot. The salver has a
chased molded rim, and the plain surface is decorated overall with flat-chased ornament composed of asymmetrical shapes filled with
matting supporting exotic foliage. The coat of
arms is engraved within a central pattern of
similar asymmetrical design. The cup rests on a
plain foot. It has a gently rounded base, straight
sides, and two S-shaped handles incorporating
female heads and scrolls. The removable flat
cover is stepped, with a plain rim and a finial in
the form of an openwork calyx. The body of
the cup is decorated overall in a pattern like that
on the salver.

CONSTRUCTION: The salver is formed from
a sheet with an applied wire border. The foot is
raised and applied. The surface of the cup,
cover, and salver is flat-chased, matted, and gilt.
The gilding, which covers the underside of the
foot, appears to have been renewed. The raised
bowl has a thickened rim and an applied cast
foot and handles. The cover is formed from a
sheet with an applied wire bezel. The finial,
which is bolted through a central post to the
cover, is composed of two cast and fabricated
sections.

This cup and salver were acquired by the
Museum from the sale of Lord Brownlow's plate from Belton House in 1963.
Many of the other objects in the sale were
from the Jewel Office and had been acquired by the first Earl Brownlow from
Rundell, Bridge, and Rundell in 1808. The
salver, which is hallmarked for 1691/2, was
presumed to have been made for the earlier
cup; both pieces are decorated with a distinctive version of the flat-chased chinoiserie popular from about 1680 to 1690.[2] Both
pieces bear the arms of the Commonwealth
under Oliver Cromwell in an early eighteenth-century style; it was suggested that
the arms had been added in the early eighteenth century following a family tradition
that they had belonged to Oliver Cromwell.

The set is problematic for several reasons. While it is not surprising to find the
1677/8 cup chased to match the later salver,
several features on the cup and the style of
the chasing itself suggest that some of the
work may be later than seventeenth-century. The cast handles on the cup have the
heads of a more common caryatid handle
form, but lack the usual Mannerist embellishments, which may have been filed off.
While the style of the flat-chased decoration appears to be in keeping with chinoiserie decoration of the 1680s, the boldly
defined abstract pattern of the matted
"ground" is unique. Also without parallel
is the absence of birds or exotically dressed
figures. A single comparison might be
made to a small two-handled cup bearing
pseudo-hallmarks for 1670.[3] It has handles
that are identical to those on the present
cup as well as flat-chased decoration with
an auricular ground and exotic foliage
without birds or people.

The engraved coat of arms on this
piece is embellished with a shell and scrolls
in the style of the early eighteenth century,

91

but the stiffness of the rendering suggests that they may be later. The treatment is similar to a small unmarked caster bearing Cromwell's arms and the inscribed date 1658[4]; the similarity extends to the illusion of shading on the right side of the armorials, and it seems possible that the caster served as the model for the engraving on the cup and salver. It is difficult to be certain when and why these two pieces were united and decorated. They may be early examples of historicist plate, or they may have been supplied to the Brownlow family in the nineteenth or even early twentieth century. There does not seem to have been a strong family tradition regarding Oliver Cromwell, but there is some evidence that Cromwell may have held some fascination for later generations.[5]

1. Incorrectly cited as belonging to the Art Institute of Chicago.
2. See cat. nos. 85 and 90.
3. The cup was included in the sale of the estate of James R. Herbert Boone, Sotheby's, New York, September 17, 1988, lot 639a. The entry was later corrected to indicate that the marks were false. I am grateful to Ian Irving for bringing this cup to my attention.
4. Sold Christie, Manson & Woods, London, July 12, 1983, lot 222.
5. Lady Elizabeth Cust, *Records of the Cust Family* (London, 1909), p. 6. Sir Edward Cust (1794–1878), brother of the first Earl Brownlow, was a military historian who published the *Lives of the Warriors of France and England* in 1867, including a chapter on Cromwell. Lady Elizabeth Cust (1909, p. 61) discusses Sir John Brownlow's (1593–1680) loyalty to the Parliamentary troups and one of their first victories, said to have been achieved about four miles from Belton House: "A local tradition still exists of a fight at Gonerby Moor close to Belton; and the old people in Belton still believe that there in the misty daybreak may be seen the shadows of ghostly armies, and heard the clang of battle sweeping across the plain." The presence of Cromwell's arms on the cup and salver might be attributable to a romantic tradition of the importance of the "Belton Fight." It may be significant that the initials *EC* are engraved on the base of both pieces; the 1963 sale catalogue suggests that they may have referred to Ethelred Cust, who married Sir John Cust in 1743, but they could equally well refer to Elizabeth or Edward Cust. Belton House inventories of 1698 and 1745 might shed light on the acquisition of the pieces; they are inaccessible at present.

• 92 •

TANKARD
London, 1691/2
Silver
55.622

MARKS: on rim near handle, maker's mark *BB* a crescent below in a shaped shield (Jackson, 1921, p. 143; rev. ed. 1989, p. 141) (repeated inside cover and on handle); leopard's head crowned; lion passant; date letter *O*

ARMORIALS: engraved on center of body, the arms of Western quartering Shirley, for Thomas Western of Rivenhall Place, Essex, son of Thomas Western, MP, by Mary, sister and co-heir of Sir Richard Shirley, Bt, of Preston, Sussex. He died in 1765, aged 56. Engraved on cover, his crest.

INSCRIPTIONS: engraved on base, *TW* in monogram; scratched on base, *25=2=0*

H. 14.9 cm (5⅞ in.); w. 17.8 cm (7 in.); diam. of base 10.8 cm (4¼ in.)

WEIGHT: 745.3 gm (23 oz 19 dwt)

PROVENANCE: E. G. Raphael, Esq., by 1929; purchased from Thomas Lumley, Ltd., London, October 20, 1955, Theodora Wilbour Fund in Memory of Charlotte Beebe Wilbour.

EXHIBITED: London, Park Lane, 1929, cat. no. 124, pl. 17 (lent by E. G. Raphael, Esq.).

DESCRIPTION: The tankard has a flat base, tapering sides, and a flat hinged cover that extends over the front edge of the vessel. The thumbpiece is in the form of a scrolling bracket. The S-shaped handle is D-shaped in section and has an applied beaded rat tail extending half way down the handle from the hinge.

CONSTRUCTION: The body of the tankard was raised and thickened at the rim. The thumbpiece was made in three sections. The handle is formed of two pieces, soldered along the edges, with a third piece forming the tailpiece. The exterior surface of the tankard has been mechanically buffed, and small pits indicate a previous engraved decoration on the cover.

This tankard appears to have been extensively altered. The form, with a flat base, sloping sides, and flat cover with a pointed front, first appeared in the 1630s. Though rare, these early examples usually have a thumbpiece that scrolls away from the hinge,[1] but otherwise have proportions very similar to the present example, which is marked 1691/2. The form was used as

92

late as the 1660s[2] but was then superseded by a larger model with an applied molded foot, usually of lighter gauge, and decorated with chasing, matting, or flat-chasing.

Since the marks on this tankard do not appear to be spurious, it may have been submitted later for assay or reworked from an earlier piece of plate. The thumbpiece, which is without parallel, as well as the beading along the spine of the handle, a common ornament of the 1680s and 1690s, may have been added at that time.

Thomas Western, whose arms and crest are engraved on the front, was born in 1709, and it is possible that the tankard was presented as a christening gift.

1. See, for example, the tankard of 1635/6 at Trinity Hall, Cambridge, maker's mark an orb and a star, h. 17.78 cm, ill. Jones, 1910, p. 34, pl. 39, no. 2. Other early examples of this form are illustrated in Clayton, 1971, p. 295, fig. 605 and in Oman, 1970, fig. 25A.
2. See the tankard of 1664/5, maker's mark *FW* a pellet above and below, h. 12.1 cm, ill. Clayton, 1985a, p. 80, fig. 2.

93

· 93 ·

DISH

London, marked 1691/2, with later alterations
Silver gilt
33.80

MARKS: on edge of dish near rim, maker's mark *II* a pellet between a fleur-de-lys below (Jackson, 1921, p. 141; rev. ed. 1989, p. 140); leopard's head crowned; lion passant; date letter *O*

ARMORIALS: engraved in center of dish, an unidentified coat of arms and crest (Per fess six escallops three and three countercharged; crest: a griffin's head erased, charged with an escallop)

INSCRIPTIONS: engraved around coat of arms in center of dish, *The gift of John Mallet upon his Admission to the place of Renter Warden *1698**

H. 3.2 cm (1¼ in.); diam. of rim 43 cm (16¹⁵⁄₁₆ in.)

WEIGHT: 2,183 gm (70 oz 4 dwt)

PROVENANCE: Anonymous Gift in Memory of Charlotte Beebe Wilbour (1833–1914), March 2, 1933.

EXHIBITED: Boston, Museum of Fine Arts, 1933 (no catalogue).

DESCRIPTION: The round dish has a shallow depression, a broad rim, and a molded edge.

CONSTRUCTION: The dish is raised from a single sheet. The molded edge is composed of two drawn wires.

The dish seems to have been substantially altered. The location of the marks on the inner curve of the depression is unusual;

94

ordinarily they appear on the edge or in the middle of the rim. There are tiny pits on the face of the dish, probably the marks of previous engraving. Furthermore, the recipient named on the inscription, John Mallet, cannot be traced as Renter Warden of any livery company, nor can any record of the arms be found. While the design of the cartouche is appropriate to about 1700, the style is tentative and the engraving thin.

· 94 ·

BOX

England?, 1692
Coquilla nut (?) with silver mounts
1978.292

Unmarked

INSCRIPTIONS: carved on back of nut, *Ano 92/ Ravel*

H. 6.6 cm (2⅝ in.); w. 5.2 cm (2¹⁄₁₆ in.); d. 5.6 cm (2³⁄₁₆ in.)

PROVENANCE: Gift of Brand Inglis in honor of Richard Alexander Inglis, September 13, 1978.

DESCRIPTION: The trilobed nut shell is cut at one end and hollowed out. The surface is carved with flowers, a scrolling vine, and a bird in low relief against a dotted ground. The rim is mounted with a plain band of silver. The flat trefoil-shaped cover has a plain rim that fits over the nut and is attached with a chain.

CONSTRUCTION: The nut is carved and polished. The silver lip is formed from a piece of wire riveted to the rim. The cover is formed of a piece of cut sheet with an applied wire rim.

Although the fascination for large silver-mounted coconut cups had waned by the seventeenth century, more modest mounted objects were still in demand. Philippa Glanville cites as an example the Scottish dealer John Clark of Penicuik who, in 1649–50, had in stock "a great variety of nuts and fruits: a 'curious flat nut well polisht; orange cullort; geryish rond little nuts; litle specklt fruit; little pomme de pins,' all mounted with silver heads or loop handles. Some were tobacco boxes."[1] Like the tortoiseshell comb and case (cat. no. 78), there remains the possibility that the mounts on this piece were applied in the West Indies or Jamaica rather than in London.

1. Glanville, 1990, p. 326.

DRESSING GLASS
London, 1692/3
Silver, walnut
60.945

MARKS: on cresting and on each of the four frame panels, date letter *p;* maker's mark *WI* a star below (Jackson, 1921, p. 139; rev. ed. 1989, p. 137); leopard's head crowned; lion passant (repeated on the four corner mounts and on the central boss on the crest)

INSCRIPTIONS: engraved on back of proper right putto, scratch weight *153–10*

H. 83.5 cm (32⅞ in.); w. 54.9 cm (21⅝ in.); d. 5.6 cm (2³⁄₁₆ in.)

PROVENANCE: purchased from Thomas Lumley, Ltd., London, September 21, 1960, Theodora Wilbour Fund in Memory of Charlotte Beebe Wilbour.

EXHIBITED: University Park, Pennsylvania, Pennsylvania State University Museum of Art, 1982, cat. no. 95, p. 69.

PUBLISHED: *Connoisseur,* American Edition, 145, no. 586 (1960), p. 27 (Thomas Lumley advertisement).

DESCRIPTION: The glass is of rectangular form with a shaped crest. The border is formed and chased with acanthus foliage, putti, and flower vases on a matted ground within gadrooned borders. The corner mounts are in the form of winged putti's heads. The arch-shaped crest consists of two putti holding a swag of fruits flanked by two vases with flowers, crowned by a winged cherub's head. The mirror is mounted with a walnut easel back; there is also a silver hook in the back from which the mirror can be hung.

CONSTRUCTION: The wood substructure of the dressing glass is made in two parts: the frame and the removable crest. The crest is covered with a single silver panel, embossed and chased. The two putti, cast in parts, and the central boss of fruits and flowers are formed separately and bolted on. The four silver panels covering the sides of the frame are embossed and chased with cast and applied borders. The joins at the corners are covered with bosses in the form of an embossed and chased putto's head. All are attached to the silver structure with original silver screws.

Almost certainly made as part of a toilet service, this mirror has an easel back with silver hinges as well as a hanging hook. The design of the frame, with a shaped crest filled with richly embossed scrolling foliage, putti, urns, and clusters of fruit, was well established by the date of the hallmark, 1692. One of the earliest dated English examples of the design belongs to a service marked in part by Jacob Bodendick in 1676.[1] In addition to the mirror, the Bodendick service includes cylindrical and rectangular boxes set with plaques chased with mythological scenes, square bottles, brushes, pomade pots, and a later pincushion marked in 1698. Another service of the 1670s with a mirror of similar design includes salvers, snuffers and a stand, candlesticks, and ecuelles.[2] Mention should also be made of the group of services by the specialist maker *WF* a knot above, which includes the Calverley Service at the Victoria and Albert Museum and a service in the Al-Tajiir Collection, both dated 1683.[3]

By the early 1690s the lush baroque foliage embossing that appears on earlier mirrors was superseded by a plainer design with Huguenot features. Though urns and putti are still incorporated into the crest, the frames are plain or gadrooned.[4]

The maker's mark on the present mirror has not been found on any individual pieces from a larger service, but it is recorded on another mirror of the preceding year described as "a small oblong toilet mirror in a plain molded frame with applied leaves at the angles and shaped cresting with a fluted border."[5] It is possible that the present mirror may have been specially made to match an existing service in an earlier style.

1. Sold, Christie's, London, May 23, 1990, lot 229.
2. Sold Sotheby & Co., London, March 28, 1946, lot 122.
3. The Calverley Service, Victoria and Albert Museum, acc. no. 240–240m-1879, ill. Oman, 1965, pls. 81–83; Toilet service, Al-Tajiir Collection, exhibited London, Christie's, 1990, cat. no. 40, pp. 60–61.
4. See, for example, the Bridgeman Toilet Service, 1691, maker's mark of Anthony Nelme, ill. Schroder, 1988, fig. 37, p. 139.
5. Christie, Manson & Woods, London, November 27, 1957, lot 97.

95

96

· 96 ·

MONTEITH
Anthony Nelme (free 1679, d. 1723)
London, 1693/4
Silver
33.84

MARKS: on underside of base, maker's mark *AN* in monogram in a shaped shield (Jackson, 1921, p. 146; rev. ed. 1989, p. 144) (repeated near rim of bowl and on removable rim); leopard's head crowned; date letter *q*; lion passant

ARMORIALS: engraved in center of bowl, the arms of Callecote

H. 18.4 cm (7¼ in.); diam. of rim 30.6 cm (12¹/₁₆ in.)

WEIGHT: 1,624.5 gm (52 oz 4 dwt)

PROVENANCE: Crichton Brothers, London, 1928; Anonymous Gift in Memory of Charlotte Beebe Wilbour (1833–1914), March 2, 1933.

EXHIBITED: London, British Antique Dealers' Association, 1928, p. 112, cat. no. 995 (lent by Crichton Brothers); Boston, Museum of Fine Arts, 1933 (no catalogue).

PUBLISHED: Hipkiss, 1933, p. 28; Lee, 1978, p. 69, fig. 13.

DESCRIPTION: The round bowl rests on a gadrooned foot. It has curved sides that are divided into cartouche-shaped lobes separated by panels of matting. The removable rim has semicircular crenellations alternating with applied shells against a matted ground.

CONSTRUCTION: The bowl is raised and chased, with a molded wire applied to the rim. The foot is formed from a single raised and chased piece. The rim is formed from a seamed piece, with cast moldings and shells applied to the border. The arms appear to have been re-engraved. The maker's mark on the detachable rim may have been let in.

CASTER
London, 1693/4
Silver
33.85

MARKS: near rim of body, maker's mark *IE* or *IF* a pellet between and below in a shaped shield (similar to Jackson, 1921, p. 135; rev. ed. 1989, p. 133) (repeated on cover); leopard's head crowned; lion passant (repeated on cover); date letter *q*

H. 19.7 cm (7¾ in.); diam. of base 8.9 cm (3½ in.)

WEIGHT: 275 gm (8 oz 17 dwt)

PROVENANCE: Anonymous Gift in Memory of Charlotte Beebe Wilbour (1833–1914), March 2, 1933.

EXHIBITED: Boston, Museum of Fine Arts, 1933 (no catalogue).

DESCRIPTION: The straight-sided caster is constructed in two pieces, with the cover secured to the base by a bayonet fitting. The caster rests on a gadrooned foot. The lower third of the base is chased with a spiraling gadrooned pattern. The sides of the cover are pierced with a symmetrical pattern of heart-shaped and other geometrically shaped openings. The top of the cover is slightly domed and has a gadrooned rim and a chased pattern of rays emanating from the central baluster finial.

CONSTRUCTION: The base and foot of the caster are formed from a single raised and chased piece. The walls are formed of an open-ended seamed cylinder soldered to the base; it is chased, punched, and matted. The pierced section of the cover is seamed, with a molded wire rim added. The gadrooned section of the cover is raised and chased. The finial is cast.

98

· 98 ·

TANKARD
London, 1694/5
Silver
42.7

MARKS: on rim and on cover, *RT* a mullet below and seven pellets in a circle (Jackson, 1921, p. 148; rev. ed. 1989, p. 145) (repeated on handle); leopard's head crowned; lion passant; date letter *r*

INSCRIPTIONS: engraved on handle, *I* over *MC*

H. 15.2 cm (6 in.); W. 18.1 cm (7⅛ in.); D. 12.1 cm (4¾ in.)

WEIGHT: 569 gm (18 oz 6 dwt)

PROVENANCE: Anonymous Gift in Memory of Charlotte Beebe Wilbour (1833–1914), January 8, 1942.

DESCRIPTION: The tankard has a flat base and a simple molded foot. It has slightly tapering sides and a flat stepped cover with a broad rim that is shaped on the front edge. The thumbpiece is in the form of a bifurcated scroll. The ear-shaped handle is D-shaped in section and has a curving tailpiece.

CONSTRUCTION: The body of the tankard is raised from a single sheet, as is the cover. The handle is formed from three pieces; the thumbpiece and hinge are cast. An engraved inscription has been removed from the inside of the cover and a coat of arms or inscription has been removed from the front of the tankard.

99

· 99 ·

TANKARD
London, 1695/6
Silver
35.1573

MARKS: on cover (indecipherable) and on rim, leopard's head crowned; lion passant; date letter *S*; indecipherable maker's mark (on rim only)

ARMORIALS: engraved on the front, the arms of Plowes of Wakefield, co. York[1]

H. 18.3 cm (7³⁄₁₆ in.); w. 20.8 cm (8³⁄₁₆ in.); d. 13.7 cm (5³⁄₈ in.)

WEIGHT: 1,032 gm (33 oz 3 dwt)

PROVENANCE: John and Richard Longman, London, purchased by Frank Brewer Bemis, 1911, Bequest of Frank Brewer Bemis, November 7, 1935.

DESCRIPTION: The tankard has a flat base with a molded rim. It has slightly tapering sides with an applied band marking the lower third of the body. The stepped cover has a broad flat rim, and it is attached to the handle by a knuckle hinge with a bifurcated scroll thumbpiece. The ear-shaped handle is D-shaped in section, and terminates in a shaped shield.

CONSTRUCTION: The tankard is raised from a single sheet with a molded wire applied to the lower third of the body. The cover is raised. The hinge and thumbpiece are cast, and the handle is formed from three pieces. The surface has been extensively worn and highly polished.

1. The arms are incorrectly blazoned and ought to feature a fess ermine instead of a chief. The arms for Plowes of Wakefield were granted in 1823, and the style of the engraving suggests that they were added in the second quarter of the nineteenth century.

100

· 100 ·

ACORN KNOP SPOON
England, possibly late 14th or early 15th century
Silver, parcel gilt
1988.291

Unmarked
L. 15.2 cm (6 in.); w. of bowl 4.7 cm (1⅞ in.)

WEIGHT: 25.5 gm (19 dwt)

PROVENANCE: purchased from How (of Edinburgh), London, May 25, 1988, Helen and Alice Colburn Fund.

DESCRIPTION: The spoon has a fig-shaped bowl and a tapering hexagonal stem. The finial is in the shape of an acorn.

CONSTRUCTION: The bowl, stem, and engraved finial of the spoon are forged from a single piece.

Though documentary sources record acorn knop spoons from the mid-fourteenth century, the precise dating of the numerous surviving examples is complicated by the absence of securely identified marks. In the form of the bowl and stem this spoon is most closely compared to an example in the Victoria and Albert Museum which is also unmarked.[1]

1. Commander and Mrs. How published Continental and English examples, categorizing the narrow hexagonal stem and rounded bowl as early fourteenth century. See How, 1952, vol. 1, p. 104. For the Victoria and Albert example, see ibid., p. 354.

· 101 ·

DIAMOND-POINT SPOON
Probably London, ca. 1470–1478
Silver, parcel gilt
47.1617

MARKS: in bowl, leopard's head above the letter B in a dotted circle; on back of stem near bowl, maker's mark a star with a dot (unrecorded)

L. 14.6 cm (5¾ in.); w. of bowl 4.5 cm (1¾ in.)

WEIGHT: 19.8 gm (15 dwt)

PROVENANCE: Charles G. Rupert, Wilmington, Delaware, sold Parke Bernet, New York, December 13, 1947, lot 217, purchased December 29, 1947, Theodora Wilbour Fund in Memory of Charlotte Beebe Wilbour.

PUBLISHED: Rupert, 1929, p. 2.

DESCRIPTION: The spoon has a fig-shaped bowl, tapering hexagonal stem, and a gilt diamond-point finial.

CONSTRUCTION: The bowl, stem, and finial are forged from a single piece. There are splits in the bowl that have been filled with lead solder.

The letters incorporated into the design of the early leopard's head punches used from about 1450 until 1478, when a date letter was introduced, have not yet been precisely interpreted.[1] The second mark on this spoon, a star with a dot, is unrecorded, but it may be related to a series of star marks published by Commander How on several late fifteenth-century spoons tentatively associated with Bristol.[2]

1. For a summary, see Jackson, rev. ed., 1989, pp. 36–37. See also How, 1957, vol. 3, p. 21.
2. How, 1957, pp. 86–87.

101

APOSTLE SPOON
London, 1504/5
Silver, parcel gilt
49.1710

MARKS: in bowl, leopard's head crowned; on back of stem near bowl, unidentified maker's mark (similar to Jackson, 1921, p. 93; rev. ed. 1989, p. 89); date letter G

INSCRIPTIONS: engraved on top of nimbus, *TS*

L. 18.9 cm (7⁷⁄₁₆ in.); w. of bowl 5.6 cm (2³⁄₁₆ in.)

WEIGHT: 62.4 gm (2 oz 1 dwt)

PROVENANCE: Marsden J. Perry, Providence, Rhode Island; Mrs. Howard Eric, Stamford, Connecticut, sold Parke Bernet, New York, December 2, 1949, lot 75, purchased December 12, 1949, Theodora Wilbour Fund in Memory of Charlotte Beebe Wilbour.

PUBLISHED: Hipkiss, 1951, p. 14.

DESCRIPTION: The spoon has a fig-shaped bowl and a slightly tapering hexagonal stem. The finial is in the form of an apostle holding a book in his right hand.

CONSTRUCTION: The bowl and stem of the spoon are forged from a single piece. The apostle figure and nimbus are cast separately and applied. The attribute in the figure's left hand has been lost.

102

· 103 ·

WRYTHEN KNOP SPOON
William Simpson (apprenticed 1499,
d. ca. 1546)
London, 1515/6
Silver gilt
47.1618

MARKS: in bowl, leopard's head crowned; on
back of stem near bowl, maker's mark a fringed
S (Kent, 1981, p. 9); date letter *s*

INSCRIPTIONS: engraved in bowl, an unidentified crest (a dragon's head erased)

L. 15.4 cm (6¹/₁₆ in.); w. of bowl 4.8 cm
(1⁷/₈ in.)

WEIGHT: 31.9 gm (1 oz)

PROVENANCE: Charles G. Rupert, Wilmington, Delaware, sold Parke Bernet, New York,
December 13, 1947, lot 219, purchased December 29, 1947, Theodora Wilbour Fund in Memory of Charlotte Beebe Wilbour.

PUBLISHED: Rupert, 1929, pl. 3, fig. 13.

DESCRIPTION: The spoon has a fig-shaped
bowl and a tapering hexagonal stem. The finial
is in the form of a wrythen knop.

CONSTRUCTION: The bowl and stem of the
spoon are forged from a single piece. The finial
is cast and applied. The gilding has been renewed.

· 104 ·

APOSTLE SPOON DEPICTING
SAINT JUDE
William Simpson (apprenticed 1499,
d. ca. 1546)
London, 1522/3
Silver gilt
49.1711

MARKS: in bowl, leopard's head crowned; on
back of stem near bowl, maker's mark fringed
S (Kent, 1981, p. 9); date letter *E*

INSCRIPTIONS: engraved on back of stem,
I.H.S.

L. 18.3 cm (7³/₁₆ in.); w. of bowl 5.2 cm
(2¹/₁₆ in.)

WEIGHT: 73.7 gm (2 oz 7 dwt)

PROVENANCE: Marsden J. Perry, Providence,
Rhode Island; Mrs. Howard Eric, Stamford,
Connecticut, sold Parke Bernet, New York,
December 2, 1949, lot 75, purchased December
12, 1949, Theodora Wilbour Fund in Memory
of Charlotte Beebe Wilbour.

DESCRIPTION: The spoon has a fig-shaped
bowl and a slightly tapering hexagonal stem.
The finial depicts Saint Jude holding a long
cross in his right hand and a book in his left.

CONSTRUCTION: The bowl and stem of the
spoon are forged from a single piece. The apostle figure and nimbus are each cast separately
and applied. The gilding has been renewed.

William Simpson, whose mark, a fringed
S, has recently been identified, is well represented by surviving apostle spoons ranging in date from 1510 to 1545.[1] In its size
and quality of modeling and chasing, this
spoon is without parallel. The saint's drapery is meticulously modeled; it is girded
at the waist and pulled back at the sleeves
in carefully defined folds. The larger figures on Bishop Fox's crozier at Corpus
Christi College, Oxford, and the figures of
Saint James the Greater and Saint Peter on
a pair of spoons in the Benson collection
show a similar attention to detail.[2]

1. Kent, 1981, pp. 9–10.
2. How, 1953, vol. 2, pp. 18–24, 62.

104

APOSTLE SPOON DEPICTING
SAINT JAMES THE LESS
William Simpson (apprenticed 1499,
d. ca. 1546)
London, 1529/30
Silver, parcel gilt
47.1616

MARKS: in bowl, leopard's head crowned; on
back of stem near bowl, maker's mark fringed
S (Kent, 1981, p. 9); date letter M

L. 18.4 cm (7¼ in.); w. of bowl 4.9 cm
(1¹⁵⁄₁₆ in.)

WEIGHT: 59.5 gm (1 oz 18 dwt)

PROVENANCE: Charles G. Rupert, New
York, sold Parke Bernet, New York, December
13, 1947, lot 211, purchased December 29,
1947, Theodora Wilbour Fund in Memory of
Charlotte Beebe Wilbour.

DESCRIPTION: The spoon has a fig-shaped
bowl and a tapering hexagonal stem. The finial
depicts Saint James the Less holding a book in
his left hand and a fuller's bat in his right. The
nimbus is pierced.

CONSTRUCTION: The stem and bowl are
forged from a single piece. The finial and nimbus are cast and applied.

105

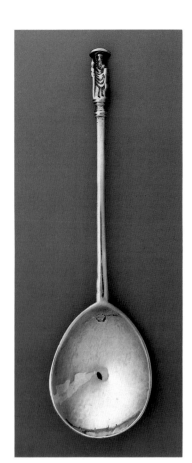

106

· 106 ·

APOSTLE SPOON DEPICTING SAINT THOMAS
Attributed to William Simpson
(apprenticed 1499, d. ca. 1546)
London, 1545/6
Silver, parcel gilt
49.1712

MARKS: in bowl, leopard's head crowned; on back of stem near bowl, maker's mark fringed *S* (Kent, 1981, p. 9); lion passant; date letter *H*

L. 17.9 cm (7 1/16 in.); w. of bowl 4.9 cm (1 15/16 in.)

WEIGHT: 42.5 gm (1 oz 8 dwt)

PROVENANCE: Reverend Thomas Staniforth, Kirk Hammerton Hall, Yorkshire, by descent to Colonel E. W. Staniforth; Crichton Brothers, London, 1898; Marsden J. Perry, Providence, Rhode Island; Mrs. Howard Eric, Stamford, Connecticut, sold Parke Bernet, New York, December 2, 1949, lot 75, purchased December 12, 1949, Theodora Wilbour Fund in Memory of Charlotte Beebe Wilbour.

EXHIBITED: London, Crichton Brothers, 1898.

DESCRIPTION: The spoon has a fig-shaped bowl and a flattened, tapering hexagonal stem. The finial depicts Saint Thomas holding a spear in his right hand. The nimbus is rayed.

CONSTRUCTION: The bowl and stem of the spoon are forged from a single piece. The apostle figure and nimbus are cast separately and applied. The finial is gilt. The bowl has been reworked.

· 107 ·

MAIDENHEAD SPOON
London?, ca. 1570
Silver
47.1429

MARKS: in bowl, maker's mark *CW* or *WC* in a dotted circle (Jackson, 1921, p. 476)

L. 16.2 cm (6 3/8 in.); w. of bowl 4.8 cm (1 7/8 in.)

WEIGHT: 31.9 gm (1 oz)

PROVENANCE: H. D. Ellis, Esq., Lt.-Col. J. Benett-Stanford, Tisbury, Wiltshire, sold Sotheby & Co., London, November 14, 1935, lot 226; J. P. Morgan (1867–1943), New York, sold Parke Bernet, October 30, 1947, lot 135, purchased November 13, 1947, Theodora Wilbour Fund in Memory of Charlotte Beebe Wilbour.

DESCRIPTION: The spoon has a fig-shaped bowl and a rectangular stem. The finial is in the shape of a bust of a maiden.

CONSTRUCTION: The bowl and stem of the spoon are forged from a single piece. The maidenhead finial is cast and attached to the stem with a lap-join. Traces of gilding remain on the finial. The bowl has been repaired.

107

APOSTLE SPOON DEPICTING SAINT ANDREW
London, 1582/3
Silver, parcel gilt
49.1713

MARKS: in bowl, leopard's head crowned; on back of stem near bowl, maker's mark a fleur-de-lys in a shaped shield (Jackson, 1921, p. 105; rev. ed. 1989, p. 101); lion passant; date letter *E*

L. 17.5 cm (6⅞ in.); w. of bowl 5 cm (2 in.)

WEIGHT: 59.5 gm (2 oz 1 dwt)

PROVENANCE: Crichton Brothers, London; Marsden J. Perry, Providence, Rhode Island; Mrs. Howard Eric, Stamford, Connecticut, sold Parke Bernet, New York, December 2, 1949, lot 75, purchased December 12, 1949, Theodora Wilbour Fund in Memory of Charlotte Beebe Wilbour.

DESCRIPTION: The spoon has a fig-shaped bowl and a tapering hexagonal stem. The finial depicts Saint Andrew holding a saltire cross. On the top of the nimbus is a dove.

CONSTRUCTION: The bowl and stem of the spoon are forged from a single piece. The figure, nimbus, and cross are cast and applied. The gilding on the finial has been renewed.

108

109

· 109 ·

SEAL-TOP SPOON
Christopher Easton[1] (active 1583–ca. 1610)
Exeter, ca. 1583–90
Silver
42.82

MARKS: in bowl, Exeter town mark; on back of stem, maker's mark *C ESTON* in a rectangular shield (Jackson, 1921, p. 331; rev. ed. 1989, p. 289)

INSCRIPTIONS: stamped on back of stem, *Breadalbane*

L. 16.5 cm (6½ in.); w. of bowl 4.8 cm (1⅞ in.)

WEIGHT: 42.5 gm (1 oz, 8 dwt)

PROVENANCE: Marquess of Breadalbane, Newick Park, Sussex; Anonymous Gift in Memory of Charlotte Beebe Wilbour (1833–1914), February 12, 1942.

DESCRIPTION: The spoon has a fig-shaped bowl and a tapering hexagonal stem. The baluster support is surmounted by a circular seal.

CONSTRUCTION: The bowl and stem of the spoon are forged from a single piece. The seal and baluster support are cast and applied. Traces of gilding remain on the finial.

1. Christopher Easton was apprenticed to John Jones, and was granted the freedom of Exeter in 1583. I am grateful to Timothy Kent for providing this information.

· 110 ·

LION SEJANT SPOON
London, 1585/6
Silver
35.1551

MARKS: on bowl, leopard's head crowned; on back of stem near bowl, maker's mark an escallop with two pellets above in a shaped shield (Jackson, 1921, p. 105; rev. ed. 1989, p. 99); lion passant; date letter *H*

INSCRIPTIONS: pricked on back of bowl near stem, partially obliterated, *EL;* engraved on back of bowl, *C* over *GE*

L. 16.3 cm (6⁷⁄₁₆ in.); w. of bowl 4.6 cm (1¹³⁄₁₆ in.)

WEIGHT: 42.5 gm (1 oz 8.8 dwt)

PROVENANCE: Reverend Thomas Staniforth, Kirk Hammerton Hall, Yorkshire, by descent to Colonel E. W. Staniforth (unverified); Crichton Brothers, New York, purchased by Frank Brewer Bemis, 1918, Bequest of Frank Brewer Bemis, November 7, 1935.

DESCRIPTION: The spoon has a fig-shaped bowl and a tapering hexagonal stem. The finial, resting upon a hexagonal baluster support, is in the shape of a lion sejant.

CONSTRUCTION: The bowl and stem of the spoon are forged from a single piece. Traces of gilding remain on the finial. The bowl has been reworked, and appears to have been struck with a forged punch.

110

· III ·

SEAL-TOP SPOON
York, 1595/6
Silver, parcel gilt
33.206

MARKS: in bowl, York town mark; on back of stem near bowl, maker's mark *WR* conjoined[1] (similar to Jackson, 1921, p. 286; rev. ed. 1989, p. 460); date letter *n*

L. 17.2 cm (6¾ in.); w. of bowl 4.9 cm (1¹⁵⁄₁₆ in.)

WEIGHT: 56.7 gm (1 oz, 19 dwt)

PROVENANCE: Anonymous Gift in Memory of Charlotte Beebe Wilbour (1833–1914), March 2, 1933.

EXHIBITED: Boston, Museum of Fine Arts, 1933 (no catalogue).

DESCRIPTION: The spoon has a fig-shaped bowl and a slightly tapering hexagonal stem. The lobed baluster support is surmounted by a circular seal. The finial is gilt.

CONSTRUCTION: The bowl and stem of the spoon are forged from a single piece; the seal and baluster support are cast separately, chased, and applied.

1. The maker's mark was attributed by Jackson to William Rawnson, who is recorded between 1562 and 1593.

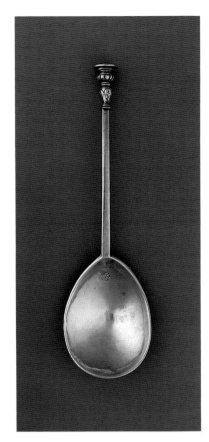

111

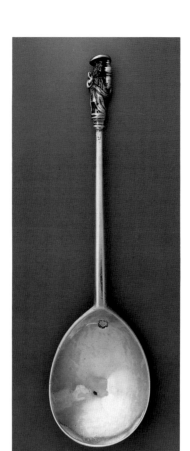

112

· 112 ·

APOSTLE SPOON DEPICTING SAINT JOHN
Probably Patrick Brew
London, 1596/7
Silver, parcel gilt
49.1714

MARKS: in bowl, leopard's head crowned; on back of stem near bowl, maker's mark a crescent enclosing a mullet[1] (Jackson, 1921, p. 106; rev. ed. 1989, p. 102); lion passant; date letter *T*

L. 18.1 cm (7⅛ in.); w. of bowl 4.9 cm (1¹⁵⁄₁₆ in.)

WEIGHT: 53.9 gm (1 oz 17 dwt)

PROVENANCE: Marsden J. Perry, Providence, Rhode Island; Mrs. Howard Eric, Stamford, Connecticut, sold Parke Bernet, New York, December 2, 1949, lot 75, purchased December 12, 1949, Theodora Wilbour Fund in Memory of Charlotte Beebe Wilbour.

DESCRIPTION: The spoon has a fig-shaped bowl and a tapering hexagonal stem. The finial depicts Saint John raising his right hand in benediction and holding a cup in his left. The nimbus is pierced and rayed.

CONSTRUCTION: The bowl and stem of the spoon are forged from a single piece. The apostle figure and nimbus are cast separately and applied. The nimbus is pierced.

1. The mark, a crescent enclosing a mullet, is a workshop mark that was in use over a long period; in 1596 it probably belonged to Patrick Brew. I am grateful to Timothy Kent for having provided this information.

· 113 ·

APOSTLE SPOON DEPICTING SAINT PETER
London, 1599/1600
Silver, parcel gilt
49.1715

MARKS: in bowl, leopard's head crowned; on back of stem near bowl, unidentified maker's mark (possibly Jackson, 1921, p. 108; rev. ed. 1989, p. 105); lion passant; date letter *B*

INSCRIPTIONS: engraved on back of bowl, *ET* over *GED;* stamped on top of stem, *T* incuse

L. 18.1 cm (7⅛ in.); w. of bowl 4.8 cm (1⅞ in.)

WEIGHT: 53.9 cm (1 oz 17 dwt)

PROVENANCE: Reverend Thomas Staniforth, Kirk Hammerton Hall, Yorkshire, by descent to Colonel E. W. Staniforth; Crichton Brothers, London, 1898; Marsden J. Perry, Providence, Rhode Island; Mrs. Howard Eric, Stamford, Connecticut, sold Parke Bernet, New York, December 2, 1949, lot 75, purchased December 12, 1949, Theodora Wilbour Fund in Memory of Charlotte Beebe Wilbour.

EXHIBITED: London, Crichton Brothers, 1898.

DESCRIPTION: The spoon has a fig-shaped bowl and an hexagonal stem. The finial depicts Saint Peter holding a book in his right hand and a key in his left. The nimbus is pierced and rayed.

CONSTRUCTION: The bowl and stem of the spoon are forged from a single piece. The apostle figure and nimbus are cast separately and applied.

113

Seal-top spoon
London, 1607/8
Silver gilt
35.1555

MARKS: in bowl, leopard's head crowned; on back of stem near bowl, maker's mark a crescent enclosing a saltire (Jackson, 1921, p. 110; rev. ed. 1989, p. 107); lion passant; date letter *K*

L. 16.9 cm (6¹¹⁄₁₆ in.); w. of bowl 4.8 cm (1⅞ in.)

WEIGHT: 45.4 gm (1 oz 11 dwt)

PROVENANCE: Philip L. Spalding, given to Frank Brewer Bemis, 1925, Bequest of Frank Brewer Bemis, November 7, 1935.

DESCRIPTION: The spoon has a fig-shaped bowl and an hexagonal stem. The baluster support is surmounted by a circular seal.

CONSTRUCTION: The bowl and stem of the spoon are forged from a single piece. The seal and chased baluster support are cast separately and applied.

The maker's mark, a crescent enclosing a saltire, has been tentatively associated with John Jermyn, who completed his apprenticeship with William Cawdell in 1595. Cawdell was among the most prolific of the London spoonmakers, and he touched off a controversy among the Wardens when he was accused of befriending the assayer and submitting large numbers of substandard spoons, a practice he continued throughout his career. Jermyn's infractions were less regular; on July 17, 1610, he was fined for submitting twenty-nine substandard spoons but was "pardoned in respect of his povertie."[1]

1. Kent, 1981, pp. 21–25.

114

115

· 115 ·

SEAL-TOP SPOON
London, 1610/1
Silver, parcel gilt
38.1641

MARKS: in bowl, leopard's head crowned; on back of stem near bowl, maker's mark two clubs in saltire in a heart-shaped shield (Jackson, 1921, p. 112; rev. ed. 1989, p. 108); lion passant; date letter *n*

INSCRIPTIONS: engraved on top of seal, *T*B*

L. 17.2 cm (6¾ in.); w. of bowl 5.1 cm (2 in.)

WEIGHT: 48.2 gm (1 oz 13 dwt)

PROVENANCE: Gift of Dr. George L. Walton, November 10, 1938.

DESCRIPTION: The spoon has a fig-shaped bowl and a tapering hexagonal stem. The baluster support is surmounted by an oval seal.

CONSTRUCTION: The bowl and stem of the spoon are forged from a single piece. The seal and chased baluster finial are cast and applied. Traces of gilding remain on the finial.

· 116 ·

SEAL-TOP SPOON
James Cluatt (free 1604, d. before 1627)
London, 1616/7
Silver, parcel gilt
38.1751

MARKS: in bowl, leopard's head crowned; on back of stem near bowl, maker's mark *C* enclosing *I* in a plain shield (Kent, 1981, p. 25); lion passant; date letter *T*

INSCRIPTIONS: pricked on top of seal, *HB* over *1617*

L. 16.19 cm (6⅜ in.); w. of bowl 4.6 cm (1¹³⁄₁₆ in.)

WEIGHT: 39.7 gm (1 oz 6 dwt)

PROVENANCE: Tiffany & Co., London, 1938; Anonymous Gift in Memory of Charlotte Beebe Wilbour (1833–1914), December 8, 1938.

DESCRIPTION: The spoon has a fig-shaped bowl and a tapering hexagonal stem. The baluster support with gadrooned lobe is surmounted by a circular seal. The finial is gilt.

CONSTRUCTION: The bowl and stem of the spoon are forged from a single piece. The seal and chased baluster support are cast and applied.

116

APOSTLE SPOON DEPICTING SAINT SIMON ZELOTES

Probably Richard Cotton (apprenticed 1590, free in 1597)
London, 1619/20
Silver, parcel gilt
49.1716

MARKS: in bowl, leopard's head crowned; on back of stem near bowl, maker's mark *RC* in a rectangle (Kent, 1981, p. 37); lion passant; date letter *b*

L. 17.9 cm (7¹⁄₁₆ in.); w. of bowl 4.6 cm (1¹³⁄₁₆ in.)

WEIGHT: 48.2 gm (1 oz 13 dwt)

PROVENANCE: Reverend Thomas Staniforth, Kirk Hammerton Hall, Yorkshire, by descent to Colonel E. W. Staniforth; Crichton Brothers, London, 1898; Marsden J. Perry, Providence, Rhode Island; Mrs. Howard Eric, Stamford, Connecticut, sold Parke Bernet, New York, December 2, 1949, lot 75, purchased December 12, 1949, Theodora Wilbour Fund in Memory of Charlotte Beebe Wilbour.

EXHIBITED: London, Crichton Brothers, 1898.

DESCRIPTION: The spoon has a fig-shaped bowl and a tapering hexagonal stem. The finial depicts Saint Simon Zelotes holding a saw in his right hand.

CONSTRUCTION: The bowl and stem of the spoon are forged from a single piece. The finial and nimbus are cast separately and applied.

117

118

· 118 ·

**APOSTLE SPOON DEPICTING
SAINT JAMES THE GREATER**
Daniel Cary (free 1604, d. 1641/2)
London, 1622/3
Silver
49.1717

MARKS: in bowl, leopard's head crowned; on back of stem near bowl, maker's mark *D* enclosing *C* (Kent, 1981, p. 26); lion passant; date letter *e*

L. 18.2 cm (7³/₁₆ in.); w. of bowl 4.8 cm (1⅞ in.)

WEIGHT: 62.4 gm (2 oz)

PROVENANCE: Mrs. Howard Eric, Stamford, Connecticut, sold Parke Bernet, New York, December 2, 1949, lot 75, purchased December 12, 1949, Theodora Wilbour Fund in Memory of Charlotte Beebe Wilbour.

DESCRIPTION: The spoon has a fig-shaped bowl and an hexagonal stem. The finial depicts Saint James the Greater holding a book in his left hand and a pilgrim's staff in his right hand.

CONSTRUCTION: The bowl and stem of the spoon are forged from a single piece. The finial and nimbus are cast separately and applied. The staff is broken above the saint's hand. There are traces of pricked initials, now illegible, on the back of the bowl near the join with the stem.

· 119 ·

APOSTLE SPOON
London, 1622/3
Silver
49.1718

MARKS: in bowl, leopard's head crowned; on back of stem near bowl, illegible maker's mark; lion passant; date letter *e*

INSCRIPTIONS: pricked on back of bowl, *G* over *EA, 1622* (?)

L. 18.3 cm (7³/₁₆ in.); w. of bowl 5.1 cm (2 in.)

WEIGHT: 56.7 gm (1 oz 19 dwt)

PROVENANCE: Marsden J. Perry, Providence, Rhode Island; Mrs. Howard Eric, Stamford, Connecticut, sold Parke Bernet, New York, December 2, 1949, lot 75, purchased December 12, 1949, Theodora Wilbour Fund in Memory of Charlotte Beebe Wilbour.

DESCRIPTION: The spoon has a fig-shaped bowl and a tapering hexagonal stem. The finial depicts a saint holding a book in his right hand. The attribute in his left hand is damaged; it may represent the bottom half of a fuller's bat, a staff, a sword, an axe, or a spear. On the top of the nimbus is a dove.

CONSTRUCTION: The bowl and stem of the spoon are forged from a single piece. The apostle figure and nimbus are cast and applied. Traces of gilding remain on the finial.

119

APOSTLE SPOON DEPICTING
SAINT BARTHOLOMEW
Probably Richard Crosse (apprenticed
1625)[1]
London, 1632/3
Silver
49.1719

MARKS: in bowl, leopard's head crowned; on
back of stem near bowl, maker's mark *RC* in a
plain shield (Jackson, 1921, p. 119; rev. ed.
1989, p. 116); lion passant; date letter *p*

INSCRIPTIONS: pricked on back of bowl near
stem, *AM* over *MS, 1633*

L. 18.7 cm (7⅜ in.); w. of bowl 5 cm (2 in.)

WEIGHT: 51 gm (1 oz 15 dwt)

PROVENANCE: Marsden J. Perry, Providence,
Rhode Island; Mrs. Howard Eric, Stamford,
Connecticut, sold Parke Bernet, New York,
December 2, 1949, lot 75, purchased December
12, 1949, Theodora Wilbour Fund in Memory
of Charlotte Beebe Wilbour.

DESCRIPTION: The spoon has a fig-shaped
bowl and a tapering hexagonal stem. The finial
depicts Saint Bartholomew holding a knife in
his right hand and a book in his left. On the top
of the nimbus is a dove.

CONSTRUCTION: The bowl and stem of the
spoon are forged from a single piece. The finial
and nimbus are cast separately and applied.
Traces of gilding remain on the finial.

1. For the association of this mark with Richard
Crosse, see Kent, 1981, p. 44.

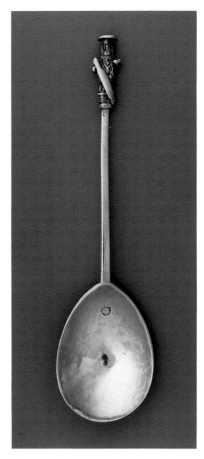

120

121

· 121 ·

SEAL-TOP SPOON
London, 1638/9
Silver
33.208

MARKS: in bowl, leopard's head crowned; on back of stem near bowl, maker's mark *HL* conjoined in a circle (Jackson, 1921, p. 121); lion passant; date letter *a*

INSCRIPTIONS: pricked on top of seal, *T* over *LS*

L. 17 cm (6¹¹⁄₁₆ in.); w. of bowl 5.1 cm (2 in.)

WEIGHT: 39.7 gm (1 oz 6 dwt)

PROVENANCE: Anonymous Gift in Memory of Charlotte Beebe Wilbour (1833–1914), March 2, 1933.

EXHIBITED: Boston, Museum of Fine Arts, 1933, (no catalogue).

DESCRIPTION: The spoon has a fig-shaped bowl and a tapered hexagonal stem. The baluster support is surmounted by a circular seal.

CONSTRUCTION: The bowl and stem of the spoon are forged from a single piece. The baluster support and seal are cast separately and applied. Traces of gilding remain on the finial.

· 122 ·

APOSTLE SPOON DEPICTING SAINT PHILIP
Daniel Cary (free 1604, d. 1641/2)
London, 1638/9
Silver, parcel gilt
49.1720

MARKS: in bowl, leopard's head crowned; on back of stem near bowl, maker's mark *D* enclosing *C* (Kent, 1981, p. 26); lion passant; date letter *a*

L. 18.1 cm (7⅛ in.); w. of bowl 5 cm (2 in.)

WEIGHT: 48.2 gm (1 oz 13 dwt)

PROVENANCE: Reverend Thomas Staniforth, Kirk Hammerton Hall, Yorkshire, by descent to Colonel E. W. Staniforth; Crichton Brothers, London, 1898; Marsden J. Perry, Providence, Rhode Island; Mrs. Howard Eric, Stamford, Connecticut, sold Parke Bernet, New York, December 2, 1949, lot 75, purchased December 12, 1949, Theodora Wilbour Fund in Memory of Charlotte Beebe Wilbour.

EXHIBITED: London, Crichton Brothers, 1898.

DESCRIPTION: The spoon has a fig-shaped bowl and a tapering hexagonal stem. The finial depicts Saint Philip holding a book in his right hand and a cross in his left.

CONSTRUCTION: The bowl and stem of the spoon are forged from a single piece. The finial is cast separately and applied. The nimbus is lacking, and the gilding on the finial has been renewed.

· 123 ·

Slip-top spoon
Jeremy Johnson (free 1640; d. 1675/6)
London, ca. 1650
Silver
33.210

MARKS: in bowl, leopard's head crowned; on back of stem near bowl *II* a mullet below in a plain shield (Kent, 1981, p. 33); lion passant; indistinct date letter[1]

INSCRIPTIONS: engraved on slip-top, *MG*

L. 16.4 cm (6⁷⁄₁₆ in.); w. of bowl 4.8 cm (1⁷⁄₈ in.)

WEIGHT: 34 gm (1 oz 2 dwt)

PROVENANCE: Anonymous Gift in Memory of Charlotte Beebe Wilbour (1833–1914), March 2, 1933.

EXHIBITED: Boston, Museum of Fine Arts, 1933 (no catalogue).

DESCRIPTION: The spoon has a fig-shaped bowl and a rectangular stem, cut at an oblique angle at the end.

CONSTRUCTION: The spoon is forged from a single piece. The surface is deeply scratched and pitted.

1. Possibly *l* for 1648/9 or *p* for 1652/3.

122

123

124

· 124 ·

PURITAN SPOON
Jeremy Johnson (free 1640; d. 1675/6)
London, 1651/2
Silver
33.209

MARKS: in bowl, leopard's head crowned; on back of stem near bowl, maker's mark *II* in a plain shield[1] (Jackson, 1921, p. 124; rev. ed. 1989, p. 119); lion passant; date letter *o*

L. 17.3 cm (6¹³⁄₁₆ in.); w. of bowl 5.2 cm (2¹⁄₁₆ in.)

WEIGHT: 53.9 gm (1 oz 17 dwt)

PROVENANCE: Anonymous Gift in Memory of Charlotte Beebe Wilbour (1833–1914), March 2, 1933.

EXHIBITED: Boston, Museum of Fine Arts, 1933 (no catalogue).

DESCRIPTION: The spoon has an elliptical bowl and a rectangular stem.

CONSTRUCTION: The bowl and stem of the spoon are forged from a single piece. The surface of the spoon is pitted overall.

1. The maker's mark is a variation of two marks attributed by Kent to Jeremy Johnson (free 1640; d. 1675/6). See Kent, 1981, pp. 33–34.

· 125 ·

APOSTLE SPOON DEPICTING SAINT BARTHOLOMEW
William Cary (free 1638)
London, 1660/1
Silver
49.1721

MARKS: in bowl, leopard's head crowned; on back of stem near bowl, maker's mark *WC* three pellets above and a rose between pellets below in a plain shield (Kent, 1981, p. 31); lion passant; date letter *C*

INSCRIPTIONS: engraved at a later date on back of bowl, *JJS*

L. 19.1 cm (7½ in.); w. of bowl 5.2 cm (2¹⁄₁₆ in.)

WEIGHT: 59.5 gm (1 oz 18 dwt)

PROVENANCE: Reverend Thomas Staniforth, Kirk Hammerton Hall, Yorkshire, by descent to Colonel E. W. Staniforth; Crichton Brothers, London, 1898; Marsden J. Perry, Providence, Rhode Island; Mrs. Howard Eric, Stamford, Connecticut, sold Parke Bernet, New York, December 2, 1949, lot 75, purchased December 12, 1949, Theodora Wilbour Fund in Memory of Charlotte Beebe Wilbour.

EXHIBITED: London, Crichton Brothers, 1898.

PUBLISHED: Hipkiss, 1951, p. 14.

DESCRIPTION: The spoon has an elliptical bowl and a tapering hexagonal stem. The finial depicts Saint Bartholomew holding a book in his right hand and a knife in his left. On the top of the nimbus is a dove on a stippled ground.

CONSTRUCTION: The bowl and stem of the spoon are forged from a single piece. The finial and nimbus are cast separately and applied. There are traces of gilding on the finial.

125

PURITAN SPOON
John King (free 1657, d. 1680)
London, 1666/7
Silver
35.1562

MARKS: in bowl, partially obliterated, leopard's head crowned; on back of stem, *IK* a rose and two pellets below in a plain shield (Kent, 1981, p. 20) lion passant; date letter *I*

INSCRIPTIONS: on back of stem, *RT to RT*

L. 18.7 cm (7⅜ in.); w. of bowl 4.8 cm (1⅞ in.)

WEIGHT: 53.9 gm (1 oz 17 dwt)

PROVENANCE: Crichton Brothers, London, purchased by Frank Brewer Bemis, 1918; Bequest of Frank Brewer Bemis, November 7, 1935.

DESCRIPTION: The spoon has an elliptical bowl and a slightly flared rectangular stem.

CONSTRUCTION: The bowl and stem of the spoon are forged from a single piece. The lower rim of the bowl is worn and dented.

126

127

· 127 ·

TREFID SPOON
John King (free 1657, d. 1680)
London, 1671/2
Silver
38.1642

MARKS: on back of stem, maker's mark *IK* a rose and two pellets below in a plain shield (Kent, 1981, p. 35); leopard's head crowned; lion passant; date letter *D*

INSCRIPTIONS: pricked on back of stem, *EW, 1682*

L. 18.9 cm (7⁷⁄₁₆ in.); w. of bowl 4.61 cm (1¹³⁄₁₆ in.)

WEIGHT: 36.9 gm (1 oz 4 dwt)

PROVENANCE: Gift of George L. Walton, November 10, 1938.

DESCRIPTION: The spoon has a deep oval bowl, a ridged rat tail, and a flattened stem with a trefid terminus.

CONSTRUCTION: The bowl and stem of the spoon are forged from a single piece.

· 128 ·

PAIR OF TREFID SPOONS
John Smith (active until ca. 1690)
London, 1673/4
Silver
33.211–212

MARKS: on back of stem, maker's mark *IS* crowned in a plain shield (Kent, 1981, p. 34); leopard's head crowned; lion passant; date letter *Q*

33.211: L. 20.3 cm (8 in.); w. of bowl 4.9 cm (1¹⁵⁄₁₆ in.). 33.212: L. 20.2 cm (7¹⁵⁄₁₆ in.); w. of bowl 4.9 cm (1¹⁵⁄₁₆ in.)

WEIGHT: 33.211, 56.7 gm (1 oz 19 dwt); 33.212, 59.5 gm (2 oz 1 dwt)

PROVENANCE: Anonymous Gift in Memory of Charlotte Beebe Wilbour (1833–1914), March 2, 1933.

EXHIBITED: Boston, Museum of Fine Arts, 1933 (no catalogue).

DESCRIPTION: The spoons are identical in form. Each has a deep oval bowl with a ridged rat tail and a flattened stem with a trefid terminus.

CONSTRUCTION: The bowl and stem of the spoon are forged and formed from a single piece.

128

129

· 129 ·

TREFID SPOON
John Smith (active until ca. 1690)
London, ca. 1678
Silver
42.83

MARKS: on back of stem, maker's mark *IS* crowned in a plain shield (Kent, 1981, p. 34); leopard's head crowned; lion passant; illegible date letter

INSCRIPTIONS: engraved on back of stem near terminus, *IM*

L. 18.4 cm (7¼ in.); w. of bowl 4.5 cm (1¾ in.)

WEIGHT: 42.5 gm (1 oz 8 dwt)

PROVENANCE: Anonymous Gift in Memory of Charlotte Beebe Wilbour (1833–1914), February 12, 1942.

DESCRIPTION: The spoon has a deep oval bowl, a ridged rat tail, and a flattened stem with a trefid terminus.

CONSTRUCTION: The bowl and stem of the spoon are forged from a single piece.

130

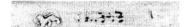

· 130 ·

TREFID SPOON

John Smith (active until ca. 1690)
London, ca. 1680
Silver gilt
19.1343

MARKS: on back of stem, maker's mark *IS* crowned in a plain shield (Kent, 1981, p. 34); leopard's head crowned; lion passant; illegible date letter

L. 19.4 cm (7⅝ in.); w. of bowl 4.6 cm (1¹³⁄₁₆ in.)

WEIGHT: 53.9 gm (1 oz 14 dwt)

PROVENANCE: Gift of Mrs. George Linder, November 6, 1919.

DESCRIPTION: The spoon has a deep oval bowl, a ridged rat tail, and a flattened stem with a trefid terminus.

CONSTRUCTION: The bowl and stem of the spoon are forged from a single piece.

· 131 ·

TREFID SPOON

London, 1688/9
Silver
33.213

MARKS: on back of stem, maker's mark *SH* in a shaped shield (Jackson, 1921, p. 140; rev. ed. 1989, p. 139); leopard's head crowned; lion passant; date letter *l*

INSCRIPTIONS: engraved on back of stem near terminus, *TA*

L. 19.7 cm (7¾ in.); w. of bowl 4.8 cm (1⅞ in.)

WEIGHT: 51 gm (1 oz 15 dwt)

PROVENANCE: Anonymous Gift in Memory of Charlotte Beebe Wilbour (1833–1914), March 2, 1933.

DESCRIPTION: The spoon has a deep oval bowl, a ridged rat tail, and a flattened stem with a trefid terminus.

CONSTRUCTION: The bowl and stem of the spoon are forged from a single piece.

131

KNIFE, FORK, AND SPOON
Peter Harache I (free 1682)
London, 1689/90
Silver gilt, steel
64.705–707

MARKS: on back of stem of fork (64.706) and spoon (64.707), maker's mark *PH* a mullet between, a crescent below and two ermine spots and a crown above in a shaped shield (Jackson, 1921, p. 150; rev. ed. 1989, p. 140), leopard's head crowned; lion passant; date letter *m*

INSCRIPTIONS: engraved on each piece: *M over GS; MK*

64.705 (knife): w. 1.9 cm (¾ in.); L. 21.1 cm (8³⁄₁₆ in.). 64.706 (fork): w. 2.5 cm (1 in.); L. 19.4 cm (7⅝ in.). 64.707 (spoon): w. 4.5 cm (1¾ in.); L. 19.5 cm (7¹¹⁄₁₆ in.).

WEIGHT: 64.705 (knife) 70.9 gm (2 oz 6 dwt); 64.706 (fork) 56.7 gm (1 oz 19 dwt); 64.707 (spoon) 56.7 gm (1 oz 19 dwt)

PROVENANCE: purchased from Firestone & Parson, Boston, May 13, 1964, Theodora Wilbour Fund in Memory of Charlotte Beebe Wilbour.

DESCRIPTION: The knife has a tapering cylindrical handle with a bun-shaped terminus. It is engraved with scrolling foliage and acanthus leaf borders. The fork has four tines, a flattened stem, and a trefid terminus. The spoon has an oval bowl, a rat tail, and a flattened stem with a trefid terminus. The handles of the spoon and fork are engraved with scrolling foliage against a striated ground.

CONSTRUCTION: The handle of the knife is formed of a seamed sheet, engraved, and gilt. The forged steel blade extends through the handle, and fits into a hole in the terminus of the silver. The spoon and fork are both forged from single pieces of silver, engraved and gilt.

132

133

· 133 ·

TREFID SPOON
London, 1690/1
Silver
38.1643

MARKS: on back of stem, indecipherable maker's mark *I?* crowned; leopard's head crowned; lion passant; date letter *n*

INSCRIPTIONS: pricked on back of stem near terminus, *AA over AS, 1692*

L. 18.6 cm (7⁵⁄₁₆ in.); w. of bowl 4.5 cm (1¾ in.)

WEIGHT: 42.5 gm (1 oz 8 dwt)

PROVENANCE: Gift of George L. Walton, November 10, 1938.

DESCRIPTION: The spoon has a deep oval bowl, a ridged rat tail, and a flattened stem with a trefid terminus.

CONSTRUCTION: The bowl and stem of the spoon are forged from a single piece. The bowl is dented and pitted.

134

· 134 ·

TREFID SPOON
Lawrence Coles (free 1667)
London, 1693/4
Silver
33.214

MARKS: on back of stem, maker's mark *LC* crowned a pellet between and a crescent between pellets below in a plain shield (Kent, 1981, p. 35); leopard's head crowned; lion passant; date letter *q*

INSCRIPTIONS: engraved on back of stem near terminus, *EH over EE, Aug 22, 1693*

L. 19.7 cm (7¾ in.); w. of bowl 4.8 cm (1⅞ in.)

WEIGHT: 56.7 gm (1 oz 19 dwt)

PROVENANCE: Anonymous Gift in Memory of Charlotte Beebe Wilbour (1833–1914), March 2, 1933.

EXHIBITED: Boston, Museum of Fine Arts, 1933 (no catalogue).

DESCRIPTION: The spoon has a deep oval bowl, a ridged rat tail, and a flattened stem with a trefid terminus.

CONSTRUCTION: The bowl and stem of the spoon are forged from a single piece.

LACE-BACK TREFID SPOON
Francis Glanville (d. 1698)
Launceston, 1693/4
Silver
1987.269

MARKS: on back of stem, a florette (?); maker's mark *GF* conjoined in a shaped shield (Jackson rev. ed., 1989, p. 318); a skull

INSCRIPTIONS: pricked on back of stem, *SH, 1693/4*

L. 20 cm (7⅞ in.); w. of bowl 4.8 cm (1⅞ in.)

WEIGHT: 42.5 gm (1 oz 9 dwt)

PROVENANCE: purchased from How (of Edinburgh), London, May 27, 1987, Gift in Memory of Kathryn Buhler from Her Friends.

DESCRIPTION: The spoon has a deep oval bowl and a ridged rat tail. The flattened stem has a trefid terminus. The back of the bowl and the end of the terminus are decorated with a scrolling relief.

CONSTRUCTION: The bowl and stem of the spoon are forged from a single piece. The decoration on the back of the bowl and the end of the terminus is die-formed. The interior surface of the bowl is pitted.

135

· 136 ·

"COLLEGE CUP"
England (?), late fifteenth-century style
Silver, parcel gilt
54.933

Unmarked
H. 22.5 cm (8⅞ in.); diam. 11.5 cm (4½ in.)

WEIGHT: 450.7 gm (14 oz 9 dwt)

ARMORIALS: engraved on cover, an unidentified crest (a lion rampant)

PROVENANCE: Purchased from John Hunt, Dublin, September 9, 1954, Theodora Wilbour Fund in Memory of Charlotte Beebe Wilbour.

DESCRIPTION: The font-shaped cup stands on three feet in the form of male busts. The stem rises from a flaring foot with a molded and crenellated rim and two stamped borders. The slightly domed cover rises to a point and is surmounted by a figure of an eagle. A foliate cresting is applied to the rim. The stem, cup, and cover are chased overall with a pattern of overlapping lobes. The interior of the cup and cover is gilt. The finial is attached on the interior with a boss in the form of a Tudor rose.

CONSTRUCTION: The body of the vessel, the cover, and the foot are raised and chased; the interior base of the cup is domed and a flat disk is applied to the top of the open stem. The three feet are cast; one has been reattached with lead solder. The foot rim is formed of two molded and stamped pieces connected with a lap join. The finial and the cresting on the cover are cast. The interior of the stem is deeply pitted and the silver is cracked and worn through in several places.

When acquired by the Museum in 1954, this cup was compared to several late fifteenth- and early sixteenth-century "college cups." The formula of a flaring stem, embossed body, and trefoil cresting around a pointed cover with a sculptural finial may be seen on the Warden's Grace Cup at New College, Oxford, the Richmond Cup in the Armourers' and Braziers' Company, and the Thomas Leigh Cup in the Mercers' Company.[1] All of these examples are considerably larger and more ambitious in design than the present cup. The small scale and disparate ornamental elements on this cup—the figural feet, crenellated rim, and oversized finial—as well as the construction of the foot and the deep pitting on the interior of the stem have since prompted the suggestion that the cup is either a forgery or substantially altered.

It is impossible to be certain which elements (if any) are authentic. The lobed chasing on the body of the cup may be compared to the spiraling decoration on the small standing cup of 1493 in the Goldsmiths' Company[2] or to the scaled pattern on an unmarked flagon at Magdalen College, Oxford.[3] The trefoil cresting on the rim of the cover is a standard feature on covered drinking cups in this category, but the motif is usually repeated around the foot.[4] The crenellated rim of the foot appears on the Huntsman Salt at All Souls College.[5] The figural form of the feet may be compared to those on the Monkey Salt at New College, Oxford,[6] which are in the form of wild men seated on cushions, and to those on the Thomas Leigh Cup, which are in the form of pilgrims' bottles.[7] The nuns' heads applied to the body of the Thomas Leigh cup are especially close in spirit to the feet on the present cup. Finally, the eagle finial may be compared to the finial on the Boleyn Cup of 1535/6.[8] A better stylistic comparison, however, is the finial on an elaborate Gothic revival inkstand of 1899. Made in the form of a castle, it incorporates many of the decorative elements mentioned above—crenellated moldings, trefoil cresting, and lobed chasing.[9]

Among the most disturbing features of this cup is the deep pitting visible on the inside of the foot. There is evidence that it once covered the exterior surface, too, which has been mechanically buffed. Such extensive corrosion could be caused if the cup were buried for a long period, or immersed in an acid to hasten the appearance of age.

The balance of evidence suggests that the cup has been substantially altered if not wholly forged, but the possibility remains that the basic structure of the cup is late fifteenth or early sixteenth century.

136

1. The Warden's Grace Cup, ca. 1480, un-marked, h. 40 cm, ill. Moffatt, 1906, pl. 31, p. 62; The Richmond Cup, ca. 1530–1550, maker's mark *E* a flower above, h. 31.8 cm, ill. Cooper, 1977, fig. 38; The Thomas Leigh Cup, 1413, maker's mark crossed implements, h. 40.7 cm, ill. Glanville, 1990, fig. 73.

2. Goldsmiths' Company, Standing cup, 1493, maker's mark an escallop below a baton, h. 14 cm, ill. Glanville, 1987, fig. 5.

3. Magdalen College, Oxford, Flagon, English or German, early sixteenth century, unmarked, h. 35.6 cm, ill. Moffatt, 1906, pl. 49. Similar decoration appears on a pair of flagons in Aachen: Flagons, Aachen, ca. 1510–1520 with later alterations, maker's mark of Hans von Reutlingen, h. 13 cm, ill. Ernst Günter Grimme, "Der Aachner Goldschmied Hans von Reutlingen (um 1465 bis um 1547)," *Aachner Kunstblätter* 49 (1980), fig. 29, p. 41.

4. The Warden's Grace Cup, mentioned above, is typical. Other examples include the Lacock Cup at the British Museum, ca. 1450–1480, un-marked, ill. Glanville, 1987, fig. 1.

5. The Huntsman Salt, fifteenth century, un-marked, exhibited Oxford, Ashmolean Museum, 1928, cat. no. 64, fig. 27; see also New College, Oxford, The Monkey Salt, ca. 1500, unmarked, exhibited ibid., cat. no. 75, fig. 31.

6. See note 5.

7. See note 1.

8. St. John the Baptist, Cirencester, The Boleyn Cup, 1535/6, maker's mark three flowers, h. 31.5 cm, ill. Glanville, 1990, fig. 128.

9. Inkstand, Dortmund, 1899, maker's mark of Carl Tewes, h. 22.4 cm, ill. Horst Appuhn, *Das Dortmunder Ratssilber, 1898–1915* (Dortmund, 1969), p. 7, pl. 4.

· 137 ·

POT

England, London, marked 1550/1 with later alterations
Porcelain with underglaze blue decoration (China, Ming dynasty, Chia-ching mark [1522–1566] with silver-gilt mounts
57.530

MARKS: on inside of cover and on neck, maker's mark a wallet hook palewise on a bend crosswise in a plain shield (Jackson, 1921, p. 98; rev. ed. 1989, p. 95) (repeated on underside of foot); lion passant; leopard's head crowned; date letter *N*

INSCRIPTIONS: engraved on cover, *LIVE TO DIE AND LIVE*

H. 19.5 cm (7¹¹⁄₁₆ in.); w. 14 cm (5½ in.); diam. of foot: 10.4 cm (4⅛ in.)

PROVENANCE: sold Christie, Manson & Woods, London, July 26, 1939, lot 140A; John Hunt, Dublin; Sotheby & Co., London, May 9, 1957, lot 123, purchased June 5, 1957 [Garrard & Co., London], Theodora Wilbour Fund in Memory of Charlotte Beebe Wilbour.

EXHIBITED: San Francisco, Fine Arts Museums of San Francisco, 1977, cat. no. 67.

PUBLISHED: Came, 1961, p. 27; Lunsingh Scheurleer, 1980, p. 178, fig. 7; Fontein, 1982, cat. no. 272.

DESCRIPTION: The bulbous porcelain jar is thrown from a fine textured paste with a gray-green hue. It is painted in underglaze blue with carp and foliage and fitted into a molded silver foot ring with a dentiled border. The foot is joined to the handle by a flat strip of foliate outline. The C-shaped handle is D-shaped in section. The silver neck of the jug flares slightly near the rim and is bordered at the base with a molded and twisted wire. The slightly domed cover is embossed with six scrolls interspersed with cornucopias and foliage against a matted ground. The inscription is engraved in a central roundel. The thumbpiece is in the form of addorsed male and female busts.

CONSTRUCTION: The foot is assembled from formed sheet and molded drawn wires. The handle is formed of two sections; the seam is split on the lower edge. The neck is raised and has an applied drawn and twisted wire. An applied lip on the inside lower rim is folded over the edge of the porcelain. The raised and embossed cover has an applied molded wire edge. The thumbpiece is cast.

This object exemplifies the problems inherent in dating silver-mounted objects. The mounts on this porcelain jar were recorded on a stoneware jug sold at auction in 1939.[1] The description of the mounts tallies with their present appearance, but the jug is listed as stoneware decorated with figures of foxes and hounds. Before the piece appeared again for sale in 1957,[2] the mounts had been altered to fit this Chinese bowl. There are no features of the silver mounts that are convincing as sixteenth-century designs, though they may well have been formed of authentic fragments. The marks on the cover are stretched and worn from reworking, and the maker's

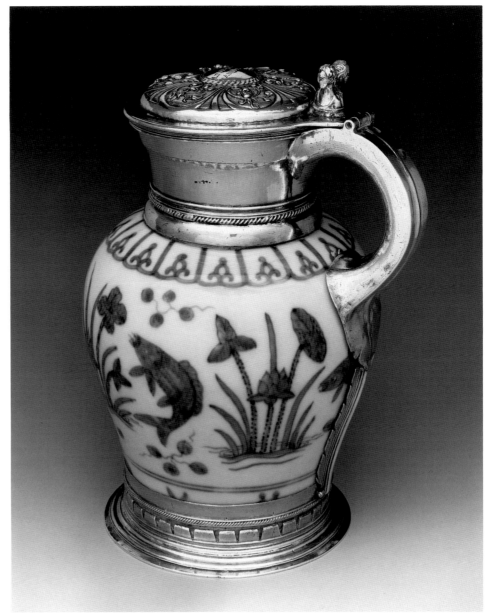

137

mark on the foot was struck with a different stamp than that used on the neck and cover. The object has several details in common with an unusual mounted jug in the Victoria and Albert Museum that has undergone considerable restoration—the thumbpieces are identical, and the large dentiled foot rims are similar.[3] The small high handle on the pot at the Victoria and Albert covers a ceramic handle, whereas the Boston pot was created from a plain bowl.[4]

1. Christie, Manson & Woods, London, July 29, 1939, lot 140A.
2. Sotheby & Co., London, May 9, 1957, lot 123.
3. Acc. no. M351–1910, Pot, lead-glazed earthenware with silver-gilt mounts, mid-sixteenth century with later additions, unmarked, ill. Glanville, 1990, cat. no. 39, p. 422.
4. The high neck and high handled profile of these pots is recorded in an engraving by Hollar after Holbein. See Glanville, 1990, p. 262.

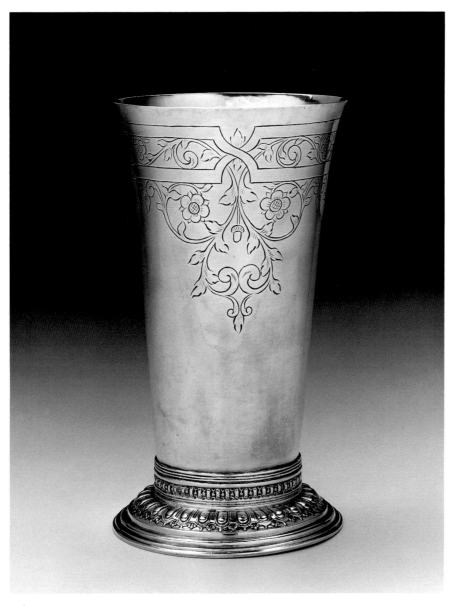

138

DESCRIPTION: The beaker rests on a spreading foot with complex molding, fluting, and, at the base of the cup, a stamped pattern of stars and ovals. The cup has high flaring sides, and an everted rim. It is chased and engraved around the rim with a band of strapwork enclosing foliage, acorns, and flowers.

CONSTRUCTION: The body of the vessel is raised. The foot is cast in one piece with applied wire molding at the juncture with the body.

The narrow proportions of the beaker are unusual, as is the broad coarsely decorated foot. The flaring section of the base is cast in one piece, a construction that should be compared to an example in the Untermyer Collection in the Metropolitan Museum of Art which is clearly assembled from several die-stamped and molded wires.[1] The maker's mark *GC* a mullet above and below is recorded by Jackson on a bottle in the Kremlin[2] and on a beaker in the Huntington Collection.[3] The latter is hallmarked on the underside of the base (as is the Untermyer example), but the maker's mark is too damaged for an accurate comparison. The marks on the present beaker should be compared to those on the communion cup of the same year by the maker *IH* a bear passant below in a circle (cat. no. 21).

1. Beaker, 1599, indecipherable maker's mark, h. 14.6 cm, ill. Hackenbroch, 1963, pl. 33, cat. no. 27. The design of the engraved floral decoration is remarkably similar. The combination of chasing and engraving in the decoration of the present beaker is unfamiliar to me.
2. Ill. Oman, 1961, pl. 25.
3. Beaker, 1608, maker's mark *GC* a mullet above and below, h. 14.9 cm, ill. Wark, 1978, cat. no. 5, p. 4.

· 138 ·

BEAKER
London, spurious marks for 1605/6
Silver
62.251

MARKS: near rim, maker's mark *GC* a mullet above and below (similar to Jackson, 1921, p. 110; rev. ed. 1989, p. 106); leopard's head crowned; lion passant; date letter *h*

H. 15.6 cm (6⅛ in.); diam. of rim 8.9 cm (3½ in.)

WEIGHT: 300.5 gm (9 oz 13 dwt)

PROVENANCE: purchased from Firestone & Parson, Boston, March 14, 1962, Theodora Wilbour Fund in Memory of Charlotte Beebe Wilbour.

· 139 ·

BOTTLE
England (?), 17th century (?)
Leather with silver mounts
54.1113

Unmarked

ARMORIALS: engraved on silver collar, the arms of George Ogilvie (d. 1663), created Lord Banff in 1642

INSCRIPTIONS: engraved above the coat of arms, the motto *HELPE VOVRE SELFE*, below the arms *DAVIDE OGELVIE, NOVA SCOTIAE; 1644/ TO ALEXANDER IRWINE OF SVTHERLAND*, and around the foot *PARECERE SVBJECTIS DEBELLARE SVPEROS*

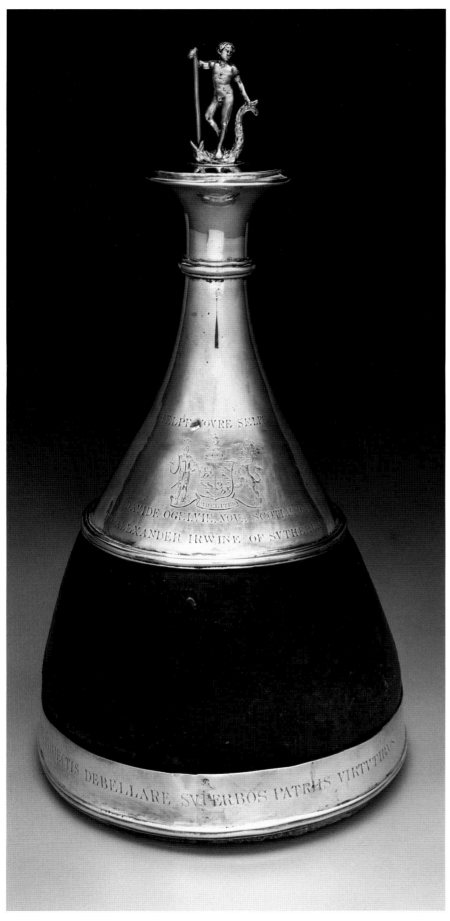

PATRIS VIRTVTIBVS (To spare the humble and to make war upon the proud with the courage of their forefathers)

H. 21.8 cm (8%16 in.); diam. 13.2 cm (5³⁄16 in.)

PROVENANCE: Earl of Altamont, by 1911; Marquess of Sligo, by 1923; purchased from Berry Hill, New York, November 9, 1954, Theodora Wilbour Fund in Memory of Charlotte Beebe Wilbour.

PUBLISHED: G. J. Monson-Fitzjohn, *Drinking Vessels of Bygone Days* (London, 1927), p. 33; Jackson, 1911, vol. 2, p. 786, fig. 1021; E. A. Jones, "Some Old Plate in the Collection of the Most Honourable Marquess of Sligo," *Connoisseur* 67 (1923), p. 66, fig.2.

DESCRIPTION: The leather bottle is in the form of an inverted funnel. It is mounted around the foot and the neck with silver that is engraved with a coat of arms and an inscription. From a molded band at the top of the neck, the neck flares to an everted rim. The opening is fitted with a small cover surmounted by a figure of Neptune astride a dolphin.

CONSTRUCTION: The leather bottle is formed of two pieces, the body, which is seamed, and the circular base, which is stitched and strengthened by a wood foot rim. The silver foot rim is seamed and has an applied drawn wire rim; the neck is raised. The finial is cast, and secured to the cork stopper with a threaded post. The inside of the neck has been repaired with a silverplated copper insert.

The inscription on this bottle indicates that it was presented to Alexander Irwine by David Ogelvie [*sic*] in 1644. The style of the engraving and the proportions of the crest and coronet, however, raise questions as to their date. In addition, errors in the engraving suggest that it may have been added later over previous decoration. The lions in the coat of arms are depicted without the imperial crown, and more significantly, the name of the donor appears to have been engraved in error. The arms are those of George Ogilvy, not David. The named recipient, engraved as Alexander Irwine of Sutherland, apparantly refers to Alexander Irvine of Drum, father of Margaret, whom George Ogilvy married in 1610. Ogilvy married secondly Mary Sutherland of Duffus. The conflation of the family names, the errors in the blazoning, and the style of the lettering suggest an historicising "improvement" to this piece, perhaps in the nineteenth century.

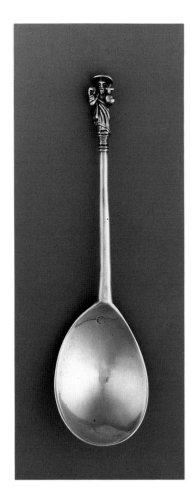

140

• 140 •

MASTER SPOON
London, marked for 1514/5
Silver
49.1709

MARKS: in bowl, leopard's head crowned; on back of stem near bowl, unidentified maker's mark (similar to Jackson, 1921, p. 93; rev. ed. 1989, p. 89); date letter *r*

L. 18.26 cm (7³⁄₁₆ in.); w. of bowl 4.93 cm (1¹⁵⁄₁₆ in.)

WEIGHT: 65.2 gm (2 oz 2 dwt)

PROVENANCE: Reverend Thomas Staniforth, Kirk Hammerton Hall, Yorkshire, by descent to Colonel E. W. Staniforth; Crichton Brothers, London, 1898; Marsden J. Perry, Providence, Rhode Island; Mrs. Howard Eric, Stamford, Connecticut, sold Parke Bernet, New York, December 2, 1949, lot 75, purchased December 12, 1949, Theodora Wilbour Fund in Memory of Charlotte Beebe Wilbour.

EXHIBITED: London, Crichton Brothers, 1898.

PUBLISHED: Hipkiss, 1951, p. 14; How, 1953, vol. 2, pp. 280–283; Hipkiss, 1953, p. 22.

DESCRIPTION: The spoon has a fig-shaped bowl and a tapering hexagonal stem. The finial is in the form of Christ holding an orb and cross in his left hand, and raising his right hand in benediction.

CONSTRUCTION: The spoon is apparently cast in one piece; the nimbus is cast separately and applied.

Commander and Mrs. How published this spoon as a cast copy of the so-called Chichester Master Spoon, which bears authentic marks for 1514/5.[1] The Boston spoon has marks in a position identical to those on the back of the Chichester spoon, and the stiffly chased drapery of the figure and absence of a solder join where the stem meets the finial confirm this hypothesis.

1. How, 1953, pp. 280–283.

• 141 •

MASTER SPOON
London, marked for 1611/2
Silver
47.1619

MARKS: in bowl, leopard's head crowned; on back of stem near bowl, maker's mark two clubs in saltire in a heart-shaped shield (Jackson p. 112; rev. ed. 1989, p. 108); lion passant; date letter *n*

L. 17.9 cm (7¹⁄₁₆ in.); w. of bowl 5.1 cm (2 in.)

WEIGHT: 62.4 gm (2 oz 1 dwt)

PROVENANCE: Charles G. Rupert, Wilmington, Delaware, sold Parke Bernet, New York, December 13, 1947, lot 217, purchased December 29, 1947, Theodora Wilbour Fund in Memory of Charlotte Beebe Wilbour.

PUBLISHED: Rupert, 1929, pl. 8, no. 38.

DESCRIPTION: The spoon has a fig-shaped bowl and an hexagonal stem. The finial depicts Christ holding an orb and cross in his left hand, and raising his right hand in benediction.

CONSTRUCTION: The spoon is cast in one piece.

The exceptional coarseness of the casting of the finial on this spoon suggests that it may be a forgery. The nimbus, orb, and cross appear to have been cast in one piece with the figure, and the mold lines are visible. There is no evidence of a solder join at the top of the stem, and there is no apparrant surface wear. The grainy quality of the marks suggests that the spoon was cast in a single piece from an authentic example.

· 142 ·

SEAL-TOP SPOON
London, marked for ca. 1640
Silver
33.207

MARKS: in bowl, leopard's head crowned; on back of stem near bowl, indecipherable maker's mark; lion passant; indecipherable date letter, possibly *a*

INSCRIPTIONS: pricked on top of seal, *H* over S*N

L. 16.7 cm (6⁹⁄₁₆ in.); w. of bowl 4.9 cm (1¹⁵⁄₁₆ in.)

WEIGHT: 36.9 gm (1 oz 4 dwt)

PROVENANCE: Anonymous Gift in Memory of Charlotte Beebe Wilbour (1833–1914), March 2, 1933.

EXHIBITED: Boston, Museum of Fine Arts, 1933 (no catalogue).

DESCRIPTION: The spoon has a fig-shaped bowl and tapered hexagonal stem. The baluster support is surmounted by an oval seal.

CONSTRUCTION: The spoon appears to have been cast in one piece. Traces of gilding remain on the upper portion of the baluster support underneath the seal. There is a large pitted area on the underside of the bowl.

141

142

Concordance

Accession Number	Catalogue Number	Accession Number	Catalogue Number
19.1343	130	40.617	73
33.60	7	42.6	86
33.61	9	42.7	98
33.62	15	42.82	109
33.63	22	42.83	129
33.64	35	42.419	37
33.65	47	46.845	18
33.66	54	46.1126	30
33.68	55	47.1427–8	21
33.69	72	47.1429	107
33.71	69	47.1616	105
33.72	83	47.1617	101
33.80	93	47.1618	103
33.84	96	47.1619	141
33.85	97	49.475	3
33.206	111	49.476	4
33.207	142	49.581	6
33.208	121	49.1709	140
33.209	124	49.1710	102
33.210	123	49.1711	104
33.211–212	128	49.1712	106
33.213	131	49.1713	108
33.214	134	49.1714	112
35.156	77	49.1715	113
35.1547	11	49.1716	117
35.1548	8	49.1717	118
35.1550	14	49.1718	119
35.1551	110	49.1719	120
35.1555	114	49.1720	122
35.1556	27	49.1721	125
35.1558	50	50.2724–5	85
35.1559	49	51.1618	10
35.1561	60	52.1835–1836	13
35.1562	126	53.2000a,b	66
35.1565	68	54.87	36
35.1566	67	54.933	136
35.1567–8	75	54.1113	139
35.1573	99	55.193	89
36.150	42	55.461	59
37.567	87	55.471	24
38.983	62	55.622	92
38.1641	115	55.930	76
38.1642	127	56.1183	17
38.1643	133	56.1184	23
38.1751	116	57.58	74
39.19	48	57.530	137
		57.533	2
		58.718	43
		59.718	31

60.117	78
60.534a,b	58
60.944	65
60.945	95
60.947a,b	82
61.184	29
61.185	71
61.654	25
61.655	61
62.167	26
62.168	63
62.251	138
62.509	88
62.672	51
62.673	44
62.979	90
62.1166	12
63.487	81
63.1252	16
63.1253	39
63.1254	52
63.1257	70
64.518–519	91
64.705–707	132
66.284a,b	79
67.601	19
67.602–603	46
67.1017	1
67.1018	32
1971.266	57
1971.640	64
1972.977	80
1972.986	28
1973.172	41
1974.563	56
1975.16–17	53
1975.711	84
1976.2a,b	45
1977.497	40
1978.226	38
1978.292	94
1979.261–262	5
1982.619	34
1984.164–166	33
1987.269	135
1988.291	100
1989.145	20

Index

Numbers indicate page references. The index includes all marks and makers represented in the Museum's collection. Works in other public collections are listed by city. All known former owners are indexed, as are armorials. For provincial plate, see town name.

Abbey Collection, Bookbinding, 109
Acorn cup, 65–66
Acorn finial, 196
Acton, John, 82
AD conjoined a pellet above a crescent below, 122
Adelaide Art Gallery of South Australia, Salt, 68
AF in a shaped shield, 117–118
AH in a rectangle, 57
Altamont, Earl of, 225
AM in monogram. See Manwaring, Arthur
American Art Galleries, New York, 160
Amsterdam, Rijksmuseum, Ewer, 128
AN in monogram. See Nelme, Anthony
Ancaster, Earl of, Pair of covered cups, 74 note 9
Andirons, 150–151
Anne of Denmark, 90–91
Apostle spoon, 197, 198–201, 204, 207–210, 212
Arcy, Mrs. N. d', 175
Argenti, Philip, 117
Armourers' and Braziers' Company
    Richmond Cup, 220
    Standing cup, 74
Ashbrook, Lord, 160
Asprey, PLC, London, 76
Audley, Christopher, 63–64

Bang, Theodor, 181
Barber-Surgeons' Company, Royal Oak Cup, 148
Barnes, J. H., 124
Bateman, Arthur, 166
BB a crescent below, 186–187
Beaker, 166, 224
Bell, John, 99
Bemis, Frank Brewer, 11–13, 56, 60, 65, 89, 123–124, 140, 152–153, 162, 166, 195, 202, 205, 213
Benett-Stanford, Lt.-Col. J., 200
Berendrecht, Michiel de Bruyn van, 128
Berkeley, Rowland, 114
Berlin, Kunstgewerbemuseum, Mounted porcelain ewer, 84
Berry Hill, New York, 225

Bird, 58–60
Bird with a branch over TI. See TI
Birmingham, Barber Institute, Butleigh Salt, 59, 87
Bleeding bowl. See Porringer
Bodendick, Jacob, 132–134, 137–139, 142, 145–151
Book cover, 107–109
Borthwick, Patrick, 111–112
Bottle, 224–225
Bowl, Covered, 183
    Standing, 63–64
    Two-handled covered, 153–154
Box, 189
    Counter, 110–111
    Sugar, 130, 164–165
    Wafer, 99–101
    See also casket
Bradbury, Frederick, 65
Breadalbane, Marquess of, 202
Brew, Patrick, 202
Bristol, 196
Bristol Museum, Mounted tin-glazed jug, 97
Browne, Francis, Viscount Montague, 101
Brownlow, Earl, 186
Bruford & Sons, Exeter, 89
Brummer, Joseph, 44, 46
Bry, Théodore de and J. Théodore de, 109
Buccleuch, Dukes of
    Andirons, 150
    Engraved plates, 51
    Elizabeth Montague, Duchess of, 94
Buhler, Kathryn Clark, 12
Bury, Colonel Howard, 86
Bury St. Edmunds, 125, note 3
    St. Andrews Castle, 124

C enclosing I. See Cluatt, James
Callecote, 192
Cambridge, Corpus Christi College, Covered cup, 44 note 7
    Fitzwilliam Museum, Footed dish, 92
    Gonville and Caius College, Tankard, 70, 82
    King's College, Bowl, 154
    Peterhouse College, Two-handled cup, 118
    Sidney Sussex College, Ewer and Basin, 80 note 4
    St. John's College, Dish, 121
    Trinity Hall, Tankard 1570/1, 70; Tankard, 1635/6, 187 note 1

Cambridge, Massachusetts, Fogg Art Museum,
    Scroll salt, 122
Candlesticks, 118–120, 162–164, 171–172
Carmarthen, Wales, 56–57
Cary, Daniel, 208, 210
    William, 212
Casket, 68–69
Caster, 193
Cats, Jacob, 132
Cawdell, William, 205
CB in monogram, 92
Cecil, William, Lord Burghley, 76
Chalice, 56, 116
Chandos-Pole, Major J. W., 134
Charles I, 92, 109–111, 126
Charles II, 101, 106, 139, 148, 158
Chicago, Art Institute of, Monteith, 173
Chichester Master Spoon, 226
Child, Sir Richard, Viscount Castlemaine, 164
Cholmondeley, Dame Mary, 72
    Sir Hugh, 72, 77
    Thomas, 77
Christie, Manson & Woods, 44, 47, 53, 54, 58,
    61, 63, 65, 70, 72, 82, 86, 92, 94, 103,
    104, 109, 114, 118, 121, 122, 124, 134,
    140, 145, 166, 170, 172, 175, 178, 181,
    184, 222
Ciborium, 148
Cirencester, St. John the Baptist, Boleyn
    Cup, 220
Clayton, Michael, London, 168
Cleveland Museum of Art
    Dish, 142, 159 note 2
    Sleeve cup, 168 note 2
Clifford, Anne, Countess of Pembroke and
    Montgomery, 51–52
Cluatt, James, 206
Clymer, Dr. George, 162
Cock, Hieronymous, 51
Coconut cup, 54–55
Coles, Lawrence, 218
Cologne, arms of, 61
    Kunstgewerbemuseum, Pewter-mounted
        stoneware jug, 62
Comb case, 166–167
Communion cup. See cup
Cook, Mrs. F. H., 82
Cooqus, Gerald, 128
Copenhagen, Nationalmuseet, Wood tankard,
    132
Cordial pot. See teapot

Cotton, Richard, 207
Counter box, 110–111
Cowdray House, 101
Crawford of Auchinames and Drumsoy, 132
Crescent enclosing a saltire, 205
    a mullet. See Brew, Patrick
Chrichton Brothers, London, 47, 51, 54, 58, 63,
    70, 94, 103, 122, 192, 200–202, 204, 207,
    210, 212–213, 226
Crichton-Stuart, John, Marquess of Bute, 58
Cromwell, Oliver, 184
Crosse, Richard, 209
Crowned cross moline, 44
Cup, College, 220–222
    Communion, 56–57, 64–66, 80, 99–101,
        111–113
    Covered, 140–142
    Spout, 124–125
    Standing, 134–135, 152
    Steeple, 94
    Two-handled, 123, 140, 162
    Two-handled, and cover, 114, 117–118, 124,
        126–128, 131, 136–137, 168–169
    Wine, 184–186

D enclosing C. See Cary, Daniel
Dehua, 170–171, 179
Delamere, Lords, 72, 74, 77
Diamond point finial, 196
Dish, 189
    Footed, 92, 104, 121
    See also basin, bowl
Dobson, W. T., 118
Dod, Robert, 76–77
Dodsworth, 178
Downame, John, 109
Dressing glass, 190
Dunham Massey, Tankards, 157
Dunn-Gardner, J., 104
Dwight, John, 171, 178

Earthenware, tin-glazed, 44–45, 97–98
Easton, Christopher, 202
Edinburgh, 111–113, 144
EG in a rectangle, 172
EI a pellet below, 162
Elizabeth I, 51–52, 90
Ellis, H. D., 56, 200
Emens, Jan, 61
Eric, Mrs. Howard, 197–198, 200–201, 204,
    207–210, 212, 226

Escallop with two pellets above, 202
Estabrook & Co., Boston, 123
Eton College
   Ewer and Basin, 80
   Salt, 122
Evelyn, John, 128
Ewer, 84–86, 157
Ewer and Basin, 51–52, 78–80
Exeter, 202

Fajardo, Diego de Saavedra, 134
Fellows, Benjamin, 158
Firestone & Parson, Boston, 88, 144, 183,
   217, 224
Flagon, 47, 74–76, 82–83, 97–98
Fleur-de-lys, 124
   in a shaped shield, 201
   incuse, 61
Flindt, Paul, 78
Fork, 217
Fort Worth, Kimball Art Museum, Cup and
   cover, 114
Four ovals, 56
Fraser, Sir Charles Craufurd, 167
Fringed S. See Simpson, William
Furness, Viscount, 118
FW in monogram, 94

Garrard & Co., London, 61, 72, 103, 137, 145,
   170, 178, 181, 184, 222
Garthorne, George, 172
GC a mullet above and below, 224
GC in monogram, 126, 137 note 2, 139 note 5.
   See also Cooqus, Gerald
Gentot, Blaise, 182
GF conjoined. See Glanville, Francis
GG a pellet below. See Garthorne, George
Glanville, Francis, 219
Glasgow Museum and Art Gallery, Commu-
   nion cup, 111
Godet, Giles, 51–52
Godfrey, William, E., New York, 56, 89, 124,
   140, 166
Goldsmiths' and Silversmiths' Company,
   London, 57, 114, 121
Gosforth, Cumberland, Tankard, 116
Greenway, Henry, 137
Gribelin, Simon, 181
Griffiths, Percival D., 167
Guest, Mrs. and Mrs. Winston F. C., 63, 150
Gunning, Peter, 162

Haddington, St. Mary, Communion cup,
   111–113
Halvorsen, Samuel, 132
Ham House, Hearth furnishings, 150
Harache, Peter I, 217
Harvey, Sebastian, 96
HB conjoined a star below, 88
Hearst, William Randolph, 44, 70, 80 note 4,
   82, 154, 158
Henrietta Maria, 109–110
Herbert, Philip, Earl of Pembroke and Mont-
   gomery, 51–52
Hesse, Langrave of, 74
Hipkiss, Edwin, 11
HK conjoined an ermine spot below. See Kayle,
   Hugh
HL conjoined in a circle, 210
Hogenberg, Remigius, 51
Holbein, Hans, 41
Holmes, John Augustus, 58
Hoo, Margaret, 175–176
Hook, 170
Hopkins, Thomas, 63
Horner, Lady, 140
Hound sejant, 114, 118, 126, 137, 142
How (of Edinburgh), London, 58, 68, 109, 129,
   132, 166, 196, 219
Howzer, Wolfgang, 128, 137, 139
Humphris, Cyril, Ltd., London, 90
Hunt, John, Dublin, 40–41, 96, 97, 126, 148,
   220, 222

I? crowned, 218
IA a pellet below. See Acton, John
IB a pellet between a crescent and two pellets below.
   See Bodendick, Jacob
ID three pellets above and a gerbe between pellets
   below, 178
IE or IF a pellet below, 178
IG a mullet below, 123
IG a crescent below, 143
IH over a bear passsant, 78, 80
   in a heart-shaped shield, 116
II a mullet below. See Johnson, Jeremy
   a pellet between a fleur-de-lys below, 189
IK a rose and two pellets below. See King, John
Inglis, Brand, Ltd., London, 101, 106, 189
IP above a bell, 70
IR between rosettes a pellet between, 161
IS crowned, 148, 214–216
IS a pellet between and a pellet below, 170

IT in a shaped shield. See Thompson, John
IW a pellet below, 170

Jamaica, 166–167, 189
James I, 90–91
Jenkins, Thomas, 153, 157
Jermyn, John, 205
Jessop, H. R., Ltd., London, 99
Johnson, Jeremy, 211–212
Jolley of Hatton garden, 183
Jones, John, 202
Jug, 53–54, 61–62, 222–223
    Malling, 44–45

Kayle, Hugh, 54, 82
Keelynge, Richard, 51
Keenleyside, R. H., 106
Kendi, 84
Kennedy, John, 99
Kilmorey, Earl of, 82
King, John, 213, 214
Kingswood, St. Andrew's, Chalice, 148
Knole, Andirons, 150 note 1
    Tray, 145
Kramarsky, Siegfried, 74

Lace-back spoon, 219
Lamb, Adam, 111
Landau, Nicolas, Paris, 84
Langworthy of Bath, 92
Launceston, 219
LC crowned a pellet between, a crescent between pel-
    lets below. See Coles, Lawrence
Lechmere-Charlton, 153
Leeds, Temple Newsam House
    Mostyn flagons, 72, 82
    Pair of cups, 181
Leeson, Earls of Milltown, 134
Legh, Colonel, 54
Leverett, John, 113–114
Levine, G. J., 124
Lewis, P. E., 181
Ley, James, Earl of Marlborough, 66, 140–142
Lincoln, 125
Lindner, Mrs. George, 216
Lion sejant finial, 202
Lisbon, Museu Nacional de Arte Antiga,
    Sandglass, 42–43
Livery badge, 76–77
Loder, Sidney, 94
London, Al-Tajiir Collection, Vases, 143

London, British Museum
    Box of weights, 110
    Engraved medallions, 90–91
    Livery badge, 76–77
    Malling Jug, 44, 60, 62 note 1
    Stapleford Cup, 65
London, Tower of London, "Queen Elizabeth
    Salt," 59
London, Victoria and Albert Museum, 12
    Acorn-knop spoon, 196
    Basin, 80 note 4
    Calverley toilet service, 190
    Candlesticks, 164
    Counter box, 111 note 1
    Engraved bowls, 51–52
    Medallions, 90–91
    Mostyn salt, 68 note 8
    Mounted jug, 223
    Mounted tin-glazed earthenware jug, 45 note
        3, 98
    Mother-of-pearl bowl, 69
    Nautilus cup, 60 note 6
    Serpentine tankard, 97 note 1
    Sleeve cup, 139, 168
    Spout cup, 125
    Stoke Prior bell salt, 90
    Studley bowl, 40
    Wax jack, 158
    Wine cup, 88 note 1
Longman, John and Richard, 195
Los Angeles, Fowler Collection, 51
Los Angeles County Museum of Art, Gilbert
        Collection
    Footed dish, 92
    Gold Box, 110–111
    Jug, Benjamin Pyne, 45
    Mazer, 40
    Rock crystal tankard, 47
    Standing salt, 68
    Tankard, 118
Lumley, Thomas, Ltd., London, 70, 82, 86,
        114, 116, 124, 136, 140, 158, 171, 186,
        190
Lytler, Robert, 77

M a line across, 64
Magniac, Hollingsworth, 98 note 1
Maidenhood finial, 200
Makower, Ernest, 92, 140, 158
Mallet, John, 189
Malling jug, 44–45, 98

Manchester City Art Gallery
  Magdalene cup, 70
  Mostyn flagons, 72, 82
Manwaring, Arthur, 116, 118, 129–130, 137
Marlborough, Mary, Countess of, 66, 142
    note 1
Master spoon, 226
Mazer, 40–41
McClary, Mrs. Andrew B., 172
Medallion, 90–91
Meline, Pembrokeshire, 57
Mercers' Company
  Dethick salt, 122
  Thomas Leigh cup, 220
Meyer, Dietrich, 168
Middle Temple, Honorable Society of the,
  Cup, 118
  Dish, 92 note 5, 121
Miller, George, 63
Mirror. See Dressing glass
Montagu, Elizabeth, Duchess of Buccleuch and
    Queensberry, 94
Monteith, 172–173, 192
Mounted ware, 44–45, 47–48, 53–55, 61–62,
    68–69, 74–76, 84–86, 157
Morgan, J. P., 51, 63, 78, 150, 200
Morrice, 66
Moscow, Kremlin Armory Museum
  Candlesticks, 120
  Flagon, 82, 84 note 4
  Livery pot, 80
  Perfume burner, 137
  Salt, 68
Mounted ware
Mug, 161, 170–171, 178–179
Munich, Schatzkammer der Residenz, Sand-
    glass, 44 note 4
Murray, Mrs. Scott, 109

Nelme, Anthony, 183, 192
New York, Metropolitan Museum of Art
  Coconut cup, 55 note 2
  Ewer and basin, 80 note 4
  Mounted porcelain, 76
  Pot, 181
  Salts, 129
  Set of twelve plates, 51
  Sleeve cup, 168 note 2
  Standing cup, 152
Newdigate, Sir Richard, 106
Noble, Andrew, John, and Michael, 61, 103,
    178

Norfolk, Dukes of, 69
Norwich, 124–125

Olgivie, George, Lord Banff, 224–225
Ostrich egg ewer, 157
Oxford, All Souls College, Huntsman salt, 220
  Ashmolean Museum
    Candlesticks, 164
    Mounted tin-glazed jug, 97
    Tankard, 72
  Christs Church College, Sugar box, 130
  Corpus Christi College, Bishop Fox's crozier,
    198
  Exeter College, Gold cup, 114 note 4, 137
    note 4, 142
  Magdalen College, Flagon, 220
  New College
    Monkey salt, 220
    Warden's Grace Cup, 220
  Wadham College, Gold cup, 114, 126, 137

Paine, Richard C., 12, 72, 94, 114
Painter Stainers' Company, 129
Parke Bernet, New York, 44, 47, 51, 63, 78,
    114, 197–201, 204, 207–209, 210, 212,
    226. See also Sotheby's
Parker, Matthew, 56, 70
Partridge, Affabel, 59. See also *Bird*
Partridge Fine Arts, London, Two-handled cup,
    128 note 11
Pasadena, Huntington Art Gallery
  Beaker, 224
  Book cover, 109
  Montieth, 176 note 3
  Mug, 179 note 3
Passe, Crispin de, 147
  Simon de, 90–91
PB a crown above a heart below. See Borthwick,
    Patrick
PD a cinquefoil below, 134
PD three pellets above a cinquefoil below, 129, 131
Peg tankard, 154
Perry, Marsden J., 197–198, 200–201, 207–210,
    212, 226
*PH a mullet between, a crescent and two ermine
    spots and a crown above.* See Harache,
    Peter I
Phillips, S. J., Ltd., London, 40, 118, 134, 157
Pick or a sythe, 51
Plowes of Wakefield, 195
Plummer, John, 154
Pomander, 60–61
Porringer, 160, 172

Porter, Jane, 102
Portland Art Museum, Sleeve cup, 139
Portuguese influence, 92, 104
Pot, 222–223
Powlett, Dukes of Bolton, 44
PR in monogram a pellet below, 158
Privy Council, 158
Puritan spoon, 212–213

Quaich, 144

Raphael, E. G., 186
Rawnson, William, 203
RB a mullet below, 99
RC a pheon below, 102
 in a plain shield. See Crosse, Richard
 in a rectangle. See Cotton, Richard
 three pellets above and below in a dotted circle,
  168, 178
Recusant plate, 116
Reid, Alexander, 144
Richmond, Agecroft Hall
 Mounted tin-glazed jug, 97
 Pendant, 111
Richmond and Lennox, Frances, Duchess of,
  99–100
RL a fleur-de-lys below, 184
RN a mullet between pellets above, 121
RN or RM a mullet below, 160
Robinson, James, New York, 82
Robinson, Sir John Charles, 65
Rockford, The Time Museum, Sandglass, 43
  note 2
Rogers, C. Coltman, 153
Rosenberg and Stiebel, New York, 74
Rous Lench Collection, 45 note 4
Roussel, Nicaise, 70, 72, 82
Roy, Henri le, 181
RP a pellet below, 140
RS a mullet below, 177
 between mullets, 152
RT a mullet below and seven pellets in a circle, 194
Rummens, F. W., 65
Rupert, Charles G., 196, 198–199, 226

Sackville, Earls of Dorset, 52, 134
Schroder Collection, London
 Coconut cup, 55 note 2
 Crystal cup and cover, 59 note 4
 Cup, 44 note 10
 Mounted cup, 47
 Salt, 82
 Tankard, 70

St. Albans, Steeple cup, 94 note 2
Salem, Massachusetts, Essex Institute, Gold
  ring, 113
Salomon, Bernard, 51
Salt, Architectural, 58–60, 86–87
 Bell, 89–90
 Pedestal, 66–68
 Scroll, 122
Salver, 175–176, 178, 184–186
Sandglass, 41–44
Seal, 101, 113
Seal-top spoon, 202–203, 205–206, 210, 227
Serpentine, 96–97
SH conjoined in a circle, 175
 in a shaped shield, 216
Ship, 86
Shirley, Sir Richard, 186
Shrubsole, S. J., New York, 51, 110–111, 117
Simpson, William, 198–199
Skottowe, Timothy, 125
Sligo, Marquess of, 225
Slip-top spoon, 211
Smedley, A. M. S., 65
Smith, John, 214–216
Smith of St. Giles, Cripplegate, 117
Solis, Virgil, 51, 69, 72 note 4
Sotheby & Co. See Sotheby's
Sotheby Parke Bernet. See Sotheby's
Sotheby's (also Sotheby & Co., Sotheby Parke
  Bernet.), 38, 60, 61, 70, 82, 86, 90, 92,
  94, 99, 104, 110, 111, 117, 132, 136–137,
  140, 148, 158, 162, 178, 222. See also
  Parke Bernet
Spalding, Philip L., 205
Spectographic analysis, 13
Spink & Son, London, 53, 66, 104, 164, 166
Standing bowl. See Bowl
Standing cup. See Cup
Standish, 102–104
Staniforth, Reverend Thomas, 200, 202, 204,
  207, 210, 212, 226
Star with a dot, 196
Sterling standard, 10
Stoneware, 53–54, 61–62, 170–171, 179, 222
Stuart, Ludovic, Duke of Lennox and Rich-
  mond, 99–101
Sugar box, 130, 164–165
Swaythling Collection, 44, 47, 70, 104, 122
Sythe, 51

Tankard, 70–71, 96–97, 106, 132–134, 137–139,
  154, 175–176, 186–187, 194–195

Taylor, Mrs. Charles H., 113
Tazza. See Bowl, standing
TE in monogram, a coronet above, 166
Tea pot, 181–182
Tempesta, Antonio, 181
Thompson, John, 154
Thyssen-Bornemisza Collection
  Dish, 120
  Tankard, 132
TI between scallops. See Jenkins, Thomas
TI three annulets and a bird with a branch in its beak above, 106
Tiffany & Co., 206
TM in monogram, 184
Toledo Museum of Art, Ewer and basin, 51
Tong Church, Shropshire, Flagon, 84
Toovey, J., 53
Torkington, Captain C., 47
Toronto, Royal Ontario Museum, Lee Collection
  Mounted Ostrich egg, 55
Tray, 145–147
Trefid spoon, 214–216, 218–219
Trefoil slipped, 60 note 2, 69, 76, 97 note 2
TS in monogram, 124
Tumbler, 86
Two clubs in saltire, 206, 226

Vase, 143
Vellert, Dirick, 51
Vertue, George, Master of, 182
Vianen, Christian van, 126–128, 136–137
Vienna, Östereichische Museum für Angewandte Kunst, Sandglass, 43 note 2
Vintners' Company
  Salt, 59
  Stoneware jug, 45 note 7

Walker, R. M. W., 86
Wallet hook palewise on a bend crosswise, 222
Walton, Dr. George L., 206, 214, 218
Wancklin, Thomas, 65–66, 142 note 1
Wavertree, Lord, 131
Wax jack, 158–159
WC above a grasshopper, 53
WC in a clipped rectangle, 124
WC or CW in a dotted circle, 200
WC three pellets above and a rose between pellets below. See Cary, William

Wells, J., 63
Westbury, All Saints' Church, 64–66
Westbury cup, 64–66
Western, Thomas, 186
WF a knot above, 190
WH a pellet and a crescent (?) below, 63
WI a star below, 190
Wickes, Forsyth, 11
Wilbour, Theodora, 11–12, 54, 57, 66, 80, 102, 104, 121–122, 130, 143, 154, 160–161, 172, 177–178, 189, 192–194, 202–203, 206, 210–212, 214–215, 218
Williamsburg, Colonial Williamsburg Foundation
  Monteith, 173 note 1
  Salt, 122
  Two-handled cup and cover, 118
Williamstown, Sterling and Francine Clark Art Institute, Tankard, 72 note 3
Willson, Walter H., 60, 82, 104, 122, 143, 152–153, 162, 178
Winchester College
  Salt, 122
  Standing cup, 106 note 2
Wine cup. See Cup, wine
Windsor, St. George's Chapel, Chalice, 116
Woodward, W. H., 104
Worshipful Company of Goldsmiths, 10, 139
  Ewer, 74 note 3
  Gibbon salt, 59, 86
  Standing cup, 120
  Standing cup, 1493, 220
  Sugar box, 130 note 3
WR an arch above a pellet below, 102
WR conjoined, 203
Wrythen-knop spoon, 198
WS a mullet and two pellets above and below in a circle, 160
WW, 146
  a fleur-de-lys and two pellets below, 140, 164
Wyatt, George, 61

X-ray fluorescence, 113, 128 note 8

Yarborough, Earl of, 157
Yong of Medhurst, 113
York, 154, 203